Teaching the New English

Published in association with the English Subject Centre
Director: Ben Knights

Teaching the New English is an innovative series concerned with the teaching of the English degree in universities in the UK and elsewhere. The series addresses new and developing areas of the curriculum as well as more traditional areas that are reforming in new contexts. Although the Series is grounded in intellectual and theoretical concepts of the curriculum, it is concerned with the practicalities of classroom teaching. The volumes will be invaluable for new and more experienced teachers alike.

Titles include:

Gail Ashton and Louise Sylvester (*editors*)
TEACHING CHAUCER

Richard Bradford (*editor*)
TEACHING THEORY

Charles Butler (*editor*)
TEACHING CHILDREN'S FICTION

Ailsa Cox (*editor*)
TEACHING THE SHORT STORY

Robert Eaglestone and Barry Langford (*editors*)
TEACHING HOLOCAUST LITERATURE AND FILM

Alice Ferrebe and Fiona Tolan (*editors*)
TEACHING GENDER

Michael Hanrahan and Deborah L. Madsen (*editors*)
TEACHING, TECHNOLOGY, TEXTUALITY
Approaches to New Media and the New English

David Higgins and Sharon Ruston (*editors*)
TEACHING ROMANTICISM

Andrew Hiscock and Lisa Hopkins (*editors*)
TEACHING SHAKESPEARE AND EARLY MODERN DRAMATISTS

Lesley Jeffries and Dan McIntyre (*editors*)
TEACHING STYLISTICS

Andrew Maunder and Jennifer Phegley (*editors*)
TEACHING NINETEENTH-CENTURY FICTION

Peter Middleton and Nicky Marsh (*editors*)
TEACHING MODERNIST POETRY

Anna Powell and Andrew Smith (*editors*)
TEACHING THE GOTHIC

Andy Sawyer and Peter Wright (*editors*)
TEACHING SCIENCE FICTION

Gina Wisker (*editor*)
TEACHING AFRICAN AMERICAN WOMEN'S WRITING

Forthcoming titles:

Heather Beck (*editor*)
TEACHING CREATIVE WRITING

Teaching the New English
Series Standing Order ISBN 978–1–4039–4441–2 Hardback
978–1–4039–4442–9 Paperback
(*outside North America only*)

You can receive future titles in this series as they are published by placing a standing order. Please contact your bookseller or, in case of difficulty, write to us at the address below with your name and address, the title of the series and the ISBN quoted above.

Customer Services Department, Macmillan Distribution Ltd, Houndmills, Basingstoke, Hampshire RG21 6XS, England

Teaching Gender

Edited by

Alice Ferrebe and Fiona Tolan
Senior Lecturers in English, Liverpool John Moores University, UK

palgrave
macmillan

First published 2012 by
PALGRAVE MACMILLAN

Palgrave Macmillan in the UK is an imprint of Macmillan Publishers Limited,
registered in England, company number 785998, of Houndmills, Basingstoke,
Hampshire RG21 6XS.

Palgrave Macmillan in the US is a division of St Martin's Press LLC,
175 Fifth Avenue, New York, NY 10010.

Palgrave Macmillan is the global academic imprint of the above companies
and has companies and representatives throughout the world.

Palgrave® and Macmillan® are registered trademarks in the United States,
the United Kingdom, Europe and other countries.

ISBN 978–0–230–25251–6 hardback
ISBN 978–0–230–25252–3 paperback

This book is printed on paper suitable for recycling and made from fully
managed and sustained forest sources. Logging, pulping and manufacturing
processes are expected to conform to the environmental regulations of the
country of origin.

A catalogue record for this book is available from the British Library.

A catalog record for this book is available from the Library of Congress.

10   9   8   7   6   5   4   3   2   1
21   20   19   18   17   16   15   14   13   12

Printed and bound in Great Britain by
CPI Antony Rowe, Chippenham and Eastbourne

Contents

Tables

Series Preface

One of many exciting achievements of the early years of the English Subject Centre was the agreement with Palgrave Macmillan to initiate the series 'Teaching the New English'. The intention of the then Director, Professor Philip Martin, was to create a series of short and accessible books which would take widely taught curriculum fields (or, as in the case of learning technologies, approaches to the whole curriculum) and articulate the connections between scholarly knowledge and the demands of teaching.

Since its inception, 'English' has been committed to what we know by the portmanteau phrase 'learning and teaching'. Yet, by and large, university teachers of English – in Britain at all events – find it hard to make their tacit pedagogic knowledge conscious, or to raise it to a level where it might be critiqued, shared or developed. In the experience of the English Subject Centre, colleagues find it relatively easy to talk about curriculum and resources, but far harder to talk about the success or failure of seminars, how to vary forms of assessment or to make imaginative use of Virtual Learning Environments. Too often this reticence means falling back on received assumptions about student learning, about teaching or about forms of assessment. At the same time, colleagues are often suspicious of the insights and methods arising from generic educational research. The challenge for the English group of disciplines is therefore to articulate ways in which our own subject knowledge and ways of talking might themselves refresh debates about pedagogy. The implicit invitation of this series is to take fields of knowledge and survey them through a pedagogic lens. Research and scholarship, and teaching and learning are part of the same process, not two separate domains.

'Teachers', people used to say, 'are born not made'. There may, after all, be some tenuous truth in this: there may be generosities of spirit (or, alternatively, drives for didactic control) laid down in earliest childhood.

But why should we assume that even 'born' teachers (or novelists, or nurses or veterinary surgeons) do not need to learn the skills of their trade? Amateurishness about teaching has far more to do with university claims to status, than with evidence about how people learn. There is a craft to shaping and promoting learning. This series of books is dedicated to the development of the craft of teaching within English Studies.

Ben Knights
Teaching the New English series editor
Director, English Subject Centre,
Higher Education Academy

The English Subject Centre

Founded in 2000, the English Subject Centre (which is based at Royal Holloway, University of London) is part of the subject network of the Higher Education Academy. Its purpose is to develop learning and teaching across the English disciplines in UK Higher Education. To this end it engages in research and publication (web and print), hosts events and conferences, sponsors projects and engages in day-to-day dialogue with its subject communities. http://www.english.heacademy.ac.uk

Notes on Contributors

Sonya Andermahr is a reader in English at the University of Northampton. She has written widely on contemporary British and American women's writing. Her publications include *Jeanette Winterson* (2009), *Jeanette Winterson: A Contemporary Critical Guide* (2007) and, with Terry Lovell and Carol Wolkowitz, *A Glossary of Feminist Theory* (2000). She is currently working on a book on narratives of maternal loss.

Brian Baker is Lecturer in English at Lancaster University. He is the author of *Masculinity in Fiction and Film: Representing Men in Popular Genres 1945–2000* (2006) and *Iain Sinclair* (2007), and he has published more widely on masculinities and genre, science and literature, and particularly science fiction.

Ros Ballaster is Professor of Eighteenth-Century Studies at Oxford University. She has published widely on topics in eighteenth-century literature, women's writing and feminist cultural studies. She holds a Postgraduate Diploma in Learning and Teaching in Higher Education and takes a special interest in the design and delivery of master's courses and the academic development of doctoral students.

Catherine Bates is a postdoctoral researcher at the university of Huddersfield. Having taught literary and cultural studies extensively at the universities of Leeds, Huddersfield, Keele and Birmingham, she has publications relating to study skills, teaching Renaissance drama, archives, subjectivity and waste, Canadian poetics, and the ethics of reading.

Steven Earnshaw is Professor of English Literature at Sheffield Hallam University. His publications include *Beginning Realism* (2010), *Existentialism* (2006), *The Pub in Literature* (2000) and *The Direction of*

Literary Theory (1996). He is Editor of *The Handbook of Creative Writing* (2007), in which his essay 'The Writer as Artist' appears.

Alice Ferrebe is Senior Lecturer in English at Liverpool John Moores University. She is the author of *Masculinity in Male-Authored Fiction 1950–2000* (2005) and the sixth volume of *The Edinburgh History of Twentieth-Century Literature in Britain, 1950–1960: Good, Brave Causes* (2012). She teaches a number of gender-related literary modules.

Stéphanie Genz is Senior Lecturer in Media and Culture at Edge Hill University. She specializes in contemporary gender and cultural theory. Her book publications include *Postfemininities in Popular Culture* (2009), *Postfeminism: Cultural Texts and Theories* (2009) and *Postfeminist Gothic: Critical Interventions in Contemporary Culture* (2007).

Ann Kaloski Naylor enjoys teaching postgraduate students at the Centre for Women's Studies, University of York. In March 2011 she instigated the first Carnival of Feminist Cultural Activism (www. feminist-cultural-activism.net) and she is currently researching contemporary cultural politics.

Rezzan Kocaöner Silkü is Associate Professor of English Literature at Ege University, İzmir, Turkey, where she received her PhD in 1996 for a thesis on Doris Lessing. She has published on George Eliot, Doris Lessing, Virginia Woolf, Joseph Conrad, Chinua Achebe, Arundhati Roy, Flora Nwapa and Caryl Phillips, and she is the author of *Industrialization, Modernity and the Woman Question* (2004).

Jane Sunderland is Senior Lecturer at Lancaster University, where she teaches gender and language to masters and PhD students and runs a weekly Gender and Language Research Group. Her most recent book is *Language, Gender and Children's Fiction* (2011). She is a past president of the International Gender and Language Association.

Fiona Tolan is Senior Lecturer in English at Liverpool John Moores University. She has published widely on contemporary British fiction, women's writing and Canadian literature, and she is the author of

Margaret Atwood: Feminism and Fiction (2007) and Co-Editor, with Philip Tew and Leigh Wilson, of *Writers Talk: Conversations with Contemporary British Novelists* (2008). She is also Associate Editor of the *Journal of Postcolonial Writing*.

Caryn M. Voskuil is Associate Professor of Literature and English at the American University of Bosnia-Herzegovina. She was Visiting Professor of Literature and Culture at the Communication University of China from 2006 to 2009 and at the Beijing International Studies University from 2005 to 2006. She lectures on literature, gender and culture, and she has published cultural analysis, literary criticism, art criticism and poetry. She has acted as consultant and speaker on gender issues for United Nations Educational, Scientific and Cultural Organization and China Central Television in China and for the European Union Police Mission and the United Nations Development Fund for Women in Bosnia-Herzegovina.

Sarah Lawson Welsh is Reader in English and Postcolonial Literatures at York St John University. Her publications include *The Routledge Reader in Caribbean Literature* (1996), *Grace Nichols* (2007) and, most recently, *Re-Routing the Postcolonial* (2010). She is also Associate Editor of the *Journal of Postcolonial Writing*. She has published widely on Caribbean and Black British literature and is currently researching food in Caribbean writing.

1
Introduction

Alice Ferrebe and Fiona Tolan

Gender provides one of the most frequently recurring theoretical frameworks taught in undergraduate English programmes. It commonly characterises literary theory survey modules, underpins Women's Studies, Queer Studies and Masculinity Studies, and informs and directs countless period and thematic modules. Indeed, it is hard to think of an English module that would not, at some point, come into contact with questions of gender, whether in discussing Shakespeare, class, poetry, Chaucer or contemporary film. Beyond the undergraduate level, masters and doctoral theses with the study of gender as their organising principle abound, encompassing numerous interdisciplinary concerns and opening up fresh fields of enquiry. Theories of gender permeate the contemporary English classroom.

At the same time, 'gender' is an almost bafflingly wide term, engaging myriad theoretical preoccupations. The ideology of first-wave, predominantly rights-based feminism remains easily discernible in contemporary liberal thought, and retains some influence within Gender Studies. It was, however, the rise of second-wave feminism and the concomitant development of an intellectually rigorous feminist theory that brought gender-based analysis to many undergraduate programmes, most typically in the form of Women's Studies courses, women's writing and dedicated language modules and feminist theory components in literary theory modules. Subsequently, the influence of postmodern theorists such as Judith Butler and Eve Kosofsky Sedgwick has extended feminist dialogues on the construction of femininity almost beyond recognition, demonstrating the constructed nature of both gender and sex. Sedgwick's work also points to the vibrant field of Queer Studies (albeit a field of tardy development in the United Kingdom) and the increasingly prevalent Masculinity Studies. To bring each of these elements under a single banner of 'gender' can be challenging, but they inarguably speak to one other, questioning the function and role of gender in society, its historical impact and cultural import, the construction and performance of sexuality and sexual identities, and the manner in which ideas about gender permeate our discourses and our classrooms as teachers of English. A focus upon a text's constructions of gender opens a productive testing ground for students, encouraging them not just to explore the power dynamics of that particular text, but simultaneously to critique the theoretical approaches with which they are being asked to work. The theorisation of gender, imbricated as it so often is with personal experience, seems peculiarly well placed to prompt our students to recognise themselves as theorisers, and to see theory itself as mutable, contextual and open to debate.

This volume brings together a number of scholars experienced in teaching gender in Higher Education (HE), specifically in the field of English Studies, and seeks to engage them in a dialogue on pedagogy. While gender as a theoretical concept has been variously contested, explored and expanded upon, relatively little has been written on the pedagogical issues it raises for teachers of English. Just as the teaching practice documented here typically asks students to consider their personal experience and its effect upon their textual responses, so a feature of this volume is a concern to share and reflect upon the teaching experiences of the colleagues it gathers together. The contributors offer a wealth of examples of useful texts and practices, from single poems and research questions to entire module structures and core teaching strategies.

The shared pedagogy that emerges is characteristically responsive to the changing intellectual cultures and needs of its student body. A number of contributors foreground this reflective practice with accounts of shaping and adjusting teaching strategies in response to regular student surveys on key ideological issues within Gender Studies. In 'Gender and the Student Experience: Teaching Feminist Writing in the Post-Feminist Classroom' (Chapter 2), an account of teaching a module on feminist fiction, Sonya Andermahr establishes the volume's emphasis on the student learning experience with a nuanced analysis of her English students' approaches to the concept of feminism and its role within literary studies. Here and elsewhere, 'teaching gender' is revealed to be a dynamic experience, demanding the repeated re-evaluation of changing student needs while simultaneously and instinctively seeking to drive forward the intellectual and political agenda of the field.

The picture of the contemporary English classroom that emerges from this volume is strikingly diverse, exemplifying a discipline that spans the study of language, literature and creative writing through a vast variety of printed, visual and digital texts. The study of gender and genre is of course inextricably linked, and this cohesiveness is represented in the range of suggested 'set texts' offered here, which spans fiction, film, theory, drama, poetry, television programmes, autobiography and polemic, pitting Shakespearean plays against twenty-first century rom-com, and even reads a dress for its construction of gender. This generic diversity can raise questions about the cultural literacy of today's English students. In 'Teaching Gender and Popular Culture' (Chapter 8), Stéphanie Genz tackles this issue, focusing on the role of popular media in shaping student perceptions of gender, and the complexities of engaging with those media representations in the classroom, particularly with regard to what she calls popular culture's 'intricate connections with feminism'. How can a teacher claim the power of enlightenment over texts with which she or he is less familiar than, and receives differently from, a 'technology-savvy and media-hungry generation of students who use digital media as a way to learn and be in touch with others and who view popular culture as a genuine expression of their identities'? The enthusiastic interdisciplinarity of English Studies is celebrated here, but it is also usefully interrogated. Lingering Leavisite anxieties about dumbing down with regard to text selection and module design are still present, together with a new risk in the current economic climate that, in embracing such a cultural span, the discipline might present itself to government and other funding bodies as simply 'not specialist enough'. Against such concerns, each of the following chapters demonstrates a shared and prized emphasis on deep pedagogical reflection, with colleagues repeatedly testing the limits, objectives and means of their teaching strategies.

Teaching gender in the twenty-first century

The bulk of the chapters in this volume follow broadly the same time-line for the development of Gender Studies in the (Western) English HE classroom. The late 1970s and 1980s are marked as a period of intense feminist activism, both political and analytical; the 1990s by a turn to theory; and the first decade of the new century by a further turn into the still more atomised deconstruction of identities within which gender forms a vital, but not dominant, focus of analysis. As editors, it had been our intention to use part of this introduction to lay out this theoretical context in more detail, but as chapter after chapter arrived with us, it became apparent that each colleague had provided, in Ann Kaloski Naylor's phrase, a 'particular framing' for their arguments and experiences, a context that in turn generates a crucial aspect of their pedagogical approach. The variance in these contexts stems from numerous influences: the gender make-up of each classroom group, including its teacher; the age and personal experiences of that teacher; their nation of origin; and the complex intellectual demands and dictats of modularisation, amongst them. The sheer diversity of the topics and texts seemed to suggest it would be better to leave each contributor to contextualise their approach to Gender Studies in their own words, just as they make a point of expounding it before their own students. As Sarah Lawson Welsh points out, 'If students can be enabled to become "active learners", agents in evaluating why context might matter to their readings (rather than being simply told that it does), their learning is likely to be considerably enriched'. In 'Teaching Gender and Language' (Chapter 7), for example, Jane Sunderland provides an admirably succinct synopsis and critique of the theoretical history of gender in English Language teaching at HE level, which should prove especially invaluable for colleagues with a more distinctly literary focus in their work.

Further reflecting on context, one particular concern for many of the contributors is the ongoing negotiation of the role of feminism in students' lives and in our classrooms. As Genz notes, although gender analysis is now a routine component of 'doing theory' on English degree courses, 'the position and understanding of feminism among teachers and/or students is more debatable and unsettled'. To this, Sunderland adds that 'young undergraduates (or at least those who have not yet had to juggle parenthood and career) ... sometimes consider that we are now living in a "Golden Age" as regards gender, that all the battles have been won, and that feminism is outdated'. Kaloski Naylor's chapter 'Teaching English to Gender Students: Collaborative Encounters with Print and Digital Texts' (Chapter 3) suggests such conflicted attitudes towards feminism might well be an issue particular to English – she can assume her Women's Studies students to be 'favourably disposed towards feminist theory'. Certainly, trouble with feminism is a common experience in the papers by English teachers collected here, most of whom voice some frustration at the paradox that, as Andermahr puts it, 'the majority of students see gender as an important category of social experience and analysis, shaping their reading choices and pleasures; at the same time, they resist the implications of the feminist concepts of structural inequality and social determination, arguing that gender "doesn't matter" or that other factors such as race signify more'. Andermahr has found, however, that her 'students are often most moved by texts which foreground gender differences in the starkest terms pointing to a deep-seated anxiety about gender and belying the positive equal rights discourse'. In meeting this challenge, all of the contributors here have developed pedagogies that are both predicated upon, as well as transformative of, students' individual experiences, with the often explicit intention of demonstrating to students that the personal is still political when it comes to gender equality. As Kaloski Naylor puts it, 'students still need to start with what they know – their own lives – in order to learn how to be empathetic, insightful critics. Then they can move out of their world', while Brian Baker asks that his students '*think differently* about constructions of gender', and hopes 'that their engagement with these ideas is so thoroughgoing that it extends beyond the boundaries of the academic discipline, still less the unit of study, and into their "real" lives'.

Engaging with student diversity

While many of the contributors reflect on the generational differences thrown up by teaching Gender Studies to students with little or no experience of second-wave feminism, other signifiers of difference also commonly play into the dynamics of the English classroom. In particular, the experience of teaching gender inevitably focuses awareness on the gender balance of a teaching group in a discipline still dominated by female students and tutors. As Ben Knights has pointed out, 'Young males who choose to study English are generally assuming a position in many ways counter-cultural, not the least of whose attractions may be an extended struggle for superiority with female teachers of reading' (Knights 2008, 3). Such dynamics form a central concern of Steven Earnshaw's chapter, ' "Men Couldn't Imagine Women's Lives": Teaching Gender and Creative Writing' (Chapter 6), at pains as he is to 'unpick possible gendered constraints on teaching creative writing' in workshops. In particular, Earnshaw seeks to find a way of teaching writing that avoids the assumption that what he calls (and the inverted commas are crucial) 'women's ways of knowing' (predicated on empathy and collaboration) are automatically and uncomplicatedly necessary and always desirable. Such assumptions of difference, motivated though they are by the best and usually feminist intentions, are aggravated in the contemporary university by the demands of the modular structure. The status of both Women and Men as separate objects of study is hotly debated in this volume: in Chapter 5, ' "Do We Need Any More Books about Men?": Teaching Masculinities', Baker is adamant that 'the *discrete* unit of study is not to be under-estimated', and accordingly, refuses a 'Masculinity Module' in favour of a wider ranging consideration of the male gender across units of study and literary genres, with science fiction forming a fruitful case study. Sunderland, in a similar vein, upholds the importance for the student of English Language of 'the recognition that understanding women's situated struggles and progress requires a full understanding and exploration of masculinity, and of gender relations'.

One of Sunderland's case studies, the reading of an International Women's Day Dress from Cameroon, emphasises another recurring concern of the colleagues collected in this volume: the exclusive association of gender theorisation, and gender equality, with the West, not least because of the extremely high standard of academic English required by the journals we look to in classrooms across the United Kingdom and United States. As Sunderland claims, and as her inventive case study exemplifies, 'This does not mean that we are stuck with this situation, but it does mean that teachers of gender and language need to try that bit harder to transcend these geographical and cultural boundaries.' She concludes: 'This is not just a question of looking at "different linguistic and cultural contexts" across the globe, but also of designing curricula and teaching materials and activities to encourage students to identify links, similarities and echoes across those contexts.'

This volume seeks to exemplify the potential for such productive links, in particular, through inclusion of reflections from colleagues working in China and Turkey. In 'The Space between Submission and Revolution: Teaching Gender in China' (Chapter 10), Caryn Voskuil recounts the necessary adjustment of her own pedagogical and theoretical 'givens' undergone in order to run successful classes on literary gender at a Chinese university. The influence of both Communism and Confucianism on her students' experience required the careful rethinking of a Western reliance within feminist and otherwise emancipatory gender discourses upon individuality and personal liberation as always-assumed goals. In 'Teaching Gender in a Turkish Context' (Chapter 11), Rezzan Kocaöner Silkü is in no doubt that, despite a long national history of political emancipation and a dominant contemporary discourse of gender equality, Turkish society remains patriarchal. The surveys she conducts amongst her students of English Literature confirm this, and the strategies she develops in response to this insight take account of ways of reading that combine ideologies from both East and West.

Together, both of these chapters work to remind us of the cultural specificity of our Gender Studies and pedagogic strategies: this impulse to 'make strange' our own critical ethnicity is also at the heart of Lawson Welsh's experience of teaching a final year 'Writing the Caribbean' module in which gender theory is used, and critiqued, in relation to postcolonial discourse. In 'Bodies, Texts and Theories: Teaching Gender within Postcolonial Studies' (Chapter 9), Sarah Lawson Welsh maps an ideal process in which her students' pre-knowledge of gender theories enables them to critique postcolonial literary texts, and then feed their readings of postcolonial writers back into a productive critique of the (Eurocentric) gender theories to which we are accustomed; thus students are encouraged to attempt a complex but highly rewarding critical reflexivity. Like Sunderland, Lawson Welsh also urges a rethinking of our currently canonical texts, both critical and literary, to allow this sort of productive undermining, hoping to 'encourage tutors as well as students to "write back" to the HE contexts in which we operate'.

English and Gender Studies on the cusp

It may well be that every era feels transitional to those living through it. As we construct our various historiographic narratives of 'where we are now', our reflections on past and recent developments inevitably leave us contemplating an uncertain future. Yet the chapters in volume return again and again to the idea that the teaching and studying of gender, and the discipline of English as a whole, has now reached a contemporary 'cusp'. This sense of transition is in part an ideological one, prompted by colleagues' efforts to engage a generation of young students from developed countries for whom gender equality seems a given; and it is also a technological one, as the digitally driven information revolution gathers pace. Addressing these related concerns, Chapter 5 suggests that a productive way to acknowledge and consider the current conceptual intermediacy of masculine selfhood – beyond the patriarchal hegemon – is through the classroom analysis of digital texts, which are at 'the leading edge of a transformation in the way in which subjectivities are produced in a digital culture'. Others also point to the digital environment as one in which the constructions and performances of gender are particularly fluid. Chapter 3 is similarly attentive to the potential of this emergent field, hymning what she calls the 'the Learning Together argument' as an example of the kind of dynamic and often risky pedagogies so characteristic of this volume. However, as Genz attests, it is probably the case that, for our younger students in particular, the digital environment is the textual field in which they are best qualified (indeed we might ruefully suspect on occasion that it is the *only* field), and their experience far exceeds our own. Like Kaloski Naylor, Genz notes approvingly how this situation 'foregrounds cooperative learning by challenging the hierarchical structure of the teacher-student relationship'. Yet she also discusses needs and strategies for maintaining authority when teaching digital and pop cultural texts, in order to guide digitally savvy students through a re-examination of the media forms and cultural practices to which they have become inured.

If we as teachers of English are on the cusp of radical digital changes in textuality, we are also experiencing a sense of transition within our discipline's critical agendas. If so many of our students are atheistic when it comes to avowing feminist beliefs, a number of the colleagues who have contributed to this volume seem at least rather agnostic. Ros Ballaster wonders 'about the extent to which one can "teach" politically or, indeed, avoid doing so', while Andermahr encapsulates a wry sense, detectable in most of the papers, that 'A nostalgic element pervades our teaching and we ourselves are no longer sure whether feminism is primarily a transformative political ideology, a part of social history or an intellectual body of knowledge with an appropriate list of learning outcomes.' Differing allegiances are in part, of course, generational, defined by the differing decades of our intellectual comings-of-age. Educational histories steeped in experiences of radical, communal political action have given way to those founded in theorisations of the power dynamics at work in the complex (a)politics of identification. Some of the colleagues represented here present themselves and their pedagogies as the prod-uct of second-wave activism; others, like Genz, commenced their academic careers 'in the backlash-ridden 1980s and 1990s when fem-inism itself became a dirty word for many and terms like "equality" and "emancipation" lost their innovative appeal and became part of our everyday vocabulary'. This is supplemented by Catherine Bates' observation in 'Teaching Queer Theory: Judith Butler, Shakespeare and *She's the Man*' (Chapter 4) that gender modules informed by third-wave theoretical thinking are no easier than feminism to 'sell' to a contemporary student clientele: 'If feminism is seen as not rel-evant *any more*', she notes, 'then queer theory can sometimes be viewed as too niche *in the first place*.' Further, as even the most radical theories – Bates discusses Butler's concept of gender as performance – become normalised, teaching gender becomes a process of repeatedly rearticulating a sense of urgency around the debates that structure our classroom engagements.

Discussing the canonising processes of literary theory anthologies, Bates points out that universities in the United Kingdom were late adopters of queer theory within their teaching of gender. Even so, if this critical paradigm was the Last Big Thing, there does seem a gen-uine uncertainty as to what the Next Big Thing might be. Earnshaw's chapter hints at the possibility that our students' apoliticism might be aggravated by a kind of 'trouble with authority' inherent in the humanities: a fundamental belief of the liberal English classroom that a single point of view should never hold total dominance. 'My assumption', he states, '... is that, politically, teaching in HE is informed by a broadly liberal attitude, which, being a default or dominant position, does not require explicit commitment in a way that might be controversial, given prevailing pedagogic norms.' As was suggested at the beginning of this introduction, and as becomes apparent in Earnshaw's reflection on the utility of examining even our most dearly held pedagogical assumptions, the debate about teaching gender conducted in this volume raises more far-reaching anxieties, about our discipline, about the purpose and value of the humanities, and about the various transitions (ideological, pedagogical, economic) that English Studies is currently undergoing.

With some of these concerns in mind, the volume concludes with Ros Ballaster's account of designing and developing a Women's Studies course at Oxford University, 'Women's Studies, Gender Studies, Feminist Studies? Designing and Delivering a Course in Gender at Postgraduate Level' (Chapter 12). In her discussion, Ballaster describes the issues raised by the different kinds of academic practice the discipline of Gender Studies brings together; by the role of theory (and its distinction from 'method' or practice) in the curriculum; the pedagogical distinctions that arise with a move to a postgraduate level; as well as the play between single discipline options and the wider field of Gender Studies. In a collection concerned with the multiple incarnations of English Studies, this final chapter points firmly towards the intimate relationship English Studies has always fostered with developmental Gender Studies, and thus the central role that English Studies is able to command within interdisciplinary engagements in gender.

We would like to thank all the contributors gathered here for their generosity in sharing their experience and expertise, and we would offer such solidarity as a model of resistance to what Andermahr, in Chapter 2, calls 'the alienated and product-driven model of education within which we now work'. The chapters bear witness to the fact that teaching, sharing and inspiring are still very much at the heart of what we do. Such mutual professional support has of course formed the basis for the work of the English Subject Centre, the future of which, in these straightened times of writing, seems bleak. In acknowledgement of their invaluable work over the past decade, we would like to thank Ben Knights and all the English Subject Centre staff, and dedicate this book to them.

Works Cited

Knights, Ben (2008) *Masculinities in Text and Teaching* (Basingstoke: Palgrave Macmillan).

2
Gender and the Student Experience: Teaching Feminist Writing in the Post-Feminist Classroom

Sonya Andermahr

This chapter examines student perceptions of gender, and feminism in particular, in the context of English Studies in Higher Education.[1] Based on my experience of teaching a third-year option in 'Feminist Fiction' at the University of Northampton since 2000, it uses the results of a long-term study of student perceptions of the module to assess students' relationship to feminist texts and their attitudes to gender as a category of literary and cultural analysis in the classroom. The questionnaire asked students what they understood by the terms 'feminism' and 'feminist text'; about the relevance of feminism today; and about the relative significance of gender as a category of analysis. I was interested to see whether students thought other vectors of social experience such as race, class and sexuality were equally, less or more important than gender.

The findings show that among students who opt for women's writing modules, there are contradictory attitudes to the concept of gender. The majority of students see gender as an important category of social experience and analysis, shaping their reading choices and pleasures; at the same time, they resist the implications of feminist concepts of structural inequality and social determinism, arguing that gender 'doesn't matter', or that other factors such as race signify more. Students are particularly resistant to feminist theories of 'difference', which they see as positing men as the other. On the whole, I identify a liberal rather than a radical feminist agenda among contemporary students. Paradoxically, however, students are often most moved by texts that foreground gender differences in the starkest terms, pointing to a deep-seated anxiety about gender and belying the positive equal rights discourse. Overall, the findings suggest that students are both drawn to and wary of feminist discourses and of privileging gender. They point to ongoing contemporary anxieties about students' own gender identities and of the continuing salience of gender in social and cultural life. The chapter concludes with a discussion of how these issues might be utilised and explored at the level of pedagogy.

Feminist fiction and social change

In 1989, when I began teaching and researching the subject, the 'feminist novel' seemed to be a more or less clearly defined category, signifying a kind of fiction inspired by and informing the women's movement of the 1960s and 1970s, and published by presses such as Virago and the Women's Press. The American classic of the genre is Marilyn French's *The Women's Room*, and I remember Margaret Atwood's *Surfacing*, Michèle Roberts' *A Piece of the Night*, Joan Barfoot's *Gaining Ground* and Gillian Hanscombe's *Between Friends* from numerous Women's Studies and women's writing courses in the late 1980s and early 1990s. Increasingly, however, the authors I teach under this heading have a more tangential relationship to the term 'feminism'; indeed, at times, they seem to actively resist it. In the contemporary genre of 'feminist' writing, there are fewer feminist role models; indeed in some texts, such as Jeanette Winterson's *The PowerBook* and Patricia Duncker's *Hallucinating Foucault*, there is no woman protagonist in the conventional sense, but rather a range of gender indeterminate narrators and characters including web-based cyborgs, cross-dressed figures, women passing as men and androgynous time-travellers. These figures do not so much tell us about women's experience, but blur gender boundaries and call sexual difference into question. Moreover, the existence of a political women's movement is no longer part of students' experience; indeed, the women's liberation movement came to an end before the current generation of students was even born.

In *Beyond Feminist Aesthetics* (1989), Rita Felski argued that 'the variety of feminist positions makes it difficult to establish absolute and unambiguous criteria for determining what constitutes a feminist narrative' (13). She suggests:

> [I]t is difficult to draw a clear line separating the 'feminist' text from any 'woman-centred' narrative with a female protagonist.... Although not all woman-centred texts are feminist, however, it is certainly true that most feminist literary texts have until now been centred around a female protagonist, a consequence of the key status of subjectivity to second-wave feminism, in which the notion of female experience, whatever its theoretical limitations, has been a guiding one. (13–14)

At the height of Anglo-American and French-oriented theories of the female tradition and *écriture féminine*, Felski was arguing against the concept of a formal aesthetic, arguing rather that the 'political value of literary texts from the standpoint of feminism can be determined only by an investigation into their social functions in relation to the interests of women in a particular historical context' (2). She focused her study on the autobiographical realist genre of feminist literature, which seemed to her to be contributing to the establishment of a feminist counter-public sphere. However, in terms of both genre and the character and focus of feminist narrative, there have been significant changes in recent years. Older feminist genres – the Bildungsroman, the confessional novel, the coming out novel – have in part been replaced by new genres such as the lesbian picaresque, historical metafiction and the postmodern novel, which foreground a multiplicity of fictional and intertextual selves. Consequently, it is much more difficult to assess what constitutes feminist fiction in the contemporary postmodern context of hybrid discourses, forms, audiences and markets, and in which there is no clearly defined feminist movement.

Having considered the centrality of feminism in my teaching, recent experience has led to a number of questions: Does it matter that designated 'feminist fiction' has no necessary relation to a feminist 'movement'? Indeed, does feminist fiction even exist as a genre category any more? And, even more pressingly, is 'feminism' a concept that is now superseded in our literary classrooms? 'Feminism' as a term certainly doesn't sell fiction any more, if it ever did; publishers avoid it, as Leslie Dick found when she published her first novel in the late 1980s: 'Serpent's Tail...adamantly refused to have either the word "feminism" or the word "psychoanalysis" anywhere near the book's cover or publicity. They thought it would "put people off" ' (Dick 205). Interestingly, they preferred to market the book as 'postmodernist'. Those of us teaching 'feminism' face similar dilemmas in the marketing of our own courses. My own, as I shall now discuss, is a case in point.

The module

The module, 'feminist fiction'[2] examines approximately ten texts in the context of contemporary feminist theory. It is divided into four paradigms, framing the fiction in terms of generic and theoretical trends within feminist literature. Table 2.1 lists the texts that have been taught since 2000/01:

Table 2.1   Third-year option module, 'feminist fiction'

- **Romance:** Jane Rule, *Desert of the Heart*; Margaret Atwood, *Lady Oracle*; Helen Zahavi, *Dirty Weekend*; Sarah Waters, *Tipping the Velvet* and *Fingersmith*; Maggie O'Farrell, *My Lover's Lover*.

- **Science fiction:** Joanna Russ, *The Female Man*; Marge Piercy, *Woman on the Edge of Time*; Margaret Atwood, *The Handmaid's Tale*; Octavia Butler, *Kindred*; Marge Piercy, *Body of Glass*.

- **Postmodernism:** Angela Carter, *Wise Children*; Jeanette Winterson, *Written on the Body*; Michèle Roberts, *Flesh and Blood*.

- **Psychoanalysis:** Alice Walker, *Possessing the Secret of Joy*; Michèle Roberts, *In the Red Kitchen*; Sarah Schulman, *Empathy*.

There are 13 featured authors from Britain and the US, writing over a period of approximately 30 years, which is broadly coterminous with second- and third-wave feminism. Apart from Rule's novel, which first appeared in 1964, the earliest was published in 1976, the most recent in 2002. The list inevitably reflects my own preferences and interests, consciously promoting stylistically and thematically challenging material, while acknowledging popular literary genres and attempting to represent the diversity of work available.

The survey

Every year during the course, I survey student responses to it.[3] As those who work in the HE sector are aware, the staff–student relationship is increasingly mediated by formulaic and standardised surveys, which serve to add to the alienated and product-driven model of education within which we now work. I wanted to use the survey to find out something of real value, hence I focused questions specifically on attitudes to feminism and the salience of gender. The questions are listed in Table 2.2:

Table 2.2   Feminist fiction questionnaire

1.	What do you understand by the term 'feminism'?
2.	Do you think 'feminism' is still relevant to women's lives today?
3.	What does the category 'feminist text' mean to you?
4.	How important is 'gender' as a category of literary analysis?
5.	Why did you enrol on the module?
6.	Would you describe yourself as a feminist?

All the questions invited open answers, except for question 5, which was multiple choice. The survey results were then used as the basis for a classroom discussion in which students were given the opportunity to elaborate on their views and debate the issues. The results are presented in Tables 2.3–2.9, accompanied by analyses of each set of data.

Regarding student understandings of the term 'feminism' (see Table 2.3), it could be argued that the responses broadly map onto the classic liberal, radical and cultural models of feminism, plus an anti-feminist viewpoint. The majority of students identified feminism with an equal rights agenda and stressed the similar interests of men and women. Typical responses included: 'Feminism is a theory

Table 2.3   Understanding the term 'feminism'

47% defined 'feminism' in terms of equality/equal rights
35% as challenging patriarchal domination
12% as a standpoint theory for women
6% as anti-male discourse

which argues equal rights for both men and women', and 'Feminism is a political movement that promotes equal rights for both sexes.' Another student viewed it as a quintessentially humanist philosophy: 'Feminism is about human rights, not only for women but for anyone oppressed by patriarchal societies.' Such responses emphasise the representativeness of feminism and downplayed differences between the sexes. However, the next biggest percentage saw feminism much more in terms of sexual difference and challenging male power. One student commented: 'Feminism looks at women in opposition to men, and aims to understand and challenge patriarchal and oppressive views.' Another stated: 'Feminism challenges the social construction of femininity.' Yet another declared: 'Feminism is above all about female empowerment.' Here, the focus is on women as a disadvantaged sex class. A smaller group identified feminism with women's perspective and/or promoting women's culture: 'Feminism represents a concern with the experience of women' and 'with the way in which being female is represented in aspects of culture and society'; it 'represents women's interests in politics, business, society, etc.' This view accords with feminist standpoint theory elaborated by sociologists such as Sandra Harding and Nancy Hartsock, in which theory is a product of praxis. A small minority were wary or even hostile to the term, viewing it as compromised by its association with anti-male attitudes and lesbianism: 'It carries the stereotype of butch, bra-burning, men-hating lesbians.' Among those who supported feminist goals, there was a similarly strong feeling that feminism had been negatively stereotyped by mainstream culture and media.

While two-thirds of students gave an apparently whole-hearted endorsement of feminism (Table 2.4), a third expressed some reservations, although no students thought it irrelevant in contemporary society.

Typical attitudes confirming feminism's continued relevance include: 'I think feminism is still relevant as I do not feel that equality

Table 2.4 Is feminism still relevant?

64% said 'Yes, definitely'
36% said 'In some ways'
0% said 'Not really'

between the sexes has been reached'; 'The media still objectifies women and feminism is important in the rejection of these images'; 'Sexism and inequality are still around – further under the surface of society than in the past'. When questioned further, students identified what they saw as the greater freedom of women and equality of the sexes in Western societies, but cited issues such as date rape, racism and unequal pay as justification for feminism's continued relevance: 'It is no longer as relevant as it has been although there are situations, such as the average wage for males and females, where equality has not been reached'; 'In countries where one race, class or caste dominates, women continue to be doubly oppressed because of their gender'.

Some students also commented on the problems caused by a greater emphasis on individualism: 'Generally women have greater independence now but they still have concerns brought about by this independence.' Students recognise that 40 years after the Equal Pay Act was passed, there is still a gender pay gap and they perceive the lack of women in key areas of the economy: 'Women are still outnumbered drastically in industry, etc.; they are paid less for the same jobs as men'; 'Women still hit glass ceilings in companies that consider them reproductive machines'. Students also thought that the 'beauty myth' has much more impact on women than men: 'There is more pressure for them to fit physical ideals'; and that women were still having to choose between their career and motherhood because the 'traditional views persist'. Misgivings about the term appeared to stem from a desire to downplay the conflict of interests between the sexes. 'There is no longer a need for radical feminism'; 'Equality within the public and private spheres is still an issue; however, positive discrimination may be a feminist step too far'. Again, there is more support for a liberal feminist agenda of equal rights, with students expressing discomfort about measures that highlight differences between the sexes.

Asking students what counts as feminist fiction gives rise to a large ragbag of texts, ranging from the anger-fuelled satire of *Dirty Weekend* to Jean Rhys' much more ambivalent *Wide Sargasso Sea*, and seemingly encompassing anything by the Brontës.[4] Students are willing to see it both as any kind of 'woman-centred' writing and as explicitly political writing. The largest single percentage conflated female-authored texts with feminist ones (Table 2.5). One student

Table 2.5 Meaning of 'feminist text'

42% defined it as texts written by and about women
29% as texts written from a feminist perspective
29% as texts offering a critique of and alternative to the gender status quo

defined feminist fiction as 'the female voice in the literary canon, which can cover all kinds of genres and political stances'. Another stated: 'It is literature that is centred on the lives and experiences of women.' Such views testify to an investment in the notion of a female protagonist, even when the texts themselves do not feature one. While the students had been taught about the anti-essentialist critiques of theorists such as Ros Coward, Toril Moi and Felski, many still wished to identify women's writing generally with feminism. In our current post-feminist or even anti-feminist climate, this gesture of identification struck me as significant and poignant. However, the two other viewpoints, amounting to nearly 60%, challenge the 'womanist' model by distinguishing feminist works as different to or critical of the mainstream. One student identified the feminist text as offering a 'critique of the role of women and representing an alternative'; similarly, another stated that feminist fiction 'denaturalizes patriarchal ideology'. Another student commented that it concerned 'sexual, intelligent, daring and/or criminal women who deconstruct stereotypes of women as vulnerable and weak'. One student identified both representativeness and political challenge as key features of the feminist text: 'It is literature written by women, foregrounding the experiences of a female protagonist. The plot usually offers an alternative to the marriage/death conclusion.' All the texts on the module were considered to be feminist texts, with the exception of O'Farrell's *My Lover's Lover*, which was seen as closer to the mainstream genre in terms of both style and politics.

Table 2.6 How important is 'gender' as an analytical category?

55% thought it was 'very important'
36% said 'not as important as other factors'
9% said 'not very important'

Over half the students surveyed underlined the significance of gender, making connections between its operation in social and cultural life: 'Gender is assigned to and controls individuals to keep them within social norms; it therefore impacts upon authors, characters and readers'; 'The study of gender is very revealing in pointing up the extent of myths of female independence'; 'Gender is important in nearly every piece of literature as it affects style and characterization. It's important to consider stereotypes which are attached to gender, and how people conform or rebel against these'. Given that the students chose the module as an option, it is not perhaps surprising that many privileged gender above other categories of analysis, stating, for example: 'For me it is the most obvious and significant aspect of a text.' While the largest group saw gender as a key category of cultural analysis, over a third thought other factors rated as or more highly. One student commented that 'gender influences individual experience; however, it is equally important to take other differences such as race, ethnicity and class into consideration in literary analysis'. Another student stated: 'Race, religion and other forms of discrimination are as important as gender.' Race was repeatedly mentioned, which perhaps reflects its heightened contemporary profile in HE, as well as in the media and society generally. In some ways students see women's writing courses as the place where 'gender' is done, while race is the proper focus of areas like postcolonialism. I think this is a problem both with our modular system, which encourages this kind of compartmentalisation, and the boundary building of the new disciplines. Students did, however, show an awareness of categorisation as posing a problem to the wider reception of feminist and women's writing: 'The category of gender can serve to segregate certain texts if they are only considered as "women's writing" – and subsequently "about" and "for" women – rather than considered for other themes and ideas.' In respect of class, although sociological studies show its continuing salience, as I point out to students, it was rarely cited as an important issue; again, this reflects more widely on educational and social trends. Teaching *Fingersmith*, a novel in which class is seen to structure the heroines' lives and desires, goes some way towards redressing this imbalance. A small minority thought that gender was no longer a significant factor. In class this often emerged as a resistance to seeing women's experience and women's writing as distinctive, and a desire to universalise the issues explored in the fiction

Table 2.7 Reasons for taking the module

91% said 'because the books looked interesting'
64% said 'to learn more about feminism'
18% said 'because I consider myself a feminist'

along the lines of: 'It's not so different for women and men.' Such views evince a desire to downplay sexual difference and foreground general human values. In seminars, they become the basis for useful discussion of texts such as *Possessing the Secret of Joy* and *Written on the Body*, which foreground and de-emphasise gender differences respectively.

The overwhelming majority of students framed their interest in the module in terms of the texts studied (Table 2.7). One student said she wanted to 'explore a different set of texts and theories from the mainstream'. Others identified a tradition of women's writing that they wanted to pursue into the present: 'I wanted to compare previously studied historical women's writing with contemporary feminist writing.'[5] Over half the students expressed a specific interest in feminism: 'I took the module because I am interested in feminism and enjoy reading books by feminist writers.' A few saw the module as addressing them as women: 'As a young woman I find women's writing easier to relate to [than other kinds of literature].' Significantly, while students could tick multiple responses for this question, most chose not to tick the 'I'm a feminist' box. This may suggest that students prefer to represent their relation to feminism as literary, textual or educational, but are less willing to make a personal identification with the term. Feminism in this view becomes just another thing you learn about, with no necessary implications for personal life. However, there is a clear hunger for women's history and for feminist knowledge; students, particularly women students, want to be given the tools to contextualise their own situations, as the following comment illustrates: 'I didn't feel that before university I had been educated in the history of women and gender. I wanted to be able to further understand the place of women in the world.'

When asked directly, the majority of students were willing to identify as feminist in some way. One student commented: 'Yes, I see

Table 2.8   Would you describe yourself as a feminist?

27% said 'Yes, definitely'
54% said 'In some ways'
19% said 'Not really'

society and culture throughout history as the causes of any differences that are supposed to exist. I support complete equality between the sexes and think the same opportunities in terms of employment or family role should be available to men and women.' Another said: 'I don't see why my gender should inhibit my life choices, hence I would describe myself as feminist.' However, given that this is a self-selecting module, it is perhaps surprising that there was not a more unequivocal identification with feminism. Nearly a fifth of students did not want to associate themselves with the term or did not think it relevant. Sometimes this was because it implied an unwanted collective identity, as in the following comment: 'I don't really feel that I have ever had cause to be feminist. I feel I have come from a generation that doesn't have gender at its heart as much as individualism. I feel I would more likely fight for my right as a person, rather than as a woman specifically.' Sometimes this was because of the stigma attached to feminism; as one student put it: 'I think feminism has become a taboo within society, with women wanting to distance themselves from radical views associated with the 1960s and 70s feminist movement. Now women need to maintain a contemporary feminist perspective, to evolve their own ideas and [challenge] stereotypes.' There was also a perception that some forms of feminism are too radical in their challenge to the status quo: 'Some of my views are feminist: I believe that women should have equal rights to men. However, I disagree with certain radical ideas such as women and men swapping roles, and the man taking the role of househusband, which would break the maternal bond.' Some students see feminism as a utopian ideal – 'I agree with the principle but it is hard to put into practice' – which underscores the importance of literature classes as a space for exploring gender issues. One comment summed up the contradictory attitude to feminism: 'I would say "no", but those who know me may disagree – I think I may be a liberal feminist!'

Feminism in the classroom

Overall, the results make interesting but inconclusive reading, high-lighting the ambiguity and fluidity of the term 'feminism' and the sophisticated nature of student negotiations of the term. The students articulate a range of positions in relation to feminist politics, and they mostly endorse the set of values it represents, just as I would expect of students on a self-chosen women's writing module. What they are not so willing to do, however, is to own the term as a way of describing themselves and their own lives. While students largely concur with the ideas associated with feminism, they are reluctant to identify as feminist, to the point of disavowing the concept. Like the Serpent's Tail publisher, they find the label 'off-putting' and old-fashioned. According to Natasha Walter in *The New Feminism*, this stance is typical of young women today, who subscribe to a feminism based on an Equal Rights agenda, in which friendships with men and therefore conflict avoidance are important factors. Although Walter optimistically sees a new confidence around sexual matters between men and women, in my classes, anxiety around an antagonistic sexual politics seems particularly strong.

Rachel Cusk, writing recently in *The Guardian*, identifies a worrying disavowal of feminism and, indeed, of the whole concept of 'women's identity' in contemporary society. The traditional female subject matter of motherhood and family life is now met with widespread intolerance, and the ideology of individualism has made it seem as if the battles of feminism have been won; in consequence,

> If a woman feels suffocated and grounded and bewildered by her womanhood, she feels these things alone, as an individual: there is currently no public unity among women, because since the peak of feminism the task of woman has been to assimilate herself with man. She is, therefore, occluded, scattered, disguised... What today's woman has gained in personal freedom she has lost in political caste. Hers is still the second sex, but she has earned the right to dissociate herself from it. (2)

My students expressed ambivalence about Cusk's argument. On the one hand, they fully agreed that individualism has made it harder for women to articulate their shared and different interests. They also acknowledged the point that women fear being labelled *as* different. Studying Atwood and Winterson, students were keen to point out that these writers do not define their work as primarily 'feminist' and are ambivalent about the category of 'women's writing'. According to Cusk, 'Women, then, might cease to produce "women's writing" not because they are freer but because they are more ashamed, less certain of a general receptiveness and even, perhaps, because they suspect they might be vilified' (2). This certainly accords with students' experiences of articulating feminist views and points up the problem of how they may express themselves without inviting charges of antagonism and inferiority. On the other hand, they rather like being individuals and are not sure that they want to 'write the book of repetition', as Cusk puts it. Their response may be to do with their age and the fact that most of them are not mothers. They are caught in painful contradictions between leading individual lives and feeling silenced as women. By exploring these issues in fictional form, the module at the very least helps students to recognise some of the contradictions of contemporary sexual politics.

In this context, it is interesting that one of the most popular texts I have taught in recent years is Helen Zahavi's uncompromising, angry and radical feminist *Dirty Weekend*. Compared with the sophisticated blurring of gender identities found in many contemporary texts, this novel returns us to a dichotomous world of sexual antagonism and violence, and it is this very visceral quality that seems to appeal to students. While its female revenge fantasy may induce a kind of guilty pleasure in some, it gives students permission to discuss latent forms of misogyny. The same can be said of Alice Walker's *Possessing the Secret of Joy*, a novel about the destructive effects of female genital mutilation in which the female protagonist undergoes a literal and grotesque form of disembodiment, and which signifies oppression rather than liberation. And, while this text arguably allows white, Western women to displace 'female oppression' onto black female bodies, it does serve to reconnect students with the global vulnerability of women. These texts say something that is absent both from the playful antagonism of 'chick lit' and from the slippery androgyny of some postmodern fiction, and perhaps articulate for students a set of issues around sexuality that have been largely repressed in today's nominally egalitarian culture. This would seem to bear out Cusk's view that women's writing 'by nature would not seek to deny equivalence in the male world. It would be a writing that sought to express a distinction, not deny it' (2). Perhaps the biggest surprise has been the student reception of Sarah Schulman's *Empathy*, a novel that explores lesbian existence as a form of symbolic abjection resulting in a 'splitting' of the subject's consciousness. Given the still-pervasive fear of 'the L word' and the students' rejection of 'radical' and 'extreme' ideas, I thought this would be an unpopular text that I would have to 'sell' heavily in terms of stylistic innovation and depicting 'marginal' experience. In fact, apart from some initial difficulty with comprehension, students displayed remarkably little discomfort with the subject matter and many found it relatively easy to 'identify' with Anna O's predicament and its radical solution: becoming a 'man' (in psychic terms) to enable her to love women within prevailing social norms.

If much contemporary fiction by radical and feminist writers seeks to go beyond gender, mainstream women's fiction – especially so-called chick lit and the romance-successor genres – continues to engage the older categories of female identity, to deal with 'female selves', however caricatured. The mainstream is where many of my students go for character identification and recognition – problems of body image, finding and losing love, and so on. This is why, despite often being embarrassed by their investment in this fiction, students often want to refer to it or do a dissertation on the feminism, post- or otherwise, of *Bridget Jones*. As tutors we should not ignore the emotional appeal of such fiction and the psychic investments being made in it. I include study of popular genres and a strand on psychoanalysis because I want students to understand the processes of desire at work in both feminist and non-feminist discourses. For the last two years I have been teaching Maggie O'Farrell's *My Lover's Lover* in the Romance category, thinking it was a good text to launch the module as it bears similarities to the mainstream genre but also explores sexual politics through its use of gothic conventions. In fact, for two years running it has been the least popular text studied; students have called it 'escapist' and 'clichéd' and tend to judge it unfavourably compared with what they see as more serious, challenging and 'literary' works. I don't fully understand this response, as I find the *Rebecca*-like relationship between the two female protagonists, Lily and Sinead, challenges simplistic definitions of female identification. What my experience teaching Schulman and O'Farrell demonstrates is the difficulty of second-guessing student reactions, and the complexity of their response to texts.

As a teacher and researcher, I am closely involved in the dissemination of feminist fiction. By adopting texts year after year, I give certain texts a profile, helping in a small way to keep them in print. I advocate and proselytise on their behalf, to persuade students of their exhilarating if not liberating content. What I wonder increasingly, as we move further away from the historical moment of the second wave, is whether I am selling, not just 'feminist fiction' but 'feminism' itself as a kind of (necessary) fiction. By this I mean not simply whether the issues raised by feminists still have purchase for today's generation, which is living in a radically different setting from that of 20 or 30 years ago; although, as I hope the survey showed, this is a valuable line of enquiry. In another sense, there is something strange about teaching a discourse that was once 'of the moment' in political and sociological terms and has now in some sense passed into history. A nostalgic element pervades our teaching, and we ourselves are no longer sure whether feminism is primarily a transformative political ideology, a part of social history or an intellectual body of knowledge with an appropriate list of learning outcomes. The contemporary contexts for feminist material in HE suggest that its discourses may be deployed in diverse ways across the syllabus, not simply as women's writing or Women's Studies, and the student body relates to it differently as a result. Sometimes it makes less sense to position Winterson with Atwood, say, rather than with Martin Amis or Salman Rushdie, or in the context of the literary fantastic. As Judith Butler reminds us, we should be wary of the regulatory function of identity categories: 'The feminist "we" is always and only a phantasmatic construction, one that has its purposes, but which denies the internal complexity and indeterminacy of the term and constitutes itself only through the exclusion of some part of the constituency that it simultaneously seeks to represent' (Butler 142). With this caveat in mind, my answer to the question 'Is there still something called feminist fiction?' would be, yes. While there may be no single entity 'feminist fiction', feminism remains an important touchstone for the kind of writing radical writers are producing. In many ways Felski's 1989 definition still holds good:

> The defining feature of the feminist text is a recognition and rejection of the ideological basis of the traditional script of heterosexual romance characterized by female passivity, dependence, and subordination, and an attempt to develop an alternative narrative and symbolic framework within which female identity can be located. (129)

Teaching strategies

In this concluding section, I would like to suggest a couple of teaching strategies for engaging students in feminist debates about the salience of gender as an analytic category.

What does feminist literature look like?

The first involves working with students to delineate what 'feminism' in a text 'looks like'. Together, we produce a list of features that reflect the variety of feminist discourses available in contemporary texts and also distinguish them from more mainstream 'commercial' fiction, asking as follows:

Table 2.9   Features of the feminist text

Does the text call normative gender ideologies into question either by

- foregrounding wo/men's oppression within patriarchy or
- foregrounding the constructedness and oppressiveness of gender categories *per se*?

Does it seek to resist that oppression through narrative form or process?

Does it engage feminist theories of gendered reality?

To what extent does it seek to transform readers' consciousness about gendered reality?

Posing such questions may lead students to conclude that contemporary feminist fiction can challenge gender ideology by focusing on women's experience, as in Atwood's work, but this is not necessarily the case: Winterson's male narrators, for example, often testify to the oppressiveness of gender norms as much as her female ones do. One learning outcome of the exercise is the recognition that contemporary feminist fiction has acknowledged Butler's insight and frequently works to complicate foundationalist notions of sexual difference.

Testing feminist theories

A second strategy involves 'testing' feminist theories of sex/gender against specific texts.[6] One practical exercise requires students to analyse a piece of women's writing in terms of these theoretical models and to evaluate what each model both permits and forecloses in terms of exploring gender identity and experience. In the 'postmodernism' and 'psychoanalysis' sections of my module, I introduce students to the concept of 'sexed embodiment' (with reference to Julia Kristeva and Luce Irigaray; see Moi (1987) and the 'performative' model of gender identity (such as that offered by Judith Butler). If the task of such feminist writing is to introduce the bodily experience of women's difference into language and writing, the task for the students is to evaluate how those categories of 'bodily experience' and 'women' operate in the critical and literary text. The students must consider whether, in setting out to demystify and deconstruct naturalised gender constructions, such theoretical models do not also place the very concept of 'woman' under erasure. This task can facilitate productive discussion. For example, some of my students concluded that, while Winterson's *Written on the Body* permits a deconstruction of the romance mode and destabilisation of gender identities, it arguably refuses an exploration of what it means to love *as* a woman inhabiting a female body. However, the text can also produce readings that exceed theoretical containment; in their presentations, students produced evidence for reading the text variously as a lesbian text, as a queer text and as an example of *écriture féminine*.

Ultimately, the study of feminist texts in the classroom offers numerous opportunities for exploring the subjects of women's history and Women's Studies. It also goes some way towards fulfilling the still-evident desire for narratives of female experience, while simultaneously questioning identity categories and foundational narratives. Seen in this way, the feminist text makes possible an exploration of the discourses of sex, gender and feminism, and in the process reasserts the value of feminist theory and pedagogy in the post-feminist English classroom.

Notes

1. Some of these data were presented in the following conference papers: 'Teaching Feminist Fiction Today' ('Teaching Contemporary Women's Writing in the 21st Century', English Subject Centre/University of Brighton, 2007); 'Selling' Feminist Fiction in the 21st Century Classroom' ('Contemporary Women's Fiction in the Marketplace', CWWN/University of Wales, Bangor, 2006).
2. The module was renamed 'Contemporary Women's Writing' in 2007–2008 to facilitate a pathway in 'women's writing' in the second and third years of study. The renamed module maintains the feminist framework of the original module and recruits similar numbers of (mainly female) students.
3. Between 2000–2001 and 2009–2010, a total of 137 students taking the module were surveyed. On average, only 1 in 15 students enrolled on the module is male. My mainly female students are concerned that so few men take the module, and discuss what their boyfriends and/or husbands think about the course.
4. Students also identified works by Mary Wollstonecraft, Mrs Gaskell, George Eliot, Mary Elizabeth Braddon, Olive Schreiner, Charlotte Perkins Gilman, Virginia Woolf and Jean Rhys as feminist.
5. The existence of a second-year module, 'Women's Writing 1750–1900', allows students to pursue a 'pathway' in women's writing.
6. Susan Watkins' *Twentieth Century Women's Writing* is very useful here; Watkins first discusses a number of feminist theories, then uses the theory to 'read' a chosen text, and finally uses the text to reveal problems or gaps in the theories.

Works Cited

Atwood, Margaret (1982) *Lady Oracle* (London: Virago).
—— (1994) *Surfacing* (London: Virago).
—— (1996) *The Handmaid's Tale* (London: Vintage).
Barfoot, Joan (1999) *Gaining Ground* (London: The Women's Press).
Butler, Judith (1990) *Gender Trouble: Feminism and the Subversion of Identity* (London and New York: Routledge).
Butler, Octavia (2004) *Kindred* (London: Bluestreak).
Carter, Angela (1992) *The Passion of the New Eve* (London: Virago).
——(1993) *Wise Children* (London: Vintage).

Coward, Ros (1980) ' "This novel changes lives": Are women's novels feminist novels? A Response to Rebecca O'Rourke's "Summer Reading" ', *Feminist Review* 5: 53–64.

Cusk, Rachel (2009) 'Shakespeare's Daughters', *Guardian Review*, Saturday 12 December, 2.

Dick, Leslie (1989) 'Feminism, Writing, Postmodernism', *From My Guy to Sci-Fi: Women's Writing in the Postmodern World*, ed. Helen Carr (London: Pandora), 204–14.

Duncker, Patricia (1996) *Hallucinating Foucault* (London: Serpent's Tail).

Felski, Rita (1989) *Beyond Feminist Aesthetics* (London: Hutchinson Radius).

Fielding, Helen (2001) *Bridget Jones' Diary: A Novel* (London: Picador).

French, Marilyn (1997) *The Women's Room* (London: Virago).

Hanscombe, Gillian (1990) *Between Friends* (London: The Women's Press).

Harding, Sandra (1986) *The Science Question in Feminism* (New York: Cornell University Press).

Hartsock, Nancy (1997) *The Feminist Standpoint Revisited* (Boulder, CO: Westview Press).

Kay, Jackie (2001) *Trumpet* (London: Picador).

Moi, Toril (ed.) (1987) *French Feminist Thought: A Reader* (Oxford: Blackwell).

—— (1992) 'Female, Feminine, Feminist', *The Feminist Reader*, eds Catherine Belsey and Jane Moore (Oxford: Basil Blackwell).

O'Farrell, Maggie (2003) *My Lover's Lover* (London: Headline Review).

Piercy, Marge (1992) *Body of Glass* (London: Penguin).

Rhys, Jean (2000) *Wide Sargasso Sea* (London: Penguin).

Roberts, Michèle (1978) *A Piece of the Night* (London: The Women's Press).

—— (1991) *In the Red Kitchen* (London: Minerva).

—— (1994) *Flesh and Blood* (London: Virago).

Rule, Jane (1986) *Desert of the Heart* (London: Pandora).

Russ, Joanna (1985) *The Female Man* (London: The Women's Press).

Schulman, Sarah (1993) *Empathy* (London: Sheba Feminist Press).

Walker, Alice (1993) *Possessing the Secret of Joy* (London: Vintage).

Walter, Natasha (1999) *The New Feminism* (London: Virago).

Waters, Sarah (1998) *Tipping the Velvet* (London: Virago).

—— (1999) *Affinity* (London: Virago).

—— (2002) *Fingersmith* (London: Virago).

Waugh, Patricia (2006) 'The Woman Writer and the Continuities of Feminism', *A Concise Companion to Contemporary British Fiction*, ed. James F. English (Oxford: Blackwell).

Winterson, Jeanette (1992) *Written on the Body* (London: Cape).

—— (2000) *The PowerBook* (London: Cape).

Zahavi, Helen (1992) *Dirty Weekend* (London: Flamingo).

3
Teaching English to Gender Students: Collaborative Encounters with Print and Digital Texts

Ann Kaloski Naylor

While much of this volume addresses the role of gender in English HE, this chapter considers the practice of teaching contemporary fiction in an environment where students have a reasonable understanding of gender and are favourably disposed towards feminist theory, but do not always see the value of 'English'. I assess two pedagogical relationships between gender and 'English': (1) the resistance to fiction by some gender students and (2) the value of teaching the new field of digital fiction. By reflecting on these two significant challenges to English Studies I identify particularly feminist interactions between 'English' and 'gender', connections that I hope will be of use to teachers in both areas. My own field is contemporary literature and culture, and I teach at the Centre for Women's Studies at the University of York, a postgraduate unit offering interdisciplinary degrees within humanities and social science.[1]

I studied for my BA in the mid-1980s. I was in my thirties when I started my degree in social studies (major) and English but soon switched to concentrate on English, as this seemed to me where the interesting questions could be asked, and where the answers were not obvious. Although my institution (University College, St John's, York) did not offer a degree in Women's Studies at that time, I was immensely lucky to take Women's Studies modules with inspirational teachers, and this rich learning environment enabled me to grasp ideas based on my experiences and my fuzzy, 'instinctive' understandings, and to develop knowledge that made sense to me 'as a woman'. I still treasure this student-centred way of learning, part of the last century's wave of radical, participatory educational theory that valued diverse experiences and different ways of knowing as both a method of teaching and a step in destabilising canonical knowledge.[2] But radical pedagogy is about more than subversion, and I like to see my teaching as 'an argument for pleasure in the confusion of boundaries and for responsibility in their construction', to borrow a phrase Donna Haraway uses to describe her famous 'Cyborg Manifesto' (150).

In my undergraduate days I experienced an energetic relationship between 'English' and 'women' gendered as authors, characters and readers. I recall the introductory lecture for a 'Women and Literature' module around 1987 when Mary Eagleton questioned not only women, not only literature, but also that pesky, complicated, adventurous 'and'. What connects 'women' and 'literature'? Does that 'and' create space for the gendered reader and gendered author and, if so, what is the landscape of that space? How far does it conceal conflicts and incongruities, and how far does it open up and question not only literature but also women, creating new and vibrant relationships between the two? A quarter of a century later I turn again to this 'and', always present as I teach and learn about 'women' and 'literature', and 'gender' and 'English', and 'feminism' and 'fiction'. How can my teaching enliven this 'and' such that students see the relevance of both 'gender' and 'English', and that old and new relationships between the two can be understood?

Resistance is fruitful

In this first section I consider ways in which resistance to fiction is articulated by Women's Studies students and offer some strategies to reduce, overturn or even exploit such opposition. Many of the key texts of Western feminism integrate readings of male texts into their ground-breaking analyses (de Beauvoir 1949/1953, Millet 1970, Greer 1970), while Women's Studies (before it became Gender Studies) would typically include literature, as students examined textual images of women, or analysed women-authored novels. So clear was the connection within this emerging field between women and literature that a US-based anthology published in 1991 was entitled *Feminisms: An Anthology of Literary Theory and Criticism*. It was a capacious and theoretically wide-ranging volume that felt free to identify its literary premise as, simply, 'feminisms', asserting a central literary space for gendered understandings. Such a claim fits well with stories told by the founders of the Centre for Women's Studies at York, who speak of the early years of CWS (mid-1980s) with deep affection for the disciplinary mixes that nurtured students, staff (and feminism),[3] and with my own impression of multi- and interdisciplinary thinking when I began my studies there in 1990 (a significant year, as I shall suggest).

Within a few years, however, it would not be possible to see 'lit crit' in such a key role within Gender Studies. I still offer *Feminisms* to my students, while recognising that even the updated 1997 volume is read in the second decade of the twenty-first century as not only partial, but also historical, and a similar volume published now would need to include the radical shifts in ideas of gender and of 'English', and probably require a more complex title and subtitle.

Once upon a time gender pedagogy was concerned with opening up students to the differences between biology (sex) and socialisation (gender), suggesting that women were not fundamentally tied to femininity, and *vice versa*, and debating ideas of difference, sameness and equality. This was stirring stuff, but many questions were unanswerable in this framework and, by 1990, this murky space was being populated by poststructuralist ideas and the related development of queer theory (from Foucault and Sedgwick, and canonised by the reception to Butler's 1990 *Gender Trouble*). Meanings of 'gender' were multiplying and the place of 'women' within such theories was not at all self-evident,[4] opening up rich debates about women's lives, femininity and queer readings.[5]

Students come into this thrilling environment of feminist theory and their resistance to reading fiction can be quite stunning. As might be expected from those who come to women's and Gender Studies in part to 'change the world', these resistances are political as well as academic. 'What's the point of fiction when so many women live under poverty and violence?' is the explicit classroom challenge, though the 'huh!' of unarticulated resistance is much trickier to handle than more strident opposition. Part of my challenge is to help these students identify and express their hostility, and then to work with their understandings: they may still want to argue for more materialism in women's and Gender Studies, but at least they will be able to argue well. For the benefit of 'English' graduates too, it is necessary to be clear about literature's role in women's and Gender Studies, as vague peer antagonism to fiction can unbalance the sense of purpose of those students who 'love reading' and who have previously enjoyed 'English'. While the resisters can be hard to handle in the classroom, at its best their explicit challenges not only enliven but also deepen understandings of 'English' and 'gender' among those students for whom delight in literature has sometimes led to an ignorance of the gendered aesthetics and politics of their beloved texts.

Thinking about this chapter, I recalled a session from my time as a Women's Studies MA student (in the early 1990s) in which our tutor, Trev Broughton, divided the class into two sub-groups who each had to discuss, then debate as a whole group, the relationship between fiction and Women's Studies. The trick was, we had to argue against our former discipline, so literature (and other humanities) students like me were forced to consider the limits of 'English' for understanding gender, while the social science graduates were challenged to identify the value of 'English' as a component of gendered knowledge. Our pre-session activity had been to browse some of the key and emerging texts of feminist literary criticism (for example, Moi 1985; Eagleton 1986; Showalter 1986), so we had all been exposed to relationships between literary criticism and Women's Studies. Social science students acknowledged that fiction can sometimes give flesh to nascent ideas (Marge Piercy's *Woman on the Edge of Time* [1976] was cited), as well as popularise controversial ideas (for example, Zoe Fairbairns' *Benefits* [1979] and Caeia March's *Three Ply Yarn* [1986]). We humanities graduates, on the other hand, were forced to argue that fiction within the academy was written from a limited spectrum of social and national groups (and we recited as many 1980s' identity groups as we could muster) and that therefore its 'situated knowledge'[6] was stuck in privileged mud. This strategy worked well to give us understanding of and respect for disciplinary differences and helped us all, I think, shine a light on a new facet of 'English'. It also gave all students a stronger foundation from which to develop interdisciplinary methods.

Looking back, I think the success of this class was partly because Women's Studies in the UK was on a disciplinary cusp: literature still mattered but there were cracks. And it is those 'cracks' I have been delving into with my students for the past 15 years or so, partly through challenging them (and myself, it has to be admitted) to read conventional fiction more carefully, with attention to words as well as context, and partly through introducing new modes of fiction (that is, digital texts) that disturb assumptions of literariness and literary meaning.

Two methods sometimes enrich this exploration: expanding feminist reader-response theory to encourage students to read the texts irreverently, and drawing out the power and pleasure of words in the development of identities and nascent political awareness. The first method is personal and unpredictable, the second academic and structured, and together they open up texts (and gender) to different meanings. One workshop I try most years is this: I give the students two short autobiographies of reading, one by Lynn Pearce (1995) and one by Alison Hennegan (1998), and ask them to write their own version focusing on a fictional text or series of texts that have made a difference to their gendered lives. Many students find this delightfully inspiring, as they identify patterns in their younger lives. One comment on the disturbing efficacy of gendered space has stayed with me: 'I've realized that my brother and I always went to different shelves in the bookshop – we wouldn't touch each other's choices'. As for texts, *Jane Eyre* is frequently cited, though rarely by UK students. The status of this Brontë novel as classic British literature has enabled its tortured explorations of girlhood and womanhood to nurture feminist desires in women from Russia, Hong Kong, Taiwan and India. There are some other obvious contenders: *Oranges Are Not the Only Fruit* (many of the heterosexual students comment on the treatment of Melanie by Winterson); Judy Blume's children's stories, of girls – *girls* – growing up in Western culture; *Little Women* (and yes, all the women are always Jo, though if the book survives new reading cultures I await a third wave, mildly camp, feminist Amy); and, latterly, the Harry Potter books ('I was Hermione'; 'I hated Hermione'; 'I was Harriet Potter'; though no one, as yet, asserting 'I am J.K. Rowling').

Yet increasing numbers of students do find it difficult to think about how their own lives are gendered – particularly young students from developed countries for whom equality for themselves seems a given. For such students the challenge is to unpick common sense, and helping them learn how to think critically about their own lives is a pivotal step. This autobiographical method makes the process personal rather than intimate, and collaborative; it enables students of different ages, cultures, sexualities and political persuasions, and from different disciplinary backgrounds, to offer part of their story to the group within a clear structure, and enables me as teacher to pick out nascent theoretical and critical strands to weave into the discussion. The essays also work as a great introduction for students unfamiliar with anglophone 'lit crit'.

There are usually one or two resisters, but I have found that even those who say that fiction has never made a difference to their lives are drawn into the stories of their peers, and *always* remember a book that once meant a lot to them, often within socialised family and community relations ('Nan read this to me', or 'This was passed around beneath the desks at school'). In this way I am able to draw out ways that fiction, through storying and imagination, activates ideas of gender, and then move from individual to more theorisable ideas. While some excellent colleagues eschew such personal pedagogy, especially for privileged white women, my teaching experience leads me to conclude that students still need to start with what they know – their own lives – in order to learn how to be empathetic, insightful critics. Then they can move out of their world. At its best, 'English' disturbs accepted logical knowledge: when fiction is valued as 'useful' it is stripped of its power to help us open up ideas – about gender in this case – that we may not even have envisaged. These two articles work well, too, as a prelude for studying fiction from many different cultures, offering insight into the value and limitations of exoticising or over-identifying gendered relationships with authors, characters and narratives; as Pearce argues, intellectually and emotionally appropriating texts via personal, imaginative readings is a temporary phase which, for mature understandings, must be replaced by a recognition that some texts speak to us more than others (90).

Digital fiction: an introduction

The years bordering the millennium were, then, a fascinating time to be teaching English literature. The 'words on the page' no longer ruled and were, in fact, often suffocated by Theory, leaving 'Reader, I married him' gasping for air. This overt recognition within some areas of the discipline that knowledge is always political was of course welcomed by those of us imbuing our pedagogy (and our lives) with gendered and other material and cultural understandings. Colleagues who teach in literature departments offer sociological, political and historiographic texts to their students alongside literary texts. I too do this. But for me, an English teacher in Women's Studies, the challenge is to help students to open up to the power of fictional knowledge. My teaching shifts and develops as theories of gender shift and develop, but sometimes I have felt the loss of text in the Text. Ironically, perhaps, it is through moving away from teaching only print fiction and bringing digital fiction into the classroom that for me (and, I think, for my students) the text has been energised. Computers and the Internet, I suggest, have reinstated the text into the study of contemporary fiction.

Yet, simultaneously, computers and the Internet have changed forever what counts as 'English'. I guess readers of this book will be persuaded, or at least prepared to be persuaded, of the connections between English Studies and gender. I am arguing that it is also not possible to teach contemporary English without adding computers to the equation, for these machines affect almost all aspects of contemporary fiction: writing, publishing, distribution, reading – and teaching, and the triangular relationship between gender and English and Information and Communication Technology (ICT) is one of the most vibrant contemporary areas of study. Because this field is so new I shall first offer a very brief summary. Teachers familiar with this area may chose to skip the next section – or, indeed, read on and critique my particular framing. The structure offered here is based on *teaching* digital fiction rather than on the more usual production (authoring, designing, media), and the relationships I invoke are by no means linear or monolithic, and in fact enable not one genre but a number of creative practices that are the result of linking text to technology.

I have identified three modes of digital textuality that require somewhat different pedagogical paths:

1. **Multimedia and Hypertexts:** This kind of teaching is the closest to conventional English Studies. Although the works often use sound and images alongside words, they can be best understood by deploying and extending a broad 'lit crit' perspective (rather than, say, film or visual studies theory, although elements from these areas can be very helpful). The works include both web-based and non-networked hypertexts published on CDs and,

increasingly, more interactive fiction that uses gaming techniques. Useful places to find early web-based women's texts and criticism are the anthology 'The Progressive Dinner Party' (Guertin and Luesebrink 2000) and the more extensive *Assemblage* (Guertin 2005), which both have a sense of newness and excitement about them, and need ferreting through for the gems (like browsing a good second-hand bookshop). If you prefer a more specialist store, consider the *Electronic Literature Collection* (Hayles *et al.* 2006) for a superb compilation of more up-to-date and ongoing texts; while this is not a specifically gendered volume, an easy key word search for 'woman authors' is a useful start. The first two sites are free to anyone, while the ELO collection is (mostly) available free for non-commercial use on a Creative Commons Licence, or the CD version is available with Hayles (2008). For hypertext CDs, search for Storyspace via the publishers Eastgate (www.eastgate.com).

2. **Textual communication and autobiography:** This encompasses two distinct methods of 'writing the self' online that are rarely connected critically: MOOs and Blogs. However, pondering this chapter has opened up connections for me, and so although, so far, I have not taught them together I now intend to use my reflections on teaching each to map out a route between the two that I will try out next year. The most famous MOO, LambdaMOO,[7] is a virtual city popular in the 1990s, where users can invent their character (with, significantly for feminist studies, ten grammatically embedded genders[8]) and interact via words, like a text-based Second Life. Blogs have three main qualities: they are chronologically written journals; they contain links to other websites and thus create networks; and they offer an open comments section, enabling direct published communication between blogger and readers (who thus become active participators).[9] Blogs are very popular amongst feminists, and a good place to read gendered blogs is at feministcarnival.blogspot.com. In contrast to Lambda's textual performance of gender, blogs encourage more direct commentary via polemic, argument and discussion. Where MOO writers express fantasies, or fictions, blog writers express opinion and are more overtly autobiographical. Blog use of the first person and the immediacy of blog writing mean that, like Lambda, blogs can be read as textual adventures in subjectivity, and it is this aspect that encourages me to draw Women's Studies

students into understandings of the relationship enacted between textuality, subjectivity and gender.

3. **Publishing:** I refer here to two trends, one commercial and one grassroots. E-readers (Kindle, iPad) have been derided critically as 'just' print texts on screen, but I include them because: (1) they will change how our students read and (2) the technology is beginning to encourage complexity via additions to the main book (for example, interviews with the author, historical background). The grassroots 'retro' trend is in paper-based publications, such as zines and radical books, and feminist publications are strong.[10] However, despite the scribbled DIY quality of many of these, self-publishing is made possible by desktop publishing software, and written zines are copied on computer-enhanced machines. Alongside the value of these texts in enlarging students' awareness of small-scale feminist fiction, the technologies also enable students to design and publish their own collaborative and individual projects.

Digital fiction: mundane and monstrous

I focus here on the first category, multimedia and hypertext, although much of my reflection, particularly about institutional availability of ICT and students' changing skills, is relevant to all digital fiction. I again interrogate implicit 'ands' through musing on the relationships between 'the digital', 'the pedagogical', 'literature' and 'Gender/Women's Studies'. I ask, specifically: in what ways might the teaching of digital fiction enable understandings of gender?

This new technology has at its heart information and communication (as clearly stated in the term Information and Communication Technology: 'ICT'). When I teach sessions on electronic media to gender students I start by adding another 'C', 'creativity'. This identification helps us assess how computer-mediated technologies enable different sorts of practices and helps us begin to read different texts differently. I have found that these three areas – information, communication and creativity – do need to be made pretty explicit. Teaching Master's students from many different disciplines, I have sometimes missed the mark in my preparation. For instance, one year I taught a single session on digital fiction to a mixed-disciplinary group. I prepared the students, as is usual, via offering reading lists and a short seminar outline in a workbook and asked the class to sample any two fictional texts from 'The Progressive Dinner Party'. In class I plunged straight in, hoping that the students would be as excited as I was about this creative menu. Alas, the feedback belied this: 'a missed opportunity to look at how we can get data for our research' was a common response. Although at first I could not understand how the students had overlooked my explanation in the workbook and interpreted 'online' as a method for generating reference lists, I came to see that the web-savvyness of some contemporary students is not always an advantage. Because they are so used to high-profile aspects of the Internet – such as social networking, online shopping and information gathering – and because the Internet is an integral part of their lives, they assume a comfortable knowledge of digital technologies that can sometimes stop them from probing further. As English teachers and students we have learned to take account of varieties of print media: the form of gossip magazines is different from car manuals, bibles from chick lit, cornflakes packets from poetry. Or, the need to find a number in a phone book requires different kinds of skills from immersing oneself in a nineteenth-century realist novel. By treating electronic technology to the same kind of process of considering different purposes we can start the class from a place of creative not-knowing and thus exploration.

But I didn't start with ICCT-savvy students nor, indeed, with an ICCT-savvy me. One strand of my teaching is with non-networked hypertext.[11] This work is sold on CDs and is therefore received as artefact, like a book, and this form has practical consequences. Our increasingly debt-burdened students spend less and less money on texts, so I loaned out my copies of these CDs, a practice that became quite expensive and a little frustrating as they were often not returned. I think this was partly because CDs are small and easily mislaid, and partly because they look like music CDs, which prior to MP3s were an easy currency for many of the students. As hypertexts became central to my teaching I asked the University library to purchase some key texts as they could keep better track of them, and the cataloguing decisions over these new forms of fiction were an interesting reflection of another fascinating 'cusp' moment – technology or fiction? Sue Cumberpatch, our ever-helpful Women's Studies librarian, arranged a licence for one of the emblematic hyperfictions,

Shelley Jackson's *Patchwork Girl*, to enable this text to be uploaded onto a number of machines. I was wary of this move. Although, as she rightly pointed out, puzzled by my reticence, the text was the same, to me the text (in its more cultural sense) was not the same, and I was keen for the students to appreciate the physicality of the CD. Of course the text needs uploading onto a computer to be read, but the fact of holding the CD and cover did (and does) seem important to me, and on reflection I think its form was part of the ease with which most students approached *Patchwork Girl*. Jackson's story is also fairly easy to place as contemporary fiction. This is how it is described:

> What if Mary Shelley's *Frankenstein* were true?
>
> What if Mary Shelley herself made the monster – not the fictional Dr. Frankenstein?
>
> And what if the monster was a woman, and fell in love with Mary Shelley, and travelled to America?[12]

Its playful gothic and feminist connotations make it a perfect companion to study alongside many Angela Carter novels. Its rich language focuses readers on the word, on the text, and it is thus an excellent introduction to feminist hypertext fiction,[13] and has quickly gained canonical status.

But, it has to be admitted, sometimes the practicalities of CDs, technology and reading on screen took over from the aesthetics of the text. Once my teaching was embedded in photocopying, now it seems that DIY IT repairs and skills are the bedrock. Some students needed help in reading: how to play with the mouse to find links, how to read for some time (say an hour) rather than for so many pages. At this time, Janet H. Murray's *Hamlet on the Holodeck* was a firm favourite with the students and helped many understand the point of hyperfiction as a 'world' rather than just 'words'. Class time was sometimes dominated by discussion of 'the reading process', a dialogue enlivened by the different paths enabled by hypertext, so that everyone read different passages. Although, with *Patchwork Girl*, 'turn to page twenty-eight' was replaced by 'let's look at lexia 28',[14] we also had to cope with the inevitable slowness or even breakdown of the technology. And deciding where to teach was not easy – large university computer rooms are noisy with machine hum and at that time accessing one computer and data projector for small seminar rooms was a challenge, even in my well-resourced institution.

Yet, I look back at those days, exploring alongside my students, with great fondness. Many of the early issues are now resolved. Students know how to 'play' their mouse, and for the past few years no one has come to class without progressing beyond the first page ('because I was waiting for the page to move, like a video') and the technology in class is (usually) quick and reliable. There is also an increasing ability among students to relate to non-physical texts, brought about, I suspect, by downloading music, videos and now books, so that reading on screen becomes naturalised, and just as no-one thinks when they get to the end of a page 'er ... how do I move on?' and needs to be shown how to turn over the paper, so the use of the mouse, screen scanning, links and clicks become an almost unnoticeable part of reading.

So, are the technological problems of teaching digital fiction worth ploughing through for the textual insights? What kinds of gendered literary practices and aesthetics make this worthwhile? I end this section with some provisional thoughts.

1. **The critical mass argument:** Women are significantly involved in many genres of digital fiction as writers, critics and readers. Many of the most interesting and critically acclaimed works are by women (see 'women authors' in Hayles 2006). Are women teaching this work? Perhaps not. The theme of the 2010 'Contemporary Women's Writing Network' conference at San Diego was 'New Texts, Approaches, and Technologies' and yet there were few papers on digital fiction. But at conferences purely on digital fiction I have usually observed a predominance of women delegates. Perhaps, as teachers, one of our jobs is to bridge that gap, and ensure our students are literate in reading both fictional forms.

2. **The temporal correlation argument:** 1990 was a key year for studies in both digital fiction and gender. That year saw the publication of the first Storyspace CD; the founding of LambdaMOO; a live, if restricted, WWW; and the publication of Butler's *Gender Trouble*. The past two decades have seen the rise of computer-mediated creativity alongside the rise of gender as a conceptual category, and they are both developments that have had a

significant academy presence. The two strands have often been intertwined and generative of each other, and it is hard to see how one can now teach Women's/Gender Studies without taking account of the other revolution.

3. **The textual argument:** Many digital texts pose challenging questions about gender via their adventurous aesthetics. Just as the development of the novel at a particular time led to a conjunction of textual form and subjectivity so, I suggest, this early digital fiction form facilitates explorations into postmodern subjectivity and, given the arguments outlined in (1) and (2) above, this is often a self of fractured gender.

4. **The learning together argument:** Although forms of digital fiction are now two decades old, the field is still developing. For most teachers it is new, and they will find themselves learning alongside and sometimes from their students, resisting the formation and dissemination of a stable feminist literary canon and benefitting from the thrill of 'not knowing', which can shoot through existing epistemological paradigms to generate previously unthought-of understandings, in this case of gender.[15] As teachers of English we know the power of art to move people – and computers have created new modes for human imagination, which we ignore at our loss.

To conclude: both the issues I have highlighted – fiction for non-literary students; digital media for non-technical teachers and students – consider times when the particular connections between gender and English are challenged. As a teacher I have a chance to keep energising the troublesome 'ands', asking: 'How might our contemporary pedagogy function as a methodology that opens up new connections between "gender" and "English" '?

Notes

1. The Centre for Women's Studies (www.york.ac.uk/inst/cws) is now the longest-standing UK Women's Studies centre; information about Women's Studies in the UK is available from The Feminist and Women's Studies Association <http://fwsa.wordpress.com>.
2. My favourites are hooks (1994) and Bal (2002).
3. As recounted in a panel discussion between three of the founders: Joanna de Groot, Mary Maynard and Jane Rendall, at Gendering East/West

Conference, July 2009, University of York, and in private conversations between myself, Nicole Ward Jouve and Haleh Afshar.

4. See Toril Moi's 2001 long essay, 'What Is a Woman?: Sex, Gender and the Body in Feminist Theory'.

5. At the same time, gender in its more straightforward sense of recognising women's place in the world as different from that of men's was playing an increasing role in Development theory and practice.

6. From Donna Haraway's 1988 essay of the same name.

7. LambdaMOO can still be visited by logging on via telnet: lambda. moo.mud.org8888. It was sites such as Lambda that gave rise to the jokes and worries that 'no-one knows who you are on the Internet' as well as to the Utopian, explosive artistic cyberfeminism of the 1990s that played fast and loose with postmodern theories of gender, identity and bodies. For a sceptical view, see Rosi Braidotti (n.d.); for a more Utopian take, see Sue Thomas (2004). Heretically, I also suggest checking out the Wikipedia entry for some useful information.

8. Female, male, neuter, either, spivak (gender ambiguous), splat (a kind of thing), plural, egotistical, royal ('we'), and second-person.

9. I am indebted to Joanna Maltby for astutely pointing out to me the different functions of links and comments.

10. For zines, see the Women's Library Collection: <http://www.londonmet. ac.uk/thewomenslibrary/searchthecollections/printed-collections/zines/ zines.cfm>, while a varied list of books and journals is listed by the Women's Institute for Freedom of the Press: <http://www.wifp.org/ DWM/DirectoryWomensMedia.html>.

11. Although much digital fiction is increasingly interactive and online, it is important, I think, to value the early CD hypertexts and not to be overwhelmed by the latest technological adventures in creativity.

12. <http://www.eastgate.com/catalog/PatchworkGirl.html>.

13. A summary by Ensslin (2010) is a useful place to start, while Hayles (2000) embeds the work in understandings of hyperfiction, and Sundén (2008) contextualises Jackson's text within cyberfeminist concerns.

14. 'Lexia' refers to a block of text (from Barthes's *S/Z*, and taken up by hypertext critics).

15. Many thanks to Helen Graham for opening me up to the epistemological power of 'the new' via supervisory discussions for her 2004 thesis *Politics, Feeling, Art: Activating Moments of the Women's Liberation Movement for Contemporary Politics* (University of York).

Works Cited

Alcott, Louisa M. (1868/1869) *Little Women* (Boston, MA: Roberts Brothers).

Bal, Miekle (2002) *Travelling Concepts in the Humanities: A Rough Guide* (Toronto: University of Toronto Press).

Barthes, Roland (1970/1974) *S/Z*, trans. R. Miller (New York: Hill and Wang).

Butler, Judith (1990) *Gender Trouble: Feminism and the Subversion of Identity* (London and New York: Routledge).

Braidotti, Rosi (n.d.) 'Cyberfeminism with a Difference' <http://www.let.uu. nl/womens_studies/rosi/cyberfem.htm>, accessed 23 September 2010.

De Beauvoir, Simone (1953), *The Second Sex*, trans. and ed. H.M. Parshley (New York: Knopf).

Eagleton, Mary (1986) *Feminist Literary Theory: A Reader* (Oxford: Basil Blackwell).

Ensslin, Astrid (2007), Section on *Patchwork Girl* extracted by johnvinder (2010) from *Canonizing Hypertext* (London: Continuum), 78–81 <http://eld. eliterature.org/node/323>, accessed 23 September 2010.

Fairbairns, Zoe (1979) *Benefits* (London: Virago).

Greer, Germaine (1970) *The Female Eunuch* (London: Paladin).

Guertin, Carolyn and Marjorie Coverley Luesebrink (February 2000), curators 'The Progressive Dinner Party', *Riding the Meridian* <http://www.heelstone. com/meridian/templates/Dinner/dinner1.htm>, accessed 23 September 2010.

Guertin, Carolyn (1999–2005) *Assemblage: the Women's New Media Gallery* (University of Toronto, Canada, and Trace Online Writing Centre) <http://tracearchive.ntu.ac.uk/traced/guertin/assemblage.htm>, accessed 23 September 2010.

Hayles, N. Katherine (2000) 'Flickering Connectivities in Shelley Jackson's *Patchwork Girl*: The Importance of Media-Specific Analysis' <http://pmc. iath.virginia.edu/text-only/issue.100/10.2hayles.txt>, accessed 23 September 2010.

Hayles, N. Katherine (2008) *Electronic Literature: New Horizons for the Literary* (Notre Dame, IN: Notre Dame University Press).

Hayles, N. Katherine and Nick Montfort, Scott Rettberg and Stephanie Strickland, eds (2006) *Electronic Literature Collection* Vol. 1 <http://www. eliterature.org/collection/1>, accessed 23 September 2010.

—— (1985/1991) 'A Cyborg Manifesto: Science, Technology, and Socialist-Feminism in the Late Twentieth Century,' *Simians, Cyborgs and Women: The Reinvention of Nature* (London and New York: Routledge), 149–81.

Haraway, Donna (1988) 'Situated Knowledge', *Feminist Studies* 14(3): 575–99.

Hennegan, Alison (1998) 'On Becoming a Lesbian Reader', *Sweet Dreams: Sexuality, Gender and Popular Fiction*, ed. Susannah Radstone (London: Lawrence & Wishart), 165–90.

Hooks, Bell (1994) *Teaching to Transgress: Education as the Practice of Freedom* (London and New York: Routledge).

Jackson, Shelley (1995) *Patchwork Girl* (Watertown, MA: Eastgate).

Joyce, Michael (1990) *Afternoon, a Story* (Watertown, MA: Eastgate).

March, Caeia (1986) *Three Ply Yarn* (London: The Women's Press).

Millett, Kate (1970) *Sexual Politics* (New York: Doubleday).

Moi, Toril (1985) *Sexual/Textual Politics: Feminist Literary Theory* (London and New York: Methuen).

Moi, Toril (2001) *What Is a Woman? And Other Essays* (Oxford: Oxford University Press).

Murray, Janet H. (1998) *Hamlet on the Holodeck: The Future of Narrative in Cyberspace* (Cambridge, MA: MIT Press).

Pearce, Lynne (1995) 'Finding a Place from Which to Write: The Methodology of Feminist Textual Practice', *Feminist Cultural Theory: Process and Production*, ed. Beverley Skeggs (Manchester: Manchester University Press).

Piercy, Marge (1976) *Woman on the Edge of Time* (New York: Knopf).

Showalter, Elaine (1986) *The New Feminist Criticism: Essays on Women, Literature and Theory* (London: Virago).

Sundén, Jenny (2008) 'What if Frankenstein('s Monster) Was a Girl? Reproduction and Subjectivity in the Digital Age', *Bits of Life: Feminism at the Intersections of Media, Bioscience, and Technology*, eds Anneke Smelik and Nina Lykke, (Seattle, WA: University of Washington Press).

Thomas, Sue (2004) *Hello World: Travels in Virtuality* (York: Raw Nerve Books).

Warhol, Robyn R., and Diane Price Herndl (1991) *Feminisms: An Anthology of Literary Theory and Criticism* (Piscataway, NJ: Rutgers University Press).

Winterson, Jeanette (1985) *Oranges Are Not the Only Fruit* (London and Boston: Pandora).

4
Teaching Queer Theory: Judith Butler, Shakespeare and *She's the Man*

Catherine Bates

Queer theory in the English Studies classroom

Teaching English in Higher Education involves encouraging and enabling students to question established assumptions, disrupt the status quo and to account for the complexity of the textualised world in which they participate. Queer theory potentially provides the opportunity to 'make trouble' (Butler 1990, vii). Developing as it did through political activism and the need to raise awareness about the existence of lifestyles and identities previously not acknowledged in mainstream culture, it opens up the opportunity for productive alternative and politicised readings of texts. As Eve Kosofsky Sedgwick eloquently points out, this body of theory owes its productivity to the 'gorgeous generativity, the speculative generosity and daring, the permeability, and the activism that have long been lodged in the multiple histories of queer *reading*' (Sedgwick 1992, viii). This creativity and commitment makes queer theory an invaluable tool for challenging particular strongly held assumptions about identity, subjectivity, personhood and society, which necessarily limit the reading of a text.

In the UK, Queer Studies is still a relatively recent addition to the literary theory canon. The core literary theory and criticism module I undertook as an undergraduate in 1996 included a concentration on feminism, Marxism, structuralism and post-structuralism. The term 'queer theory' did not become part of my vocabulary until I was a postgraduate in 1999, taking specialised modules on gendered identities. It seems that Queer Studies did not constitute an essential component of modules introducing literary theory to students in the UK until the late 1990s and the early 2000s. This is despite the fact that the groundbreaking texts of Sedgwick and Judith Butler, *Between Men* and *Gender Trouble*, were published in 1985 and 1990, respectively.[1]

The expansion of what constitutes the canon of literary theory can, to some degree, be tracked through the changes in literary theory anthologies. The set text used at the University of Leeds when I was an undergraduate was Dennis Walder's *Literature in the Modern World* (1990). Useful in many ways, the gender section contains no queer theory; the second edition, however, published in 2004, contains extracts from Sedgwick and Butler. While this establishes queer theory as a key component in the canon of literary theory, it also indicates how long it took for this to happen: Sedgwick's work had been published for 19 years before this collection was changed to include her. It is significant, I think, that this is a British publication, and that Butler and Sedgwick are added to a section entitled 'Literature and Gender'. The theory collections I have since taught from – primarily US publications – tend to include a more wide-ranging selection of queer theories. This reflects the cultural specificity of queer theory, which is a point I raise with my students in contextual lectures, pointing to the Stonewall Riots in New York in 1969 and the particular ways AIDS mobilised and defined the US gay rights movement in the late 1980s. Julie Rivkin and Michael Ryan's *Literary Theory: An Anthology* (2004), a particularly useful US anthology, provides an excellent introduction to queer theory and then moves through extracts from Michel Foucault's *The History of Sexuality*, further extracts from Butler and Sedgwick, and proceeds to include writers who contribute more specifically to an understanding of transgendered identity, such as Teresa de Lauretis and Judith Halberstam. This collection is particularly useful for enabling students to understand a kind of genealogy of Queer Studies; making connections between theorists can become a useful way of learning how widely and productively their theories can be applied.

Introducing queer theory to students

In approaching the study of queer theory with my students, I generally supplement student-led seminars with contextual lectures, which begin by describing queer theory as both a body of thinking in its own right and a necessary component of Gender Studies as a whole. *Gender Trouble* and *Between Men* are introduced as texts built on feminist foundations, and I suggest that the questions Butler and Sedgwick ask about the manner in which gender is constituted, performed and policed are continuations and expansions of the feminist project. I also emphasise the mutually productive relationship Queer Studies maintains with other theoretical disciplines; students are encouraged to consider how it influences and is influenced by cultural materialist approaches, is both a reaction to and draws upon psychoanalysis, and has both shaped and become part of the postmodern and the postcolonial. As can be demonstrated by reading Butler for example, with her direct references to Simone de Beauvoir, Michel Foucault, Jacques Derrida, Sigmund Freud and Louis Althusser, new theories are built from a rethinking of the connections between more established debates.

As well as embedding Queer Studies within larger bodies of theory, my teaching tries to discourage the application of queer theory as a means of determining a text's identity and possibilities. By this I mean, rather than labelling certain texts as 'queer' (on a theory survey module, for example), it can be far more productive to encourage students to perform queer readings. This allows 'queer' to signify beyond a term only denoting sexuality within the heterosexual/homosexual binary, thus attempting to avoid using it as a deterministic term. To support this move, I ask students to discuss Sedgwick's opening up of 'queer' to refer to 'the open mesh of possibilities, gaps, overlaps, dissonances and resonances, lapses and excesses of meaning when the constituent elements of anyone's gender, of anyone's sexuality aren't made (or can't be made) to signify monolithically' (Sedgwick 1994, 8). As part of this discussion, we consider the idea that texts, like people, are also made of this kind of open mesh. Introducing queer theory at a stage in a module when it can be interrogated by and used productively with a number of texts can become a way of allowing theories and texts to develop new meanings through the overlaps and resonances, gaps and excesses that students are able to identify and discuss.

Queer Studies presents particular challenges to the English tutor in Higher Education. While students are used to the idea of feminism (although not always willing to take it seriously or embrace it), I find that the idea of queer theory is often quite new to them, meaning they are not always prepared – at least initially – to acknowledge its significance at all. If feminism is seen as not relevant *any more*, then queer theory can sometimes be viewed as too niche *in the first place*. I have found that students can be dismissive of queer theorists' attempts to challenge essentialist assumptions about sexual identity, and/or embarrassed to discuss sexuality. Furthermore, discussion can often involve a perpetuation of stereotypes, potentially creating an 'us and them' attitude that effectively others gay and transgender identities (precluding the notion that they may well be represented in the seminar room). When first teaching queer theory I often found students using it as a way to diagnose what was wrong with the characters in the text, treating homosexuality as a kind of mystery psychosis to be solved – as if the revelation that a character is gay would explain anything else that may be understood as 'problematic' about them. A good example of this is what I find to be a common response to *Mrs Dalloway*, in which students connect Clarissa's memories of intimate feelings for Sally Seton with Septimus's mental illness and Woolf's own suicide. Of course, there are many problems with this reading, which I will not expand upon here. Suffice to say, lesbian desire becomes coupled with war trauma and mental illness as a problem to be identified and treated. Raising and interrogating such assumptions is part of the work that queer theory aims to do, and Sedgwick's more open definition of 'queer' is one way to help move students beyond this diagnostic approach.

Teaching Judith Butler: troubling gender

Judith Butler's theory of gender performativity is arguably now fundamental to the teaching of literary theory. It is useful as a way of both articulating the boundaries that police identity and contemplating the possibilities for moving beyond those limits. Students, in my experience, find the discussion of drag as a phenomenon that emphasises gender as performative a relatively easy concept to understand. Butler's ideas, however, together with her writing style, are often difficult for students to fully digest. Moreover, it is easy, if one is not focusing on the full articulation of her theory, to mix up Butler's idea of performativity with the concept of performance in general, and so become attached to an idealised notion that we are all free to simply perform the identities we would wish. I have had frustrating discussions with students who have not really questioned their own fixed, essentialist assumptions of masculinity and femininity, but instead argued that 'if men want to dress like women, that's fine, but it's nothing to do with me'.

In reflecting on some of the issues involved in teaching with Butler's work, I have, over time, amended my approach. I used to give students the theory to read in advance, letting them guide the subsequent discussion. Unfortunately much time would then be spent discussing how difficult Butler was to read; the conversation would often slide into generalised statements about how everybody performs their identity, and how identity in general is a construct. I found the more adventurous students quite attached to the idea that we are effectively walking around in drag, while other students found this off-putting and became defensive. While I remain committed to student-directed reading and discussion, this kind of general discussion does pose a danger that students will fail to approach the more nuanced understandings of complex ideas and debates such as Butler's theory of gender performativity. I have since begun to guide their reading much more carefully, highlighting key concepts and arguments, and bringing in extracts from later works, such as *Bodies that Matter*, to supplement *Gender Trouble*.[2] I find that this directed approach ensures a sound critical foundation, from which subsequent discussions and debates can develop much more freely. What follows is a description of some approaches to teaching Butler's theory that I have found fruitful within my own teaching practice.

Performativity

Commencing with a guided group discussion of the set extracts, I take the earliest opportunity to provide the students with a brief history of the performative, considering – as do both Sedgwick and Butler – Austin's original articulation of the term. We examine together Austin's distinction between constative and performative speech acts, using his example of the wedding ceremony as a culturally loaded event in which the *context* of the performance, the boundaries within which it takes place and those witnessing it, all become important.[3] From here, we can start to discuss the idea that not all performances are therefore considered to work, or considered legitimate.

Using the introduction to *Bodies that Matter* (and drawing upon Derrida if time allows), we discuss Butler's use of the performative, and the way in which it suggests that every gender performance is a *citation*. To argue this is to realise that a gender cannot be invented – it can only be reiterated, or at the very most, parodied. Once the students feel confident in their understanding of the performative, I direct them to the following much-cited paragraph from *Gender Trouble*:

> Is drag the imitation of gender, or does it dramatize the signifying gestures through which gender is established? Does being female constitute a 'natural fact' or a cultural performance, or is 'naturalness' constituted through discursively constrained performative acts that produce the body through and within the categories of sex?... gender practices within gay and lesbian cultures often thematize 'the natural' in parodic contexts that bring into relief the performative construction of an original and true sex. (Butler 1990, viii)

A collaborative close reading of this extract enables students to consider the way in which, for Butler, gender performance produces a notion of the natural, rather than the reverse. Where students find it helpful to have a discussion of what this production of the 'natural' looks like, I might question the point at which the initial gendering of an individual takes place; this can help to clarify the idea that 'doing gender' is a societal, rather than an individual process, the terms of which are socially regulated. It is also helpful here to point them towards a relevant section in *Bodies that Matter* (232) in which Butler clearly emphasises the discipline and punishment that regulate gender boundaries; this leads us on to a consideration of the regulation and policing of gender roles.

Policing

In exploring the idea that gender performances are regulated, rather than chosen, we talk, in general, about scenarios in which people experience exclusion for performing in the wrong way, and discuss how this exclusion is enacted. This usually leads to a conversation about bullying, laughter, disgust and disbelief. This allows me to point out – gently – to anyone refusing to take the discussion seriously, that they are in effect regulating gender norms by refusing to contemplate difference. In my experience, this kind of confrontation, only deployed with particularly disruptive students, has the effect of affirming the importance of what is at stake; generally, other students step in at this point to continue thinking through the processes of marginalisation (something most have experienced).

To further this discussion, we might address Butler's use of Mary Douglas's *Purity and Danger*, a text that suggests that bodily boundaries are socially established in order to naturalise cultural taboos and assumptions as to what constitutes 'the body'. Using this idea to contemplate processes of exclusion, Butler discusses the following quotation from Douglas:

> Ideas about separating, purifying, demarcating and punishing transgressions have as their main function to impose system on an inherently untidy experience. It is only by exaggerating the difference between within and without, above and below, male and female, with and against, that a semblance of order is created. (Douglas, quoted in Butler 1990, 131)

Using both Douglas's statements and Butler's reflections on their significance, the students are encouraged to consider how they might apply these ideas to literary texts. With some group collaboration, they establish a list of useful enquiries relevant to the analysis of performance and taboo. This list typically includes questions such as: What system has been put in place? What binaries (often exaggerated) is it reliant upon? What disorder threatens the order? Which 'polluting' person (one who has crossed some culturally established line) is in the wrong? How is their 'wrong position' identified and articulated in the text? What line has been crossed? Who will be put in danger as a consequence?

Polluting people in *The Merchant of Venice*: an undergraduate seminar plan

Once established, we make use of the above list in a later seminar on contested identity performances in *The Merchant of Venice*. In preparation, students are asked to read the play and re-read the relevant sections from *Gender Trouble*. In class, we set about trying to apply Douglas's theory of the polluting person to our reading of the play. Working in small groups, I find that students most commonly use the concept to discuss ethnicity and the way in which Shylock's 'wrong position' is explained by his Jewishness. However, as becomes apparent from the alternative readings suggested by other students, this analysis can miss some key issues; by sharing their contrastive approaches, the students are able to recognise the fact that the characters are subject to a number of ideologies.

Portia provides a useful example here. With her declaration, 'I may neither choose who I would, nor refuse who I dislike; so is the will of a living daughter curbed by the will of a dead father' (I.2.22–4), she immediately highlights the limits she is subjected to by a patriarchal system that constrains her freedoms. As a group, we consider how the binaries of the play become exaggerated: how outspoken and assertive (and potentially unruly) Portia is for a daughter, and how dead (and yet still controlling) is her father. The students often point to Portia's playful comments about the suitors and her clearly superior wit. Using Douglas's theory, we talk about the way in which this gender trouble is exacerbated by Portia's deciding to take control of Antonio's court case, dressing as a man and winning with her superior logic and rhetorical skill. I suggest that perhaps she is then put back in her place through a marriage in which her husband will govern her and her wealth. Quite rightly, students often point out that Portia seems too strong to simply submit, and that the play ends with an unruly marriage of three, as Bassanio is to stay with the married couple.

While the play seems to reach this conclusion relatively happily, the students (often influenced by their own critical reading) frequently identify something excessive about Bassanio's friendship with Antonio. We consider whether the strength of this relationship could reveal Portia's cross-dressing to be a limited performance, one which serves to emphasise a patriarchal gender system that will only allow her in the courtroom if everyone thinks she is male. Ultimately, I try to enable the students to think through the complexities of the text: Portia's behaviour potentially threatens the patriarchal system that would subordinate her to Antonio; however, the strong homosocial bond between Antonio and Bassanio seems to stand eventually as the most important relationship, effectively putting Portia in her place, but arguably also exposing marriage – this heteronormative union – as subordinate to friendship.[4]

In practice, I find that Butler and her use of Douglas can help students to identify the differing ideologies to which the characters are subject and their bids to move beyond those ideologies; whether Shakespeare champions or thwarts these attempts is an issue for productive discussion. In general, Butler's focus on 'regulatory regimes' works well with literary texts that incorporate transgressive or indeterminate genders; it can help students understand how identity is restricted by multiple ideologies.[5] At the same time, the issue of the text's *stance* can be difficult for students to grasp: that is, the difference between performing a feminist reading of a text and labelling a text 'feminist'. Similarly, if a text focuses on homosexuality or gender ambiguity, students tend to assume that it actively advocates the politics of Butler or Sedgwick. With this difficulty in mind, the concluding section describes my teaching of a Renaissance play alongside a twenty-first century film; this combination has proved successful in encouraging students to consider the complex relationships texts can have to queer theories.

Shakespeare's *Twelfth Night* (1601) and Fickman's *She's the Man* (2006): a case study

At Keele University I taught a final-year undergraduate English Studies module, 'Shakespeare on Film', the first section of which focused on teen Shakespeare film adaptations, including Baz Luhrmann's *William Shakespeare's Romeo + Juliet* (1996), Gil Junger's *10 Things I Hate About You* (1999) (loosely based on *The Taming of the Shrew*) and Andy Fickman's *She's the Man* ('inspired by' *Twelfth Night*). For each seminar, students were required to read the relevant Shakespearean play, watch the set film and read two critical articles: one about the play, and one about Film and/or Cultural Studies. The two-hour discussion sessions commenced with student presentations that critically analysed both play and film within the context of one of the articles.

This model of teaching has a number of advantages for engaging students with literary texts and critical theory, and the relationship between the two.[6] When undertaken with commitment, the preparatory work provides a wealth of material for discussion. The films, which students often found easier to begin talking about, provide a route into the more complex critical ideas and the trickier plays. At the same time, the critical theory demonstrates a mode of analysis that can expose the deceptively accessible American high school comedies to more complex, nuanced and productive readings.

For the session on *She's the Man*, the students were asked to read Butler's 'Bodily Inscriptions, Performative Subversions'[7] and Jean Howard's 'Crossdressing, the Theatre and Gender Struggle in Early Modern England', which provides a historically embedded analysis of *Twelfth Night* and usefully demonstrates the relevance of Butler's theory of drag to an early modern context. I often find that students consider Queer Studies anachronistic to the non-contemporary, and tend to assume that in the Renaissance period 'traditional' values were unquestioningly upheld; this can lead students to defend, dismiss or at least simplify the gender politics of Renaissance texts. A common argument would look like this: women were universally expected to be obedient, silent wives, and men strong, brave husbands – therefore it is unsurprising if transgressive characters are punished; beyond this initial observation, contemporary understandings of sexuality are irrelevant to sixteenth-century texts. Belying these assumptions, Howard's essay instead discusses clothing as a semiotic system signifying class and gender, and demonstrates that cross-dressing was a major concern during this period.

She's the Man is a particularly slapstick American high school comedy. Viola lives for soccer, but the film begins with the girls' soccer team at her school being cancelled amidst claims that girls are too weak to play. A defiant Viola decides to pose as her brother Sebastian, who is about to start at a rival school (but will be in London for the first weeks). Viola cross-dresses as Sebastian (helped by gay friend and hairdresser, Paul), joins the soccer team and falls in love with her roommate, Duke Orsino, as he helps her train for the first team and she helps him woo Olivia. Meanwhile, to please her mother, she trains to become a debutante, courting suspicion from both Sebastian's girlfriend and school geek Malcolm (also pursuing Olivia). In the film's climax, Viola reveals her 'real' identity (exposing her breasts) during a match between the rival teams, and scores the final goal. Everyone ends up at the debutante ball, mostly in pairs: Viola and Duke, Sebastian and Olivia, Viola and Sebastian's previously separated parents – the gay characters don't feature on stage, but are seen happily clapping along.

The film keeps *Twelfth Night*'s twins, finding a less tragic way to keep Sebastian out of the picture. On the surface, this gives students an opportunity to consider the film as more progressive: while Shakespeare's Viola cross-dresses to disguise her identity as an Illyrian and so survive, Fickman's Viola passes as a boy to prove a point: girls are as good at soccer as boys. However, I wanted to encourage a more sustained comparison between the play and the film that might expose other ways in which the film actually limits gender possibilities.

Viola is accepted as a man in *Twelfth Night* from the beginning (we used Howard to contextualise this, discussing clothes as such powerful signifiers that the characters cannot see beyond them). Contemplating the significance of Olivia's attraction to Viola/Cesario, I posed the question: Is it that she doesn't see beyond the clothes, or that she identifies the ineffable ambiguity of the person within them, recognises Viola's behaviour as something not typically masculine and becomes attracted to this different 'doing' of manliness which does not fit into the system? A student pointed out that Olivia also does not fit; her mourning for her brother is considered excessive and, like Hamlet's for his father, is condemned as threatening to the normal running of the state. As one of the presenters used her introduction to suggest, Butler might say she is not conforming to the expectations of reproductive heterosexuality.

Picking up on this point, we compared this excessive Olivia to her equivalent in *She's the Man*; in the film, we observed, she is only mourning the end of a relationship. This increases her desirability to the boys as she is deemed 'vulnerable'. Furthermore, when Viola/Sebastian compliments Olivia on her shoes (momentarily forgetting her masquerade), this slip seems to seal Olivia's love for Viola/Sebastian as a boy unlike other boys. This is substantiated by another change in the adaptation – a scene one of the student presenters noted: when Viola/Sebastian drops song lyrics written by her brother, Olivia finds them and is further confirmed in her love. The equivalent scene in *Twelfth Night* has Viola/Cesario using her *own* words to woo Olivia. A debate ensued as to which version was more progressive. On the one hand, the film allows a man – the real Sebastian – to articulate his sensitive emotions; in the play, Viola's poetic language confirms her womanly sensibilities. On the other hand, a woman deploys rhetorical skill in the play, whereas the film's Viola is admired only for her smile; moreover, she plays the admiring sister to her talented brother. These cross-currents provided much to consider, and even those students who were less theoretically adept felt able to contribute to the ensuing debate about the function of the comparative gender performances.

To further explore the point about excessive gender performance, I drew upon the DVD's bonus material, which includes Amanda Byne (who plays Viola) and Fickman discussing Byne's gender performance as a man. Both assert that the atmosphere on set changed when she dressed as a man – that people behaved differently around her, and she behaved differently around them. This supports the notion of performativity (in changing the performance iteration Byne revealed gender performance to be a parody). At the same time, both Byne and Fickman work hard in the clip to stress Byne's overt femininity, which seems to suggest that her successful gender performance was in danger of threatening the gender binary, so her essential 'girling' (to use Butler's term) needed to be emphasised. Ultimately, she seems to parody both femininity and masculinity. The clip prompted some useful discussion, and as a group we concluded that it was difficult to know who she was after these performances – an insightful student suggested it was as if the system was there but it had subsumed the individual.

Another particularly fruitful area of discussion that developed was an investigation into the genre of both play and film. After reflecting on the way genre might be understood in terms of Butler's notion of the performative (roles will not be recognised unless they are played within a recognised context; the genre potentially provides this context), even less confident students were able to spot the citations from other examples of the genre and begin analysing the trajectories of stock characters. Discussing generic expectations, we noted that both types of comedy (Shakespearean and teen movie) tend to work within heteronormative limitations, concluding with a satisfactory (heterosexual) union.[8] We framed the subsequent discussion in terms of social regulation and punishment, which we had examined in previous sessions.

In *She's the Man*, Orsino monitors Viola/Sebastian and initially judges her performance to be inappropriate. He and his friends discover a female signifier, a tampon, which she explains away but, more significantly, they also reject her for expressing distress over a past relationship and so behaving 'like a girl'. We analysed a subsequent scene in which Viola/Sebastian enacts a self-consciously heterosexual performance, employing her girlfriends to drape themselves over her, thus confirming her to be a desirable, controlling male. The boys are impressed with this performance, in which the girls are treated as sexual objects, and as one student observed, normative masculinity becomes associated with misogyny. Moreover, some noted the homophobia implied in a scene in which Duke and Viola spontaneously jump onto a bed to avoid a spider, hugging each other in fright. Duke jumps down, disgusted, blaming the confusion on the fact that Viola/Sebastian had been pretending to be a girl in order to teach Duke to flirt.

From these observations, we proceeded to a comparison with *Twelfth Night*, which seems more ambiguous. Orsino's relationship with Viola/Cesario is more comfortable; he enjoys playing the role of an older male mentor to her/him. Moreover, Antonio is a friend to Sebastian, as Antonio in *The Merchant of Venice* is to Bassanio: both declare themselves faithful servants willing to give their lives for their friends. Since Orsino's relationship with Viola/Cesario mirrors this though, and then becomes a romantic relationship, we discussed the opportunity the play gives for a relationship beyond the heteronormative to be imagined. It puts Sebastian and Antonio's relationship within the realm of romance, and Viola and Orsino's within the realm of the homosocial. As we discussed, this reveals both the heterosexual romantic relationship and homosocial bonds to be normative constructs.

It was when these observations were discussed that many of the students began to arrive at the belief that *She's the Man* does not give the same opportunity for exposing and questioning heteronormativity. Duke's excessive concern not to appear intimate with Viola-as-boy transforms their relationship from that of the original play; in fact much of the film's comedy stems from these homophobic anxieties. Moreover, there is no equivalent Antonio figure for Sebastian to bond with, and Sebastian moves between women, with the film's approval, as if they were interchangeable. And furthermore, his first girlfriend's excessive femininity, associated with superficiality and cruelty, is used to legitimise Viola's femininity and show it to be 'normal' (a girl *can* like soccer).

Ultimately, by providing students with a text they would find accessible, using it in comparison with a more complex literary text and supplementing both with close readings of extracts from Butler, I found queer theory to be working productively in the English seminar room. It was able to account persuasively for the complexities and potential rupture of the strict gender system in Shakespeare's play, and helped us think through the disappointingly conservative adaptation in Fickman's film. The two texts revealed queer theory to be a useful tool for developing students' understanding of not just the terms of the debate, but also the way in which the critical interrogation of gender performance can be potentially transformative, exposing and moving us beyond the processes of regulation.

Notes

1. I mention these as the two texts that still seem to dominate the teaching of queer theory in English departments in the UK, and that did much to shape the theoretical vocabulary of the field; there is of course a substantial wider body of work in Gay and Lesbian Studies.
2. The introduction to *Bodies that Matter* usefully addresses the more ambiguous moments in *Gender Trouble* and clarifies the idea of performativity; it also more clearly situates Butler's theory within the larger context of the AIDS crisis and gay rights. I also make use of Butler's 'Imitation and Gender Insubordination' (anthologised in Fuss), which troubles Butler's personal identity as a 'lesbian'. Such instances can engage students, helping them see the theorist beyond the dense theorising and potentially understand the political seriousness of the argument.
3. Austin's wedding ceremony example is used extensively by Sedgwick, particularly in her introduction to *Performativity and Performance*.
4. Sedgwick's *Between Men* is a natural choice for further reading at this point, if time allows.
5. This works particularly well on modules that also have room to address Foucault's *Discipline and Punish*.
6. I acknowledge and thank Lucy Munro as the original designer and convenor of this module and its pedagogical structure.
7. This extract, taken from *Gender Trouble*, is included in *The Judith Butler Reader* alongside a useful contextual introduction written, in retrospect, by Butler.

8. Useful further reading on this might include Burt's work on teen Shakespeare, and Osbourne, Klett and Pittman's analysis of teen adaptations of *Twelfth Night*.

Works Cited

Austin, J.L. (1962) *How to Do Things with Words* (Oxford: Clarendon Press).

Burt, Richard (2002) 'Afterward: T(e)en Things I Hate About Girlene Shakesploitation Flicks in the Late 1990s, or, Not-So-Fast Times at Shakespeare High', *Spectacular Shakespeare: Critical Theory and Popular Cinema*, eds Courtney Lehmann and Lisa S. Starks (London: Associated University Presses), 205–32.

Butler, Judith (1990) *Gender Trouble: Feminism and the Subversion of Identity* (London and New York: Routledge).

—— (1991) 'Imitation and Gender Insubordination', *Inside/Out: Lesbian and Gay Theories*, ed. Diana Fuss (London and New York: Routledge), 13–31.

—— (1993) *Bodies that Matter: On the Discursive Limits of 'Sex'* (London and New York: Routledge).

—— (2004) 'Bodily Inscriptions, Performative Subversions' extracted from *Gender Trouble*, *The Judith Butler Reader*, ed. Sarah Salih with Judith Butler (Oxford: Basil Blackwell, 2004), 90–119.

Fuss, Diana (ed.) (1991) *Inside/Out: Lesbian and Gay Theories* (London and New York: Routledge).

Howard, Jean (1988) 'Crossdressing, the Theatre and Gender Struggle in Early Modern England', *Shakespeare Quarterly* 39(4) (Winter): 418–40.

Klett, Elizabeth (2008) 'Reviving Viola: Comic and Tragic Teen Film Adaptations of *Twelfth Night*', *Shakespeare Bulletin* 26(2): 69–87.

Osbourne, Laurie E. (2008) '*Twelfth Night*'s Cinematic Adolescents: One Plot, One Play, One Setting, and Three Teen Films', *Shakespeare Bulletin* 26(2): 9–36.

Pittman, L. Monique (2008) 'Dressing the Girl/Playing the Boy: *Twelfth Night* Learns Soccer on the Set of *She's the Man*', *Literature/Film Quarterly* 36(2): 122–37.

Rich, Adrienne (1980) 'Compulsory Heterosexuality and Lesbian Existence', *Journal of Women's History* 15(3): 11–47.

Rivkin, Julie and Michael Ryan, eds (2004) *Literary Theory: An Anthology* (Oxford: Blackwell).

Sedgwick, Eve Kosofsky (1985/1992) *Between Men: English Literature and Male Homosocial Desire* (New York, Guildford: Columbia University Press).

—— (1994) *Tendencies* (London and New York: Routledge).

—— (1995) *Performativity and Performance*, with Andrew Parker, eds (London and New York: Routledge).

Shakespeare, William (1993) *The Merchant of Venice*, ed. Jay L. Halio (Oxford: Oxford University Press).

—— (2008) *Twelfth Night*, eds Roger Warren and Stanley W. Wells (Oxford: Oxford University Press).

She's the Man (2006) dir. Andy Fickman (Dreamworks).

10 Things I Hate About You (1999) dir. Gil Junger (Touchstone Pictures).

Walder, Dennis (ed.) (1990) *Literature in the Modern World* (Oxford: Oxford University Press in association with the Open University).

William Shakespeare's Romeo + Juliet (1996) dir. Baz Luhrman (Twentieth Century Fox).

5
'Do We Need Any More Books about Men?': Teaching Masculinities

Brian Baker

'Why study masculinity?', a university lecturer in English asked me, when I discussed this chapter with her; 'What do students, male and female, learn from it?' Or, as the partner of a former colleague more baldly put it, 'Do we need any more books about men?' Good questions. My answer, in short, is this: the development of masculinities as a field of study was a necessary extension of the vital importance of feminist critical theory and practice in the English academy from the 1970s onwards. Where feminism had opened a space to consider the multiple, conflicted, resistant and emergent constructions and representations of the feminine (and female), much work remained to be done in revisiting a totalised conception of masculinity, which had been unambiguously identified with patriarchal and hegemonic ideological formations.

A focus on masculinities within English Studies prompts students to interrogate such assumptions. Rather than being secondary to, or parasitic on the work of feminism, a focus upon the specific constructions of masculinity within patriarchal, late capitalist, democratic and mediated cultures *complements* it. An analysis of the dominant and subordinated forms of masculinity helps to reorganise the field of Gender Studies towards the *subject* and helps undo (or at least bring into view) problematic male/female, masculine/feminine binaries of earlier discourses on sex and gender. This chapter is organised into three sections in order to situate a discussion of contemporary Masculinity Studies in terms of (1) its informing discourses, which shape and underpin teaching of the subject; (2) its organisation in university English curricula; and (3) how the study of masculinities can be embedded within teaching units on genre fiction, particularly science fiction.

The discourses of visibility, crisis and pathology

In the course on science fiction that I teach in the Department of English and Creative Writing at Lancaster University, we study the Wachowski Brothers' *The Matrix* (1999). I include this text partly in relation to the sub-genre of cyberpunk, alongside William Gibson's first novel *Neuromancer* (1984), partly as a further articulation to the representations of the relationship between human and technology that we pursue throughout the unit, and partly because the film itself encodes the kind of critical approach to science fiction that understands it as a mode of 'estrangement' (following the pioneering work of Darko Suvin), a lens through which to understand our own world differently through representations of another. Through estrangement, the culturally and politically invisible is made visible. When Morpheus (Laurence Fishburne) talks to Neo (Keanu Reeves) about the Matrix, it is in terms that offer themselves specifically to a reading of the film as a metaphor for ideology and the processes of naturalisation and occlusion that prevent the subjects of that ideology from being able to perceive it:

> The Matrix is everywhere. It is all around us. Even now, in this very room. You can see it when you look out your window or when you turn on your television. You can feel it when you go to work...when you go to church...when you pay your taxes. It is the world that has been pulled over your eyes to blind you from the truth....Like everyone else you were born into bondage. Into a prison that you cannot taste or see or touch. A prison for your mind.

Of course, in a joking manner, this reveals my own intentions: I hope to reveal to my students things that they cannot taste or see or touch, things about their own culture that have remained invisible. This trope of cultural or political *invisibility* is one that can be found in recent writings about Masculinity Studies. In the aptly titled 'High

Visibility: Teaching Ladlit', her contribution to *Masculinities in Text and Teaching* (2008), Alice Ferrebe begins with the argument that a 'founding assumption' of contemporary Masculinity Studies is 'that the specificity of male gender constructions and experience is initially, and tactically, hidden beneath the textual surface' (220). She cites the work of Michael Kimmel, who has identified 'a similar blind spot in teaching as well as textual processes, remarking of the "educational endeavour" that "at every moment of the process, men are invisible"' (220). Furthermore, Ben Knights, the editor of the above volume, asserts in his discursive introduction that 'The formation of male subjectivity needs itself to be made visible' (4).

The problem, as Ferrebe notes, is not that masculinity is *not* present, either in the classroom, in cultural texts, or in English Studies itself; it is that is has hitherto remained 'unseen' because of the biases of institutionalised readings of canonical (English) literature (rather than literatures in English) and 'the (male) gendered particularity of purportedly "universal" themes' (220). As Sally Robinson argued in 'Pedagogy of the Opaque' in *Masculinity Studies and Feminist Theory* (2002), 'This freedom from scrutiny has enabled the white, middle-class masculine norm to remain invisible, natural, and thus unchallenged' (147). Robinson asserts that the importance of scholarship in deconstructing dominant or hegemonic masculinity is 'that by making hegemonic masculinity visible we begin to erode its power' (147). Therefore, there is an emancipatory and even politically empowering impetus behind this rendering-visible:

> This is a good way to begin initial discussions of masculinity in the classroom, for students quickly flesh out this claim by noting that while they have been studying men and masculinity all their academic lives (in the guise of literature, political science, history courses about humans in general), they have rarely if ever studied men as such. (147)

Robinson notes that the very existence of Masculinity Studies tends to belie the fact of this invisibility, and the then current 'crisis in masculinity' (which reached its year of greatest popular urgency around 1999) rendered masculinity highly visible in popular discourses. The same prevalence was repeated in critical discourse. Susan Faludi's

Stiffed (1999) suggested that contemporary American masculinity had been undermined by the paternal failures of the 'Greatest Generation' and the awareness of this failure subsequently transmitted by baby boomers; Anthony Clare's *On Men: Masculinity in Crisis* (2000) discussed the 'dying phallus', the fatal undermining of a patriarchal subject characterised by domination, aggression, power and authority. The high tide has since receded in terms of popular visibility of the 'crisis' in masculinity, but it has left its mark on the walls of the seminar room: both male and female students now take up issues of masculinity in class discussion and in assessment.

Discussion of masculinity, its increased visibility in social and cultural thought, does not mean a kind of liberation of available subject-positions, though. On the contrary, the increased visibility of masculinity renders it part of what Michel Foucault would describe as the disciplinary matrix of power/knowledge, controlled through medical, social-scientific, legal/judicial and other kinds of discourses. Masculinity Studies, then, partakes of the operation of the 'disciplinary institution' (the university) in making the 'crisis' visible. I should here acknowledge my own indebtedness to, and therefore implication in, the feminist-inspired analyses of masculinities that have re-negotiated its relationship with patriarchy and understand it to be a much more anxious and fissured subject than had previously been imagined. In my own writing on gothic masculinities, I place the masculine subject in relation to the post-Enlightenment rational subject, as does Carole Jones in her recent *Disappearing Men* (2009), who writes:

> The rational subject is therefore a masculinised one, privileging qualities traditionally associated with men: independence, self-sufficiency, control, dominance. This model underpins a dominant model of masculinity 'which establishes its hegemony partly by its claim to embody the power of reason' (Connell 1995: 164). A crisis in the rational subject, then, is a masculine crisis, a phrase that reverberates through the culture in the final decades of the twentieth century. (21)

Discourses of crisis in the field of masculinities, which have been the focus not only of the theory and criticism surrounding the cultural production of masculinities, but also what has been taught and learnt in the classroom, reflect a wider critique of the post-Enlightenment subject (going back at least as far as Freud) that implicitly pathologises the masculine subject. I would argue that contemporary Masculinity Studies in the academy seeks to bring to light a fissured male subject, deformatively produced by patriarchy and beset by internal contradictions. It seeks to articulate forms of masculinity in social and cultural representation that do not correspond to uncomplicated assumptions of masculinity's relationship to patriarchy (an unchallenged dominance): issues of race/ethnicity, class, age and sexuality cut across patriarchal constructions, creating hegemonic forms of masculinity (the 'breadwinner', for instance) as well as subordinated ones (the gay man, the boy and so on). It has been the subject of Masculinity Studies, as it is of my own teaching practice, to articulate these differences, or in the paradigm we have just revealed, to make them *visible*, while at the same not reducing them solely to the pathologised 'crisis' masculinity that was much in evidence at the turn of the millennium.

I have written about such 'crisis' texts as *Fight Club* and *American Beauty* (both 1999) and have taught both films as part of courses on Hollywood cinema and even screen adaptation, but I think that we are probably now, some decade afterwards, post-'crisis', in the sense that the moment of highest visibility of this discourse has passed. This recognition helps students to conceptualise a plurality of differing masculinities produced in a variety of historical, cultural and social contexts. Avoiding 'fixing' masculinity in the classroom (in either sense: healing it or locking it down) is crucial, as this reflects what Carole Jones suggests, in her study of Scottish fiction from the last two decades of the twentieth century, is a fundamental 'betweenness' at work in representations of men. Her notion of *transition* suggests further that the contemporary masculine subject is moving between the un-thought patriarchal hegemon of the past, and the possibility of some kind of reconstructed form of masculine subjectivity in the future (26). The teaching of masculinities should, and does, reflect this movement.

If we are post-'crisis', in some ways, the forms of masculine subjectivity present in social formations and in cultural representations are still in negotiation, and it is part of the work of Masculinity Studies in the seminar room to approach both of these areas. Here I agree with

Sally Robinson, in part: the teaching of masculinities always engages wider ideological and social frames of understanding, and should challenge cultural assumptions that students bring into the seminar room. In my experience, they are more than willing to accept this challenge. As Ben Knights stresses in his introduction to *Masculinities in Text and Teaching*, the continuum between textual masculinities and their articulation in the 'real', whether as a 'matrix' or ideological framework through which students understand and process the world (and text), or in the performance of masculinity in pedagogical situations, is a crucial issue: 'Masculinity, we propose, is an aspirational identity rather than descriptive fact. Forms for exhibiting it in the classroom (or anywhere else) do not simply exist: they are perpetually in formation, hence at least potentially changeable' (8). What follows is that 'the *study* of text [is] a social practice' (17), not disengaged from world or ideology. Towards the end of this chapter I will return to science fiction and my own experience of teaching masculinities and genre as a means by which to focus an analysis of the interconnection between social practice and pedagogical practice, within (and perhaps in negotiation with) the 'matrix' of institutional and cultural discourses surrounding masculinities, of which 'crisis' now seems a minor part.

In contemplating pedagogic practice in this field, a fundamental question must be: what do we intend Masculinity Studies students to learn? Making hegemonic or dominant masculinity visible in selected literary or filmic texts is surely not the end of the pedagogical arc. In asking students to consider representations of masculinity, surely we ask of them to renegotiate their own internal libraries of representations, their own 'naturalised' assumptions about gender, their own ideologies? When I teach a class about the basic units of film construction (as I have done many times at different institutions), I implicitly (and sometimes explicitly) ask them to see film in a different way, and when they tell me after a few weeks that their friends now despair of them because they offer a commentary about shot construction or *mise-en-scène* when watching a film, I feel a sense of satisfaction. I have successfully estranged them from their deeply acculturated viewing habits, and made them more self-conscious decoders of filmic texts. In teaching Masculinity Studies, I ask students (male and female) not so much to 'learn' about different representations of masculinities and their contexts, but to engage in a re-conceptualisation of subject-formation itself.

As a final point on this, Robinson concludes her essay with a bracingly overt politics of pedagogy:

> Masculinity studies, in my view, takes off from the deeply felt conviction – on the part of male and female scholars and teachers – not only that masculinity must be deconstructed as a cultural construct but that men, too, must be convinced to distance themselves from the dominant fictions of masculinity that do, more often than not, procure rewards within patriarchal culture. (154)

In her conception, Masculinity Studies has a fundamentally rhetorical or persuasive function: 'men ... must be convinced' to reject patriarchal masculinity. Some educationalists, still less politicians, might find themselves uncomfortable with a characterisation of an academic field that seems so close to a form of social engineering. And yet, as I have myself revealed about my own practice, I ask students to *think differently* about constructions of gender, and assume (even hope for) a possibility that their engagement with these ideas is so thoroughgoing that it extends beyond the boundaries of the academic discipline, still less the unit of study, and into their 'real' lives.

Undergraduate studies of masculinity

In the course of researching this chapter I have noted many discrete undergraduate courses in anglophone universities that focus upon masculinities in the context of literary, filmic or cultural production. In Australian, Canadian, British and US higher education institutions the *visibility* of masculinity as an area of study within a broad curricular structure is more apparent than perhaps it has ever been. These courses are often connected to the research interests of those faculty members who teach them, and therefore can be assumed to provide a detailed and rigorous investigation of contemporary issues in masculinities.[1]

These research-informed, seminar-based courses provide evidence of the increased importance of masculinities in the fields of

Gender Studies, English Studies and the intersections of literature/ film/culture, and are also clearly a development of the critical impact of feminism and women's writing courses during the last 30 years: many, if not the majority, of those convening 'representations of masculinity' modules were female faculty. This issue, as I noted above, is raised by Ferrebe in her essay 'High Visibility' and it has, Ferrebe calculates, an important (and possibly problematic) effect on the pedagogical dynamic of masculinities taught by a female lecturer, particularly to male undergraduate students. As many who have written about teaching masculinities have noted, this intensifies the already gendered experience of studying English at undergraduate level where, in the UK for instance, young men comprise 28 per cent of the student cohort studying English. In an April 2010 report by the English Subject Centre in the UK, published in their biannual magazine *WordPlay*, students from a range of different Higher Education institutions were questioned about their experiences of studying English. The study of English was assumed by the student body to be, in some sense, implicitly 'feminising'. The writer of the report, John Hodgson, notes:

> the belief (expressed in various ways) that English was a more natural subject for girls to study than for boys. 'I mean this in the nicest way,' said Becky [from a pre-1992 university], 'but I think it takes a type of guy to do English'. She thought he would be 'not the most macho kind'. (8)

I will offer some further thoughts about the pedagogical situation in the light of my own experience below, but here would like to stress another part of the report, which identifies a particular response by both male and female students to material that deals explicitly with gender issues. Hodgson notes that 'women in the focus groups expressed more awareness than did the men of the difference in numbers between the genders' (8), but the presence of 'boys' was most explicitly welcomed 'in seminars with a feminist agenda – without them, [a female student] thought, "[the discussion] becomes a bit one-sided" ' (8). While male students would try to accommodate a 'feminist position', female students (somewhat ironically but significantly) 'would shy away from being labelled as feminists' (8).

In some senses the report tends to reproduce well-worn gender binaries, including male activity and confidence (and implied female self-effacement), as well as the idea that only 'not the most macho kind' of young man would be comfortable with the study of literature at degree level. It also offers the stereotyped response of a male student who 'challenged the focus on feminist readings' of Victorian fiction (while at the same time allowing 'the legitimacy of such readings in a patriarchal world where "it's been masculine readings ever since day one" ' (7)). This echoes the reported student response in Robinson's 'Pedagogy of the Opaque'.

Little in this 2010 report really surprises in relation to gender and the student experience of university English, but even though the report attempts to differentiate with regard to the type of institution (and therefore the different modes of delivery, learning patterns, staff–student ratios and learning resources available) I think that in considering the teaching of masculinities within the contemporary context of English Studies, the importance of the *discrete* unit of study is not to be underestimated. It is my own feeling that the discrete unit is something of a double-edged sword. In my own department at Lancaster University we have recently celebrated the twenty-fifth anniversary of a full-year, consortial (lecture/seminar-based) course in women's writing, and it is vitally important to note the foundational and ongoing work of such courses to disseminate feminist critical practice and gender analysis within contemporary Literary Studies. Very many departments of English will have such a course, successfully taught over a period of decades. It is worth noting, anecdotally, that in my department this course is staffed by female faculty and the gender balance in the cohort is even more pointed towards female students than in the English cohort overall. There is no full-year consortial unit on men's writing, of course. My colleagues who are interested in the field of literary representations of masculinity are also engaged more widely with debates about gender and, yes, women's writing; if I were to teach a course on literary masculinities, I would do so as a specialist seminar-based module, on my own. I have chosen not to, a decision I will expand upon shortly.

This is not to decry the teaching interests of my colleagues in any way. I point this out to emphasise the difference between the teaching of literary representations of masculinities and the importance and much more widespread teaching of women's writing. One does not map onto the other. As Robinson noted, the 'oppressor' paradigm that informed women's writing's relation to patriarchy *cannot* be reproduced in a 'Masculinity Studies' context (142), and even if faculty teach both subjects, different approaches are required. Where women's writing courses may be informed by debates about canonicity, form, the importance of writing itself or the expression of an alternate literary tradition, a Masculinity Studies module's literary or filmic texts may be formally indistinguishable from those studied on other courses where the focus is not upon gender, but upon mode/genre, period, national categories or other connecting concept, *except* that these texts are explicitly or self-consciously focused upon male experience or on masculine subjectivity. These are often texts deeply embedded in patriarchal gender scripts but which *make these patriarchal representations visible*, often through 'crisis' or pathological modes (from *Macbeth* to *Fight Club*).

The crucial pedagogical question, I believe, relates to the opening of my chapter, where I described the model of intellectual *estrangement* at work in the teaching of masculinities and the 'making visible' of the otherwise universalised or naturalised (masculine) subject. In short, does a discrete module on masculinities, in curricular environments that tend to compartmentalise critical engagements (to a greater or lesser extent), tend to reveal the 'invisibility' of the masculine subject in other units of study, or does it tend to block this understanding by considering the issues of masculinity as a separate, and thereby contained, area of literary interest? For the male student who challenged 'feminist readings of Victorian fiction' in the *WordPlay* study, the implications of these readings to a broad referential frame of literary production (Victorian literature) are clear, and must surely have been one of the reasons why his resistance was stirred: the implications are *not* compartmentalised. If literary masculinities in broad, consortial courses are not pathologised nor made visible through 'crisis', are they visible to students at all?

I ask this question because I have always approached the teaching of literary masculinities through embedding these issues in broader units of study: American literature, Hollywood cinema, Edwardian literature, science fiction. In part, this has been determined through the curricular structures of the institutions at which I have taught, but it has also been a conscious decision to try to break through the compartmentalisation of knowledge that seems to have been the corollary of modularisation, and the pressures towards a utilitarian attitude towards study encouraged by reorienting the British university student as a consumer. Just as, in trying to get Film Studies students to alter their viewing habits so that *all* films are watched differently, so, in trying to estrange students from naturalised assumptions about gender scripts, pedagogical practice must always extend beyond the primary focus of a module in terms of its stated aims and learning outcomes.

Teaching masculinities and genre: a case of science fiction

In her essay on teaching masculinities and the gothic, Ranita Chatterjee notes that:

> in the academy, and especially in our pedagogical practices, though we acknowledge that gender is socially constructed, we tend to resurrect a two-gendered, two-sexuality model and ignore, or worse, forget about the existence of transgendered and transsexual individuals. (77–8)

This is not the case in my experience of researching and teaching in the field of science fiction. Other modes of popular fiction (particularly *noir* thrillers and romance fiction) have become the critical site of much analysis of popular representations of gender, and persuasive deconstructions of (particularly white) masculinity, but it is science fiction (sf) that offers both a literary and critical history in which concepts of subjectivity, as well as constructions of gender, have been interrogated. It is an especially fruitful field of study in this regard because it offers both feminist readings of patriarchal sf *and* feminist rewritings of sf tropes to deconstruct constructions of femininity and masculinity from within the fictional frame, in texts written by men and by women.

It is the first task of a course in science fiction to challenge the gendering of the genre in popular reception: the belief that it is a 'boy's genre' (unlike fantasy or the recent phenomenon of the 'dark romance'). Anecdotally, I have found that the gender balance in science fiction classes tends more towards an equal division between male and female students rather than the 70/30 split commonly found in British university departments of English, and that more female students self-confess to having little experience of reading sf and having taken the course because they were interested in studying what, for them, is a 'new' area. Students are sometimes surprised to learn that gender has been a long-standing issue in science fiction at the very level of the writing of sf texts. I have asked the students to read texts by, and talk about the case of, James Tiptree, Jr, an sf writer most famous for short stories such as 'The Girl Who Was Plugged In', published in 1973 (and seen as a forerunner of the 1980s sub-genre of cyberpunk, of which Gibson's *Neuromancer*, mentioned above, was the first major novel) and 'Houston, Houston, Do You Read?' (1976). Tiptree published sf in the late 1960s and 1970s and 'his' writing, in line with the universalised male writer-subject and reader-subject assumed within the sf community at the time, was received as unproblematically 'masculine' in both its 'hard' (technology and science-oriented) and 'soft' (sociologically oriented) sf modes. By the mid-1970s, hints about the gender of 'Tiptree' had begun to surface, and in 1976 the obituary of one Mary Bradley revealed that her daughter, Alice Sheldon, had had a writing career that was essentially identical to that of Tiptree. Tiptree was 'outed' as Sheldon, male as female. This productive 'cross-dressing' had no negative impact upon the reception of her works and, even after Sheldon's death in 1987, her works still provide one of the genre's most visible cases of the problematic of gender-and-genre identifications in Literary Studies. I will return to the idea of productive transvestism below, but I cite Sheldon's case here to indicate that an instability of gender and subject categories, embedded within science fiction texts themselves, can be highly productive as a means by which to engage student discussion of issues of gender and of subjectivity itself.

The literary history of science fiction also offers many examples of science fiction that explicitly attempt to, in Fredric Jameson's words, 'project the Other of what is' (77). The importance of feminist sf to the genre's post-war history cannot be overstated: the works of Ursula Le Guin, Joanna Russ, Marge Piercy, Suzy McKee Charnas and others in the late 1960s and 1970s focused particularly upon gender constructions and upon women's experience within the frames of science fiction world-creation. Some texts had an overtly Utopian intention, in imagining other forms of societal organisation or, in the case of Le Guin's *The Left Hand of Darkness* (1969), alternate modes of (human) sexual biology that, through estrangement, encourages students to reconsider their naturalised (and therefore *invisible*) assumptions about gender. When, in *The Left Hand of Darkness*, Le Guin famously writes 'the King was pregnant', she encapsulates the way in which her imagination of a hermaphroditic society (where oestrous cycles determine a change from potentiality to sexual potency, from 'neuter' subjectivity to *either* male or female sexual organs depending upon the partner) challenges our conceptions of the implications of social order, biology and gender role. It is, in Le Guin's own words, a 'heuristic device, a thought-experiment' (9). When I have taught *The Left Hand of Darkness* to undergraduates, it is not the challenge to representations of gender that students sometimes find uncomfortable. It is the very 'science-fictional' character of the text that some find problematic, set as it is in an alien world, with neologisms (such as *shifgrethor*, a concept of honour and respect that regulates social interaction) or with what Suvin calls a *novum*: a fictional novelty that determines how the world is extrapolated (like the *ansible*, a communications device that enables instantaneous communication between far-distant worlds). I must confess at this point that I have achieved very mixed results with *The Left Hand of Darkness* as a teaching text, more so than any other, and feedback from the students tends to confirm my sense that it is the form of this novel and its linguistic density that they find off-putting, but I also suspect that the very strong traces of the Utopian form in *The Left Hand of Darkness* also meet resistance from the students, who tend to find dystopia (and a strong degree of narrative dynamism) more congenial.

Returning to Chaterjee's lament that Literary Studies often fails to 'break the binary' in terms of gender representations, a text such as *The Left Hand of Darkness* indicates that this is not so within the study of science fiction. Science fiction provides a literary *and* conceptual model to break the binary, to imagine other constructions of gender and the subject, let alone other constructions of the masculine and feminine. The interface between the human and the machine, for instance, is a recurrent motif in sf and indicates its proximity to (and pedagogical usefulness in teaching) current debates about the subject and the post-human. I have usefully cross-fertilised my unit on science fiction with that of a colleague which deals more directly with the theory of post-humanism, a field that many students seem to find fascinating, perhaps unsurprisingly in a digital age.

In the field of science fiction, these debates go back to the importance of cyberpunk in the 1980s and 1990s and the critical figure of the 'cyborg' in rethinking constructions and representations of gender. In Donna Haraway's now famous 'A Cyborg Manifesto', a text which is available online and to which I direct students, she uses the figure of a cyborg race – of 'creatures simultaneously animal and machine, who populate worlds ambiguously natural and crafted' – to construct an 'ironic political myth faithful to feminism, socialism and materialism' that rethinks social reality as a 'world-changing fiction', privileging hybridity and 'pleasure in the confusion of boundaries' (149–50). These boundaries include the public and private, the technological and biological, and the physical and non-physical. Haraway imagines a resistant politics in which 'people are not afraid of their joint kinship with animals and machines, not afraid of permanently partial identities and contradictory standpoints' (154). The cyborg then becomes not a figure of assimilation by machinic systems (*Star Trek*'s Borg) but one of *resistance to* ideological fixity.

This is not to say, however, that the cyborg figures in cyberpunk – including the 'razorgirl' Molly Millions in William Gibson's aforementioned *Neuromancer* – have been held up by feminist critics of sf as indicating a new and progressive form of representations of gender: far from it. Feminist students have often taken issue with such representations in seminars I have taught. Indeed, the rather problematic sexualisation and objectification of these figures instead bespeaks a cyborg fetishism, and along with the deployment of 'hard-boiled' masculine subjectivities suggests that the cyberpunk 'revolution' was not much of a revolution at all. However, in texts like *Neuromancer*, gender binaries are cut across by cyborg discourses in a more Haraway-like sense, particularly in the imagination of non-human subjectivities, and it is here that seminar discussion is often focused. In *Neuromancer* and in subsequent sf (for instance, in Iain M. Banks's 'Culture' novels, a galaxy-spanning story-world) the sentient machines or Artificial Intelligences (AIs) are of as much psychological interest as the human (or quasi-human) actants, if not more so. I have organised my curriculum more recently in such a way as to foreground the issues of sentience, subjectivity or 'humanity', which contemporary students seem to find particularly urgent and interesting. Here, the very centrality of the human as a categorical imperative in defining subjectivity is displaced. If the study of literary masculinities (as could also be said of literary femininities) is really about the processes, practices and discourses of subject-formation, then science fiction foregrounds, in terms of the material available to be discussed in the seminar room, what is ideologically invisible in terms of masculine *and* feminine: that we, as individual subjects, are constructed as such.

Ruth Page, in 'Gender and Narrative Form', writes of a pedagogical project wherein students were asked to respond to a hypertext narrative in terms of a piece of creative writing. What Page suggests is that her students imaginatively approached the status of a Haraway-like cyborg, where partial, hybrid and contingent subjectivities can be produced not out of science fiction alone, but also out of the students' experience of everyday life. In the same vein, as long ago as 1992, Allucquere Rosanne Stone, in her essay 'Will the Real Body Please Stand Up?' identified in early online virtual spaces the phenomenon of what she calls 'computer crossdressing' (84), the use of an online persona or avatar that is of the opposite gender. She wrote: 'On the nets, where *warranting*, or grounding, a persona in a physical body, is meaningless, men routinely use female personae whenever they choose, and vice versa' (84).

In early virtual environments the absence of embodiment guaranteed the opportunity for a kind of virtual transvestism. In the virtual environment *Second Life*, such plasticity remains. It seems clear that the kinds of interactivity offered by contemporary digital and online technologies have disrupted the assumption of a 'natural' and unitary subjectivity for some people, who are happy to embrace a contingent and multiple sense of selfhood. In the age of Facebook and Twitter, however, where there seems a conversely powerful impetus to suture the gap between online and 'real', public and private, personae (through the uploading and publication of personal data, photographs and so on), perhaps it is folly to trumpet the possibility that digital technologies may be enabling of a different, more progressive mode of thinking about subject-formation and gender.

What interests me about Ruth Page's findings is that it was the opportunity to *write* creatively within the pedagogical framework that enabled the (male) students to imagine 'the Other of what is', that is, post-human or cyborg subjects. Knights suggests that it is not only the *production* but also the *reception* or cultural negotiation of texts that must remain in view with regard to Masculinity Studies in the classroom. Page's essay suggests to me the reverse: that it is the possibility of *production* of gendered subjectivities (and possible alternatives to the naturalised hegemon) that is engaged in the writing assignments. It is here, I think, that the possibly transformative implications of the development of digital culture, and online discursive practices regarding gender and the subject, can be brought into considerations of the teaching of masculinities. As I wrote above, the mode of *estrangement* is one that I have used not only in teaching science fiction, but also in Film Studies and other subjects where a reorganisation of students' acculturated behaviours or assumptions is central to the pedagogical process. If the production of gender performances in digital culture is now fairly commonplace, this offers the opportunity to use the students' own life experiences and cultural practices to make the invisible visible.

In moving towards a conclusion, I will once again draw upon my own teaching experience. Some ten years ago, I taught a course entitled 'Gender and Representation' that considered representations of femininity and masculinity in film, television, advertising and other forms of popular media and culture. In one session, I asked students to look at some examples of 'fan fiction', including some 'slash' fiction, alongside Constance Penley's groundbreaking essay, 'Feminism, Psychoanalysis and Popular Culture', which analysed these para-literary forms in the light of a feminist politics of appropriation and resistance. The students seemed stunned by such material: not shocked by its content, but completely unaware of the existence of such texts and the kind of cultural sensibility that informed their production. Since then, I have been involved in several postgraduate supervisory roles in which fan fiction (or 'fanfic') has been the focus of the research, and where the postgraduate student's own critical practice was informed by being a fan fiction writer themselves, with their own assumed online 'identity' under which they posted in the LiveJournal community.[2]

A recurrent problem that these postgraduate students have encountered is their ability to forge a meaningful connection between two types of writing, two modes of discourse: the creative and the critical. Quite clearly, what is also at stake here is two kinds of persona or subject, the 'writer' and the 'academic', and an apparent incompatibility between the two. One student confessed herself unable to 'come out' as an academic within the fanfic community, fearing that this would involve a kind of delegitimisation in the eyes of her peers. Clearly, some forms of digital transvestism are more problematic than others, and here I think we also find anxiety about a reduction of the plurality and diversity of the fanfic community when assimilated into the critical discourse of the academy.

These postgraduate students are perhaps on the leading edge of a transformation in the way in which subjectivities are produced in a digital culture, and their struggles to formalise and theorise their positions as writers/academics look forward to a time when this kind of 'cyborgism' is less troubled, and much more commonplace. There has been a rapid alteration in the relationship between production and consumption in the everyday lives and practices of young people in developed economies with popular access to online digital networks. In 'remix culture' (a term derived from the 'remix' or alternative version in dance music, which has now become a more general term for the production of appropriative or recombinatory texts), in fan fiction, in the blogosphere, on Wikipedia: the consumers (our students) have become producers, reworking and appropriating and collaging existing media texts and scripts as well as generating their own. In the realm of teaching practice, the concept of the 'liquid book' – a kind of plural, collaboratively produced and open online text(s) – has been fruitfully introduced by the editors of the online journal *Culture Machine*, and I have experimented with such Virtual Learning Environment (VLE) spaces in the teaching of my science fiction unit.

It is my suspicion, and my hope, that digital culture will shortly have a profound effect upon the pedagogical relationship, not only in terms of delivery of teaching materials, online books or articles, discussion threads and VLEs, all of which are now fairly commonplace, but in ultimately arriving at a situation where students become co-producers of knowledge; where the fluidity and potentiality of the cyborgised digital subject extends outwards to an enriched discursive and conceptual terrain; and where we, as teachers of 'masculinities', not only make the patriarchal and ideological formations of gender and the subject *visible* to students, but encourage them to engage with their own everyday experiences and practices as part of their university studies.

Notes

1. At the end of Robinson's 'Pedagogy of the Opaque', there is appended a four-part syllabus on 'American Masculinities' that, we can also assume, forms the structure for the experience of teaching masculinities that Robinson writes about so incisively.
2. LiveJournal is a long-standing virtual community and blog-hosting site, which incorporates social-networking functions with blog, journal or diary publication. It has been an important site for fanfiction communities and the dissemination of fanfiction texts.

Works Cited

Baker, Brian (2006) *Masculinity in Fiction and Film 1945–2000* (London and New York: Continuum).
——— (2007) 'Gothic Masculinities', *The Routledge Companion to Gothic*, eds Catherine Spooner and Emma McEvoy (Abingdon: Routledge), 164–73.
Brod, Harry (1995) 'Masculinity as Masquerade', *The Masculine Masquerade: Masculinity and Representation*, eds Andrew Perchuk and Helaine Posner (Cambridge, MA and London: MIT Press), 13–19.
Chatterjee, Ranita (2008) 'Charlotte Dacre's Nymphomaniacs and Demon-Lovers', *Masculinities in Text and Teaching*, ed. Ben Knights (Basingstoke: Palgrave Macmillan), 75–89.
Clare, Anthony (2000) *On Men: Masculinity in Crisis* (London: Chatto and Windus).
Cohan, Steven (1997) *Masked Men: Masculinity and Movies in the Fifties* (Bloomington and Indianapolis: Indiana University Press).
Connell, R.W. (1995) *Masculinities* (Cambridge: Polity).
Dooley, Mark (2008) 'Queer Teaching/Teaching Queer', *Masculinities in Text and Teaching*, ed. Ben Knights (Basingstoke: Palgrave Macmillan), 59–74.
Faludi, Susan (1999) *Stiffed: The Betrayal of Modern Man* (London: Vintage).
Ferrebe, Alice (2008) 'High Visibility: Teaching Ladlit', *Masculinities in Text and Teaching*, ed. Ben Knights (Basingstoke: Palgrave Macmillan), 220–34.
Foucault, Michel (1990) *The History of Sexuality, Volume 1: An Introduction*, trans. Robert Hurley (Harmondsworth: Penguin).
——— (1991) *Discipline and Punish: the Birth of the Prison*, trans. Alan Sheridan (Harmondsworth: Penguin).
Gibson, William (1995) *Neuromancer* (London: Voyager).

Haraway, Donna (1991) 'A Cyborg Manifesto: Science, Technology, and Socialist-Feminism in the Late Twentieth Century', *Simians, Cyborgs and Women: The Reinvention of Nature* (New York: Routledge), 149–181, available at <http://www.stanford.edu/dept/HPS/Haraway/CyborgManifesto.html>, accessed 20 March 2011.

Hodgson, John (2010) 'Student Voices', *WordPlay* 3 (April), 6–14.

Jameson, Fredric (1998) 'Of Islands and Trenches: Neutralization and the Production of Utopian Discourse', *The Ideologies of Theory: Essays 1971–86, Vol. 2: The Syntax of History* (London and New York: Routledge), 75–101.

Jeffords, Susan (1994) *Hard Bodies: Hollywood Masculinity in the Reagan Era* (New Brunswick, NJ: Rutgers University Press).

Jones, Carole (2009) *Disappearing Men: Gender Disorientation in Scottish Fiction 1979–1999* (Amsterdam and New York: Rodopi).

Kimmel, Michael (1987) *Changing Men: New Directions in the Study of Men and Masculinity* (London: Sage).

—— (1996) *Manhood in America: A Cultural History* (New York: Free Press).

Knights, Ben (1999) *Writing Masculinities* (Basingstoke: Macmillan).

—— (2008) 'Masculinities in Text and Teaching', *Masculinities in Text and Teaching*, ed. Ben Knights (Basingstoke: Palgrave Macmillan), 1–36.

Le Guin, Ursula (1989) 'Is Gender Necessary? Redux,' *The Language of the Night: Essays on Fantasy and Science Fiction* (London: The Women's Press), 7–16.

—— (2001) *The Left Hand of Darkness* (London: Orion).

MacKinnon, Kenneth (1997) *Uneasy Pleasures: The Male as Erotic Object* (London: Cygnus Arts).

The Matrix (1999) dir. The Wachowski Brothers (Warner Brothers/Village Roadshow Pictures).

Neale, Steve (1993) 'Masculinity as Spectacle: Reflections on Men and Mainstream Cinema', *Screening the Male: Exploring Masculinities in Hollywood Cinema*, eds Steven Cohan and Ina Rae Hark (London and New York: Routledge), 9–20.

Page, Ruth (2008) 'Gender and Narrative Form', *Masculinities in Text and Teaching*, ed. Ben Knights (Basingstoke: Palgrave Macmillan), 109–25.

Penley, Constance (1992) 'Feminism, Psychoanalysis and Popular Culture', *Cultural Studies*, eds Lawrence Grossberg, Cary Nelson and Paula A. Treichler (New York and London: Routledge), 479–500.

Robinson, Sally (2000) *Marked Men: White Masculinity in Crisis* (New York: Columbia University Press).

—— (2002) 'Pedagogy of the Opaque', *Masculinity Studies and Feminist Theory: New Directions*, ed. Judith Kegan Gardiner (New York: Columbia University Press), 141–60.

Schoene-Harwood, Berthold (2000) *Writing Men: Literary Masculinities from Frankenstein to the New Man* (Edinburgh: Edinburgh University Press).

Stone, Allucquere Rosanne (1992) 'Will the Real Body Please Stand Up?: Boundary Stories about Virtual Cultures', *Cyberspace: First Steps*, ed. Michael Benedikt (Cambridge MA and London: MIT Press), 81–118.

Suvin, Darko (1979) *Metamorphoses of Science Fiction: On the Poetics and History of a Literary Genre* (New Haven and London: Yale University Press).

Tiptree Jr., James [Alice Sheldon] (2004a) 'The Girl Who Was Plugged In', *Her Smoke Rose Up Forever* (San Francisco, CA: Tachyon), 43–78.

—— (2004b) 'Houston, Houston, Do You Read?', *Her Smoke Rose Up Forever* (San Francisco, CA: Tachyon), 163–216.

6
'Men Couldn't Imagine Women's Lives': Teaching Gender and Creative Writing

Steven Earnshaw

It is perhaps possible to write neutrally on gender, but rather point-less. The question I want to put is: 'How should the creative writing workshop operate in a society that favours men over women?', rather than framing a more balanced question: 'In what ways does gender impact on the teaching of creative writing?'[1]

We need to be more subtle, of course, than this, since recent research emphasises how gender can affect men adversely as well as women, and not all men have access to the 'gender dividend', but we should not lose sight of the overriding inequality. Politically, global power is male (UN 2008, Table 4), as is world business and finance (Connell 2009, 2; Holmes 2007, 8), as is science and technol-ogy (Connell 2009, 7) and men continue to get paid more (UN 2008, Table 4). Religion is everywhere patriarchal (Connell 2009, 7). Edu-cationally, yes, boys tend to underachieve at school in the area of writing and literacy, and to underperform with respect to girls (Brown 1999, 178–81; Fletcher 2006). But when we get to adult-level creative writing teaching, the issue seems more obviously to reflect general social prejudices, that is, gender bias is imported from the world at large into the creative writing workshop in a variety of ways: teaching styles; expectations about writing; genre and literary tradition; work-shop politics and egos; gender perception. In the UK, the existence of the Orange Prize, a major award for women authors only (founded 1996), and *Mslexia*, a magazine aimed primarily at female writers and readers, suggests that there is a continued and firm belief in the need for an appreciation of the way in which gender affects the production and reception of women's writing, and that modes of redress in the writing world can be, and may have to be, political.

This chapter is not confined to women's writing, but it is nevertheless written in the context of gender inequalities on the global stage and within the sphere of writing and publication. What should the creative writing workshop be offering against this backdrop? What research there is on the creative writing workshop and gender suggests that for a number of reasons female students are disadvantaged (McCabe 1994; Brown 1995; Orellana 1995; Thomas 1995, 125–7; Weiser 1999). Yet the majority of books on creative writing and creative writing pedagogy do not specifically address gender, including, most recently: Mills (2006); Morley (2007); Earnshaw (2007) – *mea culpa*; and Harper and Kroll (2008). Julia Casterton in *Creative Writing: A Practical Guide* (2005) claims that women experience 'relentless denial of their powers, which begins as soon as they speak, if not before, and makes the act of writing for them primarily an act of rebellion' (Casterton 2005, 3–4), but this does not noticeably inform the advice that follows.

Should tutors be obliged to introduce gender as a topic, or do they simply need to be 'aware' and act accordingly? Or do they need to imagine students and writers as 'genderless' or 'gender-neutral': gender-transcenders?[2] Because, having said all of this, the *raison d'être* of the creative writing workshop is, and has to be, to improve students' writing, not make them and their tutors 'better people'.

So the question we really have is: 'How can attention to gender improve everybody's writing?'

The workshop 1: class dynamics

In the context of creative-writing teaching my instinct is to subordinate politics to aesthetics. The concern is with writing, not consciousness-raising. The workshop is obviously a good forum to discuss politics, and some students (and tutors) may put politics first, but surely the creative writing takes precedence in this environment. If politics in any guise crops up, fine, but do not engineer the workshop around political issues. And yet, I confess, this does not seem to me an entirely acceptable position.

What work there is on the gender dynamics of the creative writing workshop points to the reproduction of gender inequality that exists in the broader sociocultural context. Nancy McCabe's participant-observer study of an American graduate creative writing workshop found that, despite the male tutor's attempts to create a 'non-hierarchical, student-centered environment', it was the male students who spoke most (McCabe 1994, 2) and it was male values that received recognition (9). It is not that there was a deliberate attempt on the part of the males to behave in this way, but by conforming to the gendered behaviour patterns in force outside of the work-shop, both the men and the women in this dynamic contributed to the recreation of the gender hierarchy, or, to use more recent terminology, 'gender order'. McCabe also makes a point about the way pedagogical practice is managed. For instance, in other studies she draws on, it is seen that women learn differently from men in a manner termed 'connected learning'. This is based primarily on 'empathy, listening and believing rather than doubt, antagonism, competitive turn-taking, and the dissection of arguments' (Belenky, *Women's Ways of Knowing*, cited in McCabe 1994, 6).

However, there is an assumption here on McCabe's part that what needs to change in the workshop is a move towards 'women's ways of knowing' and that what is construed as female-gendered learning is preferable to male-gendered learning. A tutor could indeed accept this view, and most guides to teaching would probably endorse it. However, this does privilege a particular teaching strategy and could be challenged at the theoretical level: if gender is indeed 'learned', then gendered learning can certainly be constructed differently. Lib-eral empathy may not always be the most valuable approach, and workshops can fall flat as students and tutor wrestle with new ways of being polite. An alternative therefore might be one that encour-ages disagreement amongst students, and is deliberately provocative. This may seem to run counter to the spirit of work currently wishing to address (and redress) gender inequity by focusing on 'empathy' and 'collaboration', but I think the alternative sketched here can be seen as a natural extension of wishing to unpick possible gendered constraints on teaching creative writing. A tutor might want to mix up teaching strategies in any case, although the mainstream position is no doubt one that urges 'empathy, listening and believing' first and foremost rather than the airing of sharply differing views.

There is another issue McCabe raises, and which is endorsed by Elizabeth Weiser's article, 'Can Women Writers Survive the Creative

Writing Workshop?' (1999). The dismissal of women's experiences as valid and valuable for creative writing is sometimes a feature of the creative writing workshop, and this derives not just from the broader sociocultural denigration of women's lives, but is part of the dominant aesthetic that frequently operates within the creative writing workshop. This view suggests that the autobiographical and confessional modes do not have the artistic credibility necessary for proper art, and so (the argument goes) when female students wish to discuss work based on their personal experiences it is dismissed, both on the grounds that men's lives are more significant than women's, and on the grounds that aesthetics should transcend individual experience. Judy Brown's essay, 'The Great Ventriloquist Act: Gender and Voice in the Fiction Workshop' shows how female students have a tendency to reproduce male-oriented narratives because they are 'valued', whereas stories relating to their own lives are not (Brown 1995, 311–13).

The remedies at this level may seem rather obvious. The tutor, aware of tendencies to drift into inequitable scenarios, should ensure that all the students are given a voice, using strategies familiar to teaching in general: males should be encouraged to listen more and females to speak out more, if this is the perceived problem in the group. The tutor should also open up discussion around aesthetics, with an eye to what may be gender-inflected judgements. There is a further issue here around aesthetic modes and genres. Weiser quotes a student, and supports the student's view, that realism is favoured over fantasy, and this intrinsically disadvantages women:

'My impression is that stories by women get dissed [*sic*] not because of gender issues per se, but because of differences in writing style [across genders]. Workshops here seem to prefer 'realistic,' plot-driven fiction. The fantastic, the mystical, the outside-of-time is less accepted.' I believe we have only to look at the infamous list of the 'Best 100' English-language novels of the 20th century published by the Modern Library division of Random House in July 1998 to see the dearth of successful female-authored texts resulting from an aesthetic based on straightly realistic, male-centered, male-populated literature. (Weiser 1999; no pagination)

Although I am not convinced by the specifics of this argument – on the contrary, the novel genre has often favoured a domestic realism where women's lives are central – the passage does illustrate how an argument around gender and writing encompasses genre, and how what has value – particular genres, particular subject matter – informs our creative writing sensibilities at different levels. I will discuss this in relation to the novel and to poetry further in the chapter.

Identity and intersections

I would suggest that what is most readily observable in the workshop is a power dynamic based on intersections between gender, age, sexual orientation, class and race, and of these it is the intersection between age and gender that is the determining feature. Creative writing groups in HE are more likely to have a diverse age range than a typical English literature class, which will tend to have students coming straight from school or college. Consequently, where a creative writing group does have mature students, it is often the older students who dominate because of their greater social confidence, and because of the tendency of younger students to defer to their elders. In such a class, *age* is the determining factor rather than gender. At the same time, I have taught older students coming to creative writing in HE who may not have had much contact with education since their school days, and such students do feel at a disadvantage compared with students who have gone straight from A Levels to an undergraduate English or creative writing degree, and then straight on to a writing Masters. Young, middle-class students may feel more at home speaking up in group situations than older, working-class students, and in these intersections between class and age it is arguable that gender may not exert much influence. Again, this is a question of classroom management – tutors keen to give everybody a fair hearing will have to negotiate all of these complex power exchanges as a matter of course.

A different, less 'liberal' approach might be one which overtly acknowledges one or more of the political contexts around identity (gender, sexual orientation, age, class, educational background, wealth, race, disability) and proceeds in this manner throughout the course of teaching. It is perfectly possible that provoking conflict, rather than seeking to nullify it, is a more constructive, or creative strategy, as I have already suggested. A tutor who sees his or her teaching as falling within the area of political commitment may indeed feel obliged to teach in this way. My assumption here is that, politically, teaching in HE is informed by a broadly liberal attitude, which, being a default or dominant position, does not require explicit commitment in a way that might be controversial, given prevailing pedagogic norms.

These are preliminary comments about the workshop, mainly in response to work already done and my own experience of teaching (and being taught) creative writing and literature. I will return to the workshop scene and scenarios after looking at an issue specific to creative writing and gender.

Gender and genre

Genres often bring their own gender-alignments. I will concentrate on just two here, the novel and poetry, but hopefully the ideas will transfer across to consideration of other genres.

The novel

> Men couldn't imagine women's lives, they seemed to believe, as in a religion, that women were numbed by an instinctive craving to fill the wet mouths of babies, predestined to choose always the petty points of life on which to hang their attention until at last all ended and began with the orifices of the body. She had believed this herself. And wondered in the blue nights if what she truly felt now was not the pleasure of driving but being cast free of Mink's furious anger. He had crushed her into a corner of life. (Proulx 143)

The scenario is not an unusual one. A woman comes to the realisation that her life has been circumscribed by the man she has lived with for many years, and that this in turn is the fate of women *en bloc*. Jewell Blood's self-awareness focuses on men's perceptions of women as biologically determined. It also identifies men as constitutionally unimaginative with respect to understanding the lives of women, with the implication that the imagination of women is superior in this respect – women can and do imagine the lives of men in a fashion that is not reciprocated. When we consider that here is a novel whose author is female, and whose central character is male, there is a further suggestion that female novelists hold the upper hand in characterisation: women can do both sexes, men can only do their own. This constitutional lack of male imagination is presumably also a biological judgement, but of women on men, although all of these elements are bound up with social circumstance or consequence.

In one way, of course, it redresses an older criticism that women have a narrower knowledge of the world than men, and so cannot write significant books. As Virginia Woolf once noted, imagining the values of a male critic: 'This is an important book, the critic assumes, because it deals with war. This is an insignificant book because it deals with the feelings of women in a drawing room. A scene in a battlefield is more important than a scene in a shop' (quoted in Russ 1984, 41). Annie Proulx's point is Woolf's – women's lives are different, but just as significant as men's – but taken further: women can write from both gender perspectives.

Another approach to the writing of novels in terms of gender can be seen in the history of the novel. Ian Watt's *The Rise of the Novel* (1957), which has set the terms of the debate ever since, placed three male novelists centre-stage: Daniel Defoe, Samuel Richardson and Henry Fielding. Unsurprisingly, given the impact Watt's book has had, there have been many criticisms, including one suggesting that this is the male-centred view of the literary novel canon. And it is not just the novels themselves, since the question of which (sub-)genres are valuable and which are to be placed further down the hierarchy of literary value often depends upon the way in which genres are gendered, such that 'romance' (regarded as solely for women) becomes the 'other' of the novel form. In the nineteenth century, George Eliot bemoaned 'silly novels by lady novelists' (*Westminster Review* 1856), at the same time as she wrote under a male pseudonym, and the case of the Brontës using gender-neutral anonymity with which to promote their work is well known[3]. Still today, there is a gendered contemporary genre – 'chick lit' – that suggests a certain type of novel which will appeal to women only, just as there are 'chick flicks': in essence, stories about women, for women.

Although it is unlikely that a course on 'writing a novel' will devote much, if any time to the novel as a genre,[4] it is certainly worth bearing in mind some of the above points (both in this section, and the preceding mention of (sub-)genres such as fantasy and memoir in relation to realism) in the presentation of the novel. It is most likely that the question of gender will arise when addressing narrative voice in fiction, especially if the writer chooses a voice that is not his or her own gender (see especially Brown 1995). It might, however, be worth specifically addressing the presentation of 'character' in relation to what Connell calls 'character dichotomy', the idea that 'Women are supposed to have one set of traits, men another' (Connell 2009, 60). Will writers, of both sexes/genders, unconsciously duplicate these dichotomies? This might be introduced directly for consideration, or could be part of the general exploration of character in relation to identity. A session, or part-session, based on exercises around imagining characters of opposite gender to the writer is bound to be productive.

The poem

If the question of gender in relation to the novel can seem rather forced when bringing it into the creative writing workshop (but fruitful, I would suggest), when it comes to poetry the issue can become quite divisive. This is partly down to (contemporary) formal taste, in that poetry tends towards the short lyric, and this makes for the possibility of representative anthologies which, in presenting a particular profile, can work politically. Hence, I would argue, the politics of gender and poetry are more overt. A case in point is Deryn Rees-Jones's critical book, *Consorting with Angels*, which looks at how female poets in the twentieth century have contested a male-dominated tradition, and is accompanied by her anthology volume, *Modern Women Poets*. A book such as Jane Dowson's *Women's Poetry of the 1930s* (1995) acted, and continues to act, as a direct challenge to Robin Skelton's *Poetry of the Thirties* (1964): for three decades Skelton's book had defined the poetic landscape of the thirties as masculine (the only female poet included was Anne Ridler). At the other end of the timescale, Robyn Bolam's *Eliza's Babes: Four Centuries of Women's Poetry in English, c. 1500–1900* provides another counterweight to male dominance. There has thus been, and continues to be, a visible promotion of a tradition of poetry by women. Vicki Bertram's *Gendering Poetry: Contemporary Men and Women's Poetry*, for instance, sees poetry as a whole permeated by the question of gender. Rees-Jones asserts that 'the poet has a very different physical relationship to the poem than the novelist has to the novel because, despite its appropriation by the printed page, poetry has always been and remains an oral and performed art . . . written to be spoken, and heard, if only in the reader's head'. As such, Rees-Jones argues, there is a performative aspect to poetry, and in this line of thought we can see that poetry is intrinsically embodied (implicitly at least) and will thus always involve 'negotiation of gender' (Rees-Jones 2005, 12–13).

The consequences of this for teaching poetry writing are unclear, however. The genre is more gender-politicised than the novel, and it is also obvious that the lives of women significantly contribute to the subject matter of poetry by women. That is, reflections on 'this life' are both individual expressions *and* take part in the body of thought and feeling that adds up to the tradition of women's poetry. In my experience, it is more likely that a creative writing poetry class might set time aside, wholly or in part, to explore contemporary women's poetry, in a way that is unlikely for contemporary women's novels.

Rather than introducing gender-related material into creative-writing workshops in a 'secondary' fashion, the fact that poetry already has a gender-political element makes it easier to offer the intersection of gender and poetry as the main focal point. For example, Helen Farish established the module 'Kiss and Tell' for the BA English Studies degree at Sheffield Hallam University. The module mixes creative writing with a critical focus on American women poets such as Denise Levertov, Adrienne Rich, Anne Sexton and Sharon Olds. Students opting to do this module know that they are undertaking both critical and creative work that has a strong gender focus (discussed below, and see Appendix). Creative writing modules established on these lines enable the exploration of gender and poetry in any number of ways.

The workshop 2: raising awareness

If people *do* gender they have to engage with ideas about how it 'should' be done, even if they find ways to do it differently. People also have to do gender within conditions not of their own making, so they have far from a free rein. (Holmes 2007, 61)

An article by Rindfleish *et al.*, 'Creating an "agora" for storytelling as a way of challenging the gendered structures of academia' (2009, pre-print) suggests that the sharing of stories – in themselves, 'sense-making tools' – allows for a raising of awareness of systemic practice (4–5). In other words, what otherwise would be experienced from the perspective of the individual becomes recognisable as part of a wider patterning of experience within certain structures and cultures. The article uses an interesting phrase, 'psychological contract' – the university within which these researchers work promotes gender equity and has won awards for it, yet the experience of female members of staff is contrary to what the university says it offers as a working environment (the reference point here is work by Robinson and Rousseau 1994). This part of the chapter – raising awareness – is a tool for guarding against the replication of gender divisions beyond the workshop, and challenging them within the creative-writing space.

To raise the issue is immediately to politicise the workshop, and this may be a problem, as described here:

> After McCabe discussed her findings with the women in her workshop, they decided to support each other in speaking up about classroom communication and about characterizations of females in stories. Tensions rose, the workshop leader accused the women of 'ruining the workshop by "politicising" it,' and McCabe hypothesized that by rejecting their traditional role of creating connection in the class, the women had forced a breakdown in class cohesion (7). Her experience suggests that women are relied upon in graduate workshops to mediate between artistic male egos, perhaps to the detriment of their own artistic progress. (Weiser 1999)

It is possible to see how this would play out in a workshop that had 'gender' as one of its themes. The starting position, as I outlined at the beginning of this essay, is that the world is gender unequal. Any workshop with this as its starting point automatically puts males on the defensive and women in the morally superior position. The situation will become additionally complex if the issue of sexual orientation is thrown into the mix and an implicit hierarchy becomes established, in the order of most valued to most criticised: lesbian; homosexual male; heterosexual female; heterosexual male. What are the tutor's options? And even here the tutor might be challenged on his or her categorisations. What about 'transgender', 'transsexual', 'homosocial', 'same-sex' rather than 'homosexual'? And whatever happened to 'androgyny'?

Raewynn Connell boldly states that 'the development of social science has provided a solution' to the general perception that gender is intrinsically divided along male/female and masculine/feminine lines: 'gender must be understood as a social structure. It is not an expression of biology, nor a fixed dichotomy in human life or character. It is a pattern in our social arrangements, and in the everyday activities or practices which those arrangements govern' (Connell 2009, 10). This would be quite a useful way in, I think, since it asks us to look at gender as a set of social relations. Although Connell's own take on this is that these relations are structured around male and female reproductive systems – differently in different cultures, but nevertheless the structural centre is the same – and a tutor (and students) might find this narrow, the presentation of the real nature of social relations, as opposed to commonplace surface apprehensions, often lies at the heart of artistic endeavour. Does this dilute the political nature of gender?

I think that the most productive way is to understand gender as 'something we do' (Holmes 2007, Chapter 3; West and Zimmerman 1987) within the constraints of gendered social structures and expectations: we are people with a certain amount of autonomy relating to gender as a social structure, as we simultaneously live and construct our selves. We 'do' gender and 'perform' gender in the workshop by default, and, if we are not careful, we might reproduce normative gender structuring in our creative writing, falling into stereotypical characterisations, voicings, writing styles and modes. This can only be bad writing, clichéd writing in a number of different aspects. Here are some suggestions:

Module ideas

'Kiss and Tell' (See Appendix)

In 'Kiss and Tell' (mentioned above) students have to write a critical essay and submit 4–5 poems. It has a specific remit around American female poets from the 1960s onwards. Students know precisely what the agenda is and can explore the politics of gender and creative writing. In terms of creative writing, such a module helps expand the poetry-writing repertoire of the student, and alerts them to the ways in which gender and genre are intertwined, for example, in confessional poetry. A module such as this allows a tutor to offer a clear, gender-focused approach to creative writing.

'Writing and Difference'

'Writing and Difference' is a module devised by the poet and critic Harriet Tarlo. This has a broader remit than 'Kiss and Tell', with the intention to introduce creative writing students to a more diverse range of literature than they might otherwise encounter, and to attend specifically to the question of difference. This means that students are asked to engage with some or all of those intersections discussed above and to think critically and creatively around them. Such a module may have a broader appeal than 'Kiss and Tell', but has a less-focused political agenda. It does however mean that most if not all students will experience both sides of the 'insider/outsider' divide and perhaps feel more 'comfortable' as a result. Suggested literature and themes are 'dialect and the spoken word'; Jean Rhys's *Wide Sargasso Sea*; 'from margin to centre'; immigrant writing, for example, Kazuo Ishiguro's *The Remains of the Day*; 'the politics of genre', for example, Louise Erdrich's 'Tracks'; Ntozake Shange's *For Coloured Girls who have Considered Suicide when the Rainbow is Enuf*.

Workshop 3: practical suggestions

'The Contest' from *Seinfeld* (Season 4, Episode 11). This Emmy award-winning episode broaches a fairly taboo subject (for mainstream television at least – male and female masturbation) in a way which recognises gender differences and yet constantly undercuts them. It also has the advantage of being funny and is one of the best examples of intricate plotting. The episode could either be presented directly as a starting point for discussion of gender-related issues around characterisation – the way Elaine is always on an equal footing with the men – or it could form the starting point for technical craft in scriptwriting.

'Home': The dynamics within a domestic set-up could be used as a neutral topic that is likely to naturally raise many of the above issues. Writing male and female characters, deciding on certain relationships within the home and then voicing characters within the relationship (and then with 'intersections' of race, class, ethnicity, age, sexual orientation). The topic is well suited for most genres of writing (adapted from an idea by Jill LeBihan).

'Gender and genre': I have discussed gender mainly with respect to poetry, the novel and scriptwriting, since these are the dominant genres for writing courses. Other genres might include memoir, a mode of writing that might have distinct gender-political motivation, for example in reclaiming 'lost voices'. 'Fictocriticism' is a genre that mixes creative writing and critical theory (see Smith 2005). Its audience is probably mainly academic, but a piece like Rachel Blau du Plessis's 'For the Etruscans' might be a starting point, or the work of Hélène Cixous and Luce Irigaray, or Donna Haraway's 'Manifesto for Cyborgs'. Discussion of *écriture féminine* could form part of this, or could be used in conjunction with other genres. Students could be asked to 'write in the style of' Woolf (for example, *Mrs Dalloway*) or James Joyce (Molly Bloom versus the rest of *Ulysses*?).

Language use: The idea that language is inherently gendered is a vexed one. However, one way of stimulating a class could be to take the list of words that appears in this passage on masculinities:

> At a lay level, one can recognize the attraction of biological explanations for understanding gender, for much of our everyday language is permeated with explicit or implicit gender(ed) interpretations. For example, words such as passive, active, sensitive, aggressive, emotional, caring, controlling, warrior, nurse, captain, leader, manager, director, cleaner, virile, frigid, impotent can be read in gendered ways, and interpreted within dualistic but dominant understandings of what it means to be a man or a woman ... Thus language not only informs concepts of masculinity, it is a tool through which to perform, label, and interpret our gender identities ...
> (Whitehead and Barrett 2001, 11)

The tutor could ask the class to write something that involves at least five of these terms. Since the words are largely gender-sensitive, this could easily raise issues around gender and language. Or the tutor could begin directly with Julia Casterton's assertion: 'Women and men stand in a different relationship to writing' (3).

There is a section in Marx and Engels's *The Communist Manifesto* that calls for the family to be abolished and replaced by a community of women (240). Either taking this passage as the starting point, or simply introducing the idea of abolition of the family as the prime social unit, would give the opportunity for future-oriented writing. Again, this could apply to most genres.

Masculinities: something from *Fight Club* would certainly open things up – perhaps look at the film rather than the book, and ask for creative responses to it; here is a work which represents the idea that there is a crisis in masculinity; some critics challenge this thesis, suggesting it has parallels with equally false claims that we are now (happily) in a post-feminist world (see Whitehead and Barrett 2001, 4–10). Other possibilities: something from Ernest Hemingway's *The Sun Also Rises* (*Fiesta*), Chinua Achebe's *Things Fall Apart* or Alan Sillitoe's *Saturday Night and Sunday Morning*.

Jean Rhys's *Wide Sargasso Sea* might be a good choice for 'recommended reading', with plenty of potential for discussion of gender, power, identity, race, literary canons and, certainly not least, writing and writing styles.

A final point for this section is that the workshop most likely does not exist in the kind of splendid isolation the above suggests. For example, a student may experience formal critical approaches to literature elsewhere if the creative writing component is part of an undergraduate degree programme, in which case the introduction of issues around gender is not likely to be contentious, even if the discussions prove to be so. Nor is the creative writing workshop the only place where the student develops his or her writing. Essential to development are the feedback sessions, usually one-to-one tutorials, and this gives plenty of scope for dealing with issues specific to a student's writing that the tutor will not want to air publicly.

Conclusion

I began by asserting that whatever is said needs to take into account the fact of gender inequality. We have seen the complexity of this as it intersects with other 'forces of identity': class, race and age in particular. But I also believe that a creative writing class has to be firstly about the writing. Students will not thank a tutor who purports to help them improve their writing, only to find themselves discussing social and political affairs at the expense of all else. Within the delivery of a lone creative writing module I think the opportunities for engineering the workshops around issues of gender are limited – and should be limited. An undergraduate degree devoted to creative writing, however, offers plenty of space within which to devise modules that combine critical and creative activity, with the political and social dimensions visibly part of the approach to creative writing.

Appendix

'Kiss and Tell: Female Sexuality in American Poetry, 1960–2000'

(Module Leader: Harriet Tarlo, Sheffield Hallam University. Level 6/ Year 3, Undergraduate. Reproduced with module leader's permission. Originally established by Helen Farish.)

Week 1 Introduction to the module: American women's poetry 1960–the present

Week 2 The new generation of women poets. **Text:** *New Selected Poems of Denise Levertov*

Week 3 Confessionalism and female sexuality. **Text:** *The Selected Poems of Anne Sexton*

Week 4 The challenge to 'compulsory heterosexuality'. **Text:** Adrienne Rich, *The Fact of a Doorframe: Poems, Selected and New 1950–1984*

Week 5 The challenge to white feminism. **Text:** Audre Lorde, *Undersong: Chosen Poems Old and New*

Week 6 Consolidation of ideas and guided creative writing workshop

Week 7 Experimental poetry and female sexuality. **Text:** Kathleen Fraser, *Il Cuore: The Heart Selected Poems 1970–1995*

Week 8 Reading Week

Week 9 Contemporary poets in the black experimental tradition. **Text:** Harryette Mullen, *Recyclopedia: Trimmings, S∗PeRM∗∗K∗T, and Muse and Drudge*

Week 10 Contemporary poets in the confessionalist tradition. **Text:** Sharon Olds, *Selected Poems*.

Week 11 Tutorials.

Week 12 Creative writing workshop of student work and final questions re assignments.

Sample essay questions

Discuss the significance of one of the following common motifs in women's poetry 1960–2000: silence; the mask; the witch.

Is there a 'common language' (Adrienne Rich) with which women talk about female sexuality and the body in their poems?

What specific challenges does confessionalist poetry about female sexuality pose to the reader?

What specific challenges does experimental poetry about female sexuality pose to the reader?

What characterises the most successful erotic poetry by women in your view?

Marge Piercy argues that women's poetry, far more than men's, is poetry 'of the body, the brain, the emotions fused'. Do you agree?

What challenge to mainstream feminist poetry was posed by black and/or lesbian poets of the 1970s onwards and how is this relevant to female sexuality?

Which of the poets studied in the course of this module have you found the most challenging and why?

How is the personal political in women's poetry 1960–2000?

How important to women's poetry about the body are the roles of mother and/or daughter.

Alicia Ostriker wrote that 'to be a creative woman in a gender-polarized culture is to be a divided self'. Do you see evidence of this in the poetry we have studied?

What poetic techniques are most successful for the exploration of female sexuality?

Why was there an explosion in women's poetry in the latter half of the Twentieth Century and why was so much of it concerned with identity and the body?

Notes

1. In researching this chapter I took the opportunity to discuss the topic with tutors and students on various occasions. I would very much like to thank Liz Barrett, Suzanne Batty, Chris Jones, Jill LeBihan, Shelley Roche-Jacques,

Harriet Tarlo and Linda Lee Welch. It has also benefited from previous discussions with Helen Farish.

2. There is no general agreement on what 'gender' is. The tenor of this article draws mainly from the feminist-sociological perspective but does recognise the strength, and potential in this context, of feminist-psychoanalytical approaches. A strategy favouring the phenomenological (subjective) dimension of gender would probably be the most broadly attractive to creative writing classes, both from the point of view of personal experience and from the necessity of writing characters who possess individual psychologies. See Holmes (2007, 104–8) for a discussion of 'Phenomenology and Habitus: Experiencing the Body', and the article 'Throwing like a Girl: a Phenomenology of Feminine Body Comportment, Motility, and Spatiality' (Young 1990).

3. Charlotte Brontë explained the use of Acton, Currer and Ellis Bell as pseudonyms for Anne, Charlotte and Emily in her Biographical Notice to the 1850 edition of *Wuthering Heights*: 'we did not like to declare ourselves women' (31).

4. An exception is Susan Hubbard's module 'Fiction and Gender' (see Hubbard, especially 137–40).

Works Cited

Bertram, Vicki (2005) *Gendering Poetry: Contemporary Women and Men Poets* (London: Pandora).

Bolam, Robyn (2005) *Eliza's Babes. Four Centuries of Women's Poetry in English, c. 1500–1900* (Tarset: Bloodaxe).

Brontë, Charlotte (1977) 'Biographical Notice', *Wuthering Heights*, ed. Emily Brontë (London: Penguin), 30–6.

Brown, Anne (1999) *Teaching Writing at Key Stage 1 and Before* (Cheltenham: Stanley Thornes).

Brown, Julie (1995) 'The Great Ventriloquist Act: Gender and Voice in the Fiction Workshop', *American Women Short Story Writers: A Collection of Critical Essays*, ed. Julie Brown (New York: Garland), 311–22.

Casterton, Julia (2005) *Creative Writing: A Practical Guide*, 3rd edn (Basingstoke: Palgrave Macmillan).

Connell, Raewyn (2009) *Gender*, 2nd edn (Cambridge: Polity).

Dowson, Jane (1995) *Women's Poetry of the 1930s* (London: Routledge).

Earnshaw, Steven (ed.) (2007) *The Handbook of Creative Writing* (Edinburgh: Edinburgh University Press).

Eliot, George (1856) 'Silly Novels by Lady Novelists', *Westminster Review*, July and October.

Fight Club (1999) dir. David Fincher (Twentieth Century Fox).

Fletcher, Ralph (2006) *Boy Writers: Reclaiming Their Voices* (Markham, ON: Pembroke).

Haraway, Donna (2001) 'A Manifesto for Cyborgs: Science, Technology and Socialist Feminism in the 1980s', *Modern Literary Theory*, eds Philip Rice and Patricia Waugh, 4th edn (London: Arnold), 465–83.

Harper, Graeme and Jeri Kroll (2008) *Creative Writing Studies: Practice, Research and Pedagogy* (Bristol: Multilingual Matters).

Holmes, Mary (2007) *What Is Gender?* (London: Sage).

Hubbard, Susan (2005) 'Gender and Authorship: How Assumptions Shape Perceptions and Pedagogies', *Power and Identity in the Creative Writing Classroom*, ed. Anna Leahy (Bristol: Multilingual Matters), 130–40.

Marx, Karl and Friedrich Engels (2005) *The Communist Manifesto* (London: Penguin).

McCabe, Nancy (1994) 'Gender Inequity in the Workshop: Methods Which Silence Women Writers', *Conference on College Composition and Communication* (ERIC ED 379 678) <http://www.eric.ed.gov/PDFS/ED379678.pdf>, accessed 8 September 2010.

Mills, Paul (2006) *The Routledge Creative Writing Coursebook* (Oxford: Routledge).

Morley, David (2007) *The Cambridge Introduction to Creative Writing* (Cambridge: Cambridge University Press).

Orellana, Marjorie Faulstich (1995) 'Good Guys and 'Bad' Girls: Gendered Identity Construction in a Writing Workshop', *Conference of the American Educational Research Association* (ERIC ED 390 852) <http://www.eric.ed.gov/PDFS/ED390852.pdf>, accessed 8 September 2010.

Proulx, E. Annie (1994) *Postcards* (London: Flamingo).

Rees-Jones, Deryn (2005) *Consorting with Angels. Essays on Modern Women Poets* (Tarset: Bloodaxe).

Rindfleish, Jennifer May, Alison Jane Sheridan and Sue-Ellen Kjeldal (2009) 'Creating an 'Agora' for Storytelling as a Way of Challenging the Gendered Structures of Academia', *Equal Opportunities International*, 28(6): 486–99.

Robinson, Sandra L. and Denise M. Rousseau (1994) 'Violating the Psychological Contract: Not the Exception but the Norm', *Journal of Organizational Behavior* 15: 245–59.

Russ, Joanna (1984) *How to Suppress Women's Writing* (Austin, TX: The Women's Press).

Skelton, Robin (1964) *Poetry of the Thirties* (Harmondsworth: Penguin).

Smith, Hazel (2005) *The Writing Experiment: Strategies for Innovative Writing* (NSW, Australia: Allen and Unwin).

Thomas, Sue (1995) *Creative Writing: A Handbook for Workshop Leaders* (Nottingham: University of Nottingham, Department of Adult Education).

United Nations Human Development Indices (2008) <http://hdr.undp.org/en/statistics/data/hdi2008/>, accessed 8 September 2010.

Watt, Ian (1957) *The Rise of the Novel* (Berkeley, CA and London: University of California Press).

Weiser, M. Elizabeth (1999) 'Can Women Writers Survive the Creative Writing Workshop?' <http://www.womenwriters.net/editorials/Weiser1.htm>, accessed 8 September 2010.

West, Candace and Don H. Zimmerman (1987) 'Doing Gender', *Gender and Society* 1(2): 125–51.

Whitehead, Stephen M. and Frank J. Barrett, eds (2001) *The Masculinities Reader* (Cambridge: Polity).

Young, I.M. (1990/2003) 'Throwing like a Girl: A Phenomenology of Feminine Body Comportment, Motility, and Spatiality', *Identities*, eds Linda Alcoff and Eduardo Mendietta (Oxford: Blackwell), 163–74.

7
Teaching Gender and Language

Jane Sunderland

The gender and language field

Although sociolinguistic and other work had been done on language and gender at various points in the twentieth century (for example, Jespersen 1922; Labov 1972; Trudgill 1972), 'Gender and Language' as a field really came into being with the second wave of the 'Western' women's movement (the 'women's liberation movement'), in the very late 1960s and early 1970s. Language was seen as one of the many ways (most) women were oppressed by (most) men. Early foci were 'sexist language' and ways in which men dominated women in private conversational talk. While there was much concern about gender representation – for example, in newspapers and children's books – linguistic studies of these had yet to be done.

Since then, the curricular content of Gender and Language Studies has expanded and developed apace, as has the scholarly reputation of the field. It is taught with increasing prevalence at undergraduate and postgraduate levels in universities across the world,[1] both as a unit of a module (or several units) and as a module in its own right (usually, but not always, an 'option choice'). It forms part of different degree programmes and accordingly is taught in different departments, not only those with linguistics, English language and/or communication in their titles, but also Gender Studies, Women's Studies and anthropology. To my knowledge, there is currently no 'MA in Language and Gender' programme anywhere in the world, but there is, I believe, no intellectual or epistemological obstacle to this. Indeed, there exists a vast body of literature on the topic, including monographs as well as edited collections, articles in a wide range of refereed journals and a dedicated *Gender and Language Journal*; the International Gender and Language Association (IGALA[2]) has been in existence since 2000 (taking over from the Berkeley Women and Language Group); and gender–language relationships constitute the basis of many PhD theses.

This development has come about in part because of a substantial widening of topics encompassed by Gender and Language. There is now as much work on written as on spoken texts, and the range of genres is vast, encompassing personal ad. columns, 'lad mags', parentcraft texts and spam e-mail messages. Public contexts – such as parliamentary sessions, tribunals, classrooms and workplaces – are now investigated as much as, if not more than, private ones. The notion of masculinity has shifted: firstly, from being marginalised (or stereotyped), to having a special focus; and secondly, from having a special focus to being integrated fully into (some) language and gender programmes. The field now also extends to sexuality, which is entirely appropriate given (1) the shared early political challenges faced by feminists and gay people (all of whom were seen as 'rocking the gender order boat'); (2) the important relationship between heterosexual attraction and gender (Hollway 1995); (3) hegemonic masculinity (of which a cornerstone is heterosexuality); and (4) the emergence of Queer Studies, which aims to interrogate all 'institutionalised' relationships, in particular those that are normative, and perceived as such (see Livia and Hall 1997; Cameron and Kulick 2003; Sauntson 2008).

The field has also developed *methodologically*: many approaches are available and utilised (see Harrington *et al.* 2008). Early empirical work on Gender and Language not prompted by the women's movement (for example, Labov 1972; Trudgill 1972) was associated primarily with sociolinguistics (and hence the variationist paradigm, which traditionally entailed the collection and comparison of spoken data from large groups of women and of men). In contrast, one of the pioneers of Gender and Language study *per se*, Robin Lakoff, very controversially used and defended her use of introspection[3] (as a speaker of English as a first language) as the basis of the first monograph in the field: *Language and Woman's Place* (1975). Gender and language research is now carried out through the more systematically empirical approaches of corpus linguistics, ethnography, stylistics, pragmatics and conversation analysis (as well as sociolinguistics). Most centrally, I suggest, it is associated with *discourse*, that is, the way things are talked and written about, and Gender and Language relationships are now explored through, *inter alia*, discursive psychology (see Edley and Wetherell 2008), feminist post-structuralist discourse analysis (Baxter 2003) and critical discourse analysis (Wodak 2008). Not only has discourse broadened the potential database for the field of language and gender – any text, written or spoken, has the potential to be gendered – the notion of discourse entailed new theory, and hence has brought about a radical paradigm shift for the field, as I will show below.

Prompted by the burgeoning women's movement, the 1970s' and 1980s' research agenda of Gender and Language could be said to have been in large part a scholarly exploration of 'gender differences' in talk, with a view to exposing linguistic (and hence social) disadvantage of women and girls in contexts such as private homes and classrooms. Curricular content followed this agenda, with language and gender sessions in the 1980s being devoted to the comparison and evaluation of what came to be known as the '(male) dominance' and '(cultural) difference' approaches to such 'differences' (see Litosseliti 2006). This often proved popular, with female students recognising some of the findings of these 'gender differences in talk' studies in their own (heterosexual) relationships. This was not surprising, given the strength of the globally popular 'gender differences' discourse: consider such notions (often unproblematised) as *'vive la différence'* and the 'battle of the sexes'. Closer to home, Deborah Tannen's *You Just Don't Understand: Women and Men in Conversation* (1990) was an international bestseller, and John Gray's *Men are from Mars, Women are from Venus* (1992) included a chapter on language.

However, retrospective examination of 'gender differences' as an approach has widely critiqued the associated studies as entailing (1) overgeneralisations and absolutes; (2) an overemphasis on inter-group variation, and an associated underplaying of similarities between women and men and of intra-group variation (that is, diversity among women, and among men); (3) a lack of appreciation of the importance of context (including 'Community of Practice', where 'practices' are both linguistic and material; see Eckert and McConnell-Ginet 1992); and, most importantly, (4) seeing language as a reflection of gender ('women speak like this because ... ') rather than as something that constructs gender, in ways I show below (see Cameron 1992; Litosseliti and Sunderland 2002). Deborah Cameron (1992) also made the political point that focusing on gender differences ironically bolsters a social division that most feminists and feminist linguists are ultimately striving to end. Corresponding social and political changes have also meant that 'gender differences' in *occupational* roles are in many world contexts much less marked than hitherto, and overt discrimination less evident, although this has brought with it a new concern with 'subtle sexism' (Lazar 2005; Mills 2008) in language (and beyond).

Accordingly, in the late 1980s and 1990s, with the advent of post-structuralism, the focus shifted in various ways. The most radical shift was to see gender not so much in terms of *who* (speaks or writes, and how) but *what* (they speak or write, and how), that is, the construction of gender, in talk and written text (see Sunderland 2004): discourse on gender. Rather than seeing talk as something that people did in ways that reflected their gender, the recognised importance of discourse and (a measure of) agency in talk and elsewhere entailed an understanding that people can *perform* different identities for themselves in the way they talk, including their gender identity, or, in other words, can *construct themselves* as gendered women/men, in part by drawing on particular gendered discourses. Doing so (in repeated and socially recognisable ways) can also be seen as constructing gender *itself*, as sets of normative and marginal ideas about women and men. This theoretical shift, which of course concerns both *language* and *gender*, is intellectually more challenging (and, to many students, less attractive) than the previous 'person-focused' emphasis on gender differences.

Teaching gender and language

This 'theoretical turn' raises all sorts of issues for pedagogy, in particular, how best to help students understand the idea of language as constitutive (but not determinist), rather than simply reflective, and the idea of gender as going beyond 'differences' between women and men, boys and girls. Students also have to familiarise themselves with the accompanying and often confusing and inconsistently used terminology (*subject position, construction, constitutiveness, performance, performativity* ...).

My approach to the notion of the construction of gender in talk includes discussion of an extract of data collected by a Lancaster University MA student, Kay Wheeler (2002), the topic of whose dissertation was 'How do we know gender is being constructed?' The extract, which is from an informal conversation between friends, two male and two female students (Romeo and James, Annie and May, all native speakers of English) is as follows:[4]

Romeo:	can I say and this might not apply to you two
	[probably addressing Annie and May] but (.) in
	my experience (.) when you're out with a bunch
	of people (.) people most likely to get you into
5	trouble are women hh
James:	really? (.) I've not seen that happen
Annie:	hh
May:	[***] witnessed that before?
Romeo:	I I I've been out like in a sort of group yeah (.)
10	like someone's come up to you in the street and
	started mouthing off (.) and
	you're like oh fair enough they're pissed and
	then the women start saying oh but you're not
	[well we're like no no we] won't we just want
15	to go
James:	really? [*************]
Annie:	hh
Romeo:	to the pub
James:	I sorry I I do not agree sorry yeah I've never had
20	that happen (.) it's always from the guys who are
Annie:	[**************] start it
Romeo:	I must hang around with some really bad
	women then
All:	[laughter]
25 May:	trust you (.) your choice of friends
James:	I don't know maybe it's just my experience but
	I've never had (.) never had that happen
Romeo:	I suppose the other thing is if you're around
	with a group of
30	women (.) you're more likely to act macho than
	you would be with just [***]

James: [yeah] but there's certainly an argument for that
(.) although I did have a friend it was quite
humorous his girlfriend was talking all this trash
35   to this other girl about my boyfriend will
beat up your boyfriend

All: [laughter]

James: you know and seriously she was (.) and he's sit
he's sitting there right behind her going [makes
40   gesture?]

All: [laughter]

James: no I'm not gonna beat that guy up I don't even
know him he (.) he hasn't done anything to me
(.) he was just basically and finally and finally the
45   only way he could resolve it (.) he couldn't think
of any other way to resolve it it's not the best
way but it (.) was all he could think of at the time
he said look
(.) if you two girls wanna fight

50 All: [laughter]

James: you can fight [long pause] that's the only time
I've ever really seen that happening (.) and I was
quite amused by that to be honest hh [long
pause] um

55 Romeo: I can't [?] really remember mates getting me into
fights um

This extract nicely illustrates how different forms of femininity (and accordingly masculinity) can be constructed: in this case, by men, and indeed, male friends in the same conversation. Here, Romeo is sustaining a construction of women as the cause of men getting into trouble (and hence men as innocent victims). James, however, is resisting the construction of women as troublemakers in a way that is equally sustained (ll. 6, 16, 26). He does provide an example in the shape of a story that would appear to support Romeo's construction, but importantly concludes his story with 'that's the only time I've ever really seen that happening' (l. 51–2), that is, the story functions as the exception that proves the rule. Romeo can be said to be drawing on a socially recognisable discourse that we might call 'Women as trouble-makers', James to be producing an equivalent *resistant* discourse.

In class, I ask students to role-play this extract. We then discuss the different but recognisable constructions of femininity (and of masculinity), noting that these contradictory constructions both come from young men. This rather neatly makes the point that *what* is said about gender, and how, is at least important as who is speaking, and how. A research question along the lines of 'How is gender constructed in the talk of these speakers?' is much more productive and interesting than 'What are some gender differences in the talk of the above speakers?', which would tell us little more than the men speak more (in this particular extract) than the women. (Additionally, because this data was collected, transcribed and analysed by a student, and was included in a successful MA dissertation, this endows it with not only epistemological weight but also pedagogic value.)

But what, then, to do about the dated, but often attractive, notion of 'gender differences in talk'? Although not much time may be devoted to this in a current programme of Gender and Language study, it should not be ignored, for historical reasons, and can of course be (and usually is) addressed critically. Further, I would add that it is not completely outdated: there is still gender discrimination, and not only in those contexts (or Communities of Practice) across the globe in which gender differentiation is extreme and disadvantageous to women. It surely remains sometimes appropriate to explore linguistic as well as social differences between women and men. But if 'gender differences' (or better, 'gender tendencies') is to be included in a programme of study, at what point? Prior to a discussion of gender and discourse? This 'historical' approach may allow students to appreciate the latter through the perceived deficiencies of 'gender differences'. Or after a discussion of gender and discourse, as a sort of 'historical aside'? This may put the notion of 'gender differences' in their place, but may also be less clear.

There is a more general, curricular design issue here: organisation of a language and gender programme of study. This includes topic selection – which requires one, difficult set of decisions; and sequencing, including the question of where to include 'gender differences in talk'. There are different possible organising principles, with the

chronological unfolding of the field (including theoretical developments) being just one. A programme of study could also be arranged
by theme or topic (such as 'advertisements', or 'parliamentary talk');
or by theoretical and/or methodological approach (for examples,
see Sunderland and Swann 2007[5]). Criteria for decision making will
include not only the type and length of the programme, but also the
level of the students, and their academic background more generally
(see below).

To return to 'differences', there is a further epistemological com-
plication, which is that the field of Gender and Language is not
only concerned with naturally occurring talk (in both public and
private contexts), or even elicited talk (for example, in interviews,
which are beyond the scope of this chapter) but also with *representation*, of women, men, boys and girls (and accordingly gender
relations) in a range of genres: fiction, advertisements, magazines,
newspapers, films, plays, television programmes, songs, textbooks,
graffiti, jokes, self-help manuals, proverbs, wedding invitations,
travel guides...the list goes on. This is something very different
in kind from talk. As Alison Easton reminds us: 'it is important
to distinguish between our experiences and the images we meet
of these in the arts, media and other cultural texts' (6). These
'images' are often written (or multimodal), but not all need be 'delivered' in writing (consider, for example, songs and scripted political
speeches).

In research projects on gender representation, the prototypical
research question, I suggest, is something like: 'How are women [or
men, or women and men] linguistically represented in [a specific
instance of a particular genre]?' This is, of course, to explore *gender
differences* in representation. Is this more defensible than the exploration of gender differences in naturally occurring talk? I would argue
that it is. We may not be able to draw a clear line between representation and naturally occurring talk: talk of course also 'represents'
given its medium of language, which *always* 'represents', and certain spoken genres will bear distinct intertextual relationships with
representational written texts (a party political debate with a corresponding party political leaflet, for example). However, by and large,
we can make a distinction between spontaneous, situated, dynamic
informal talk, on the one hand, and designed (and often static) 'representations' on the other. The justification for exploring gender

differences in representations is then precisely that they are *not* differences in the 'who' of language use (that is, speakers) but rather in the 'what' (that is, discourse). Further, as this language is created in a society that is still sexist in many ways (again, see Lazar 2005; Mills 2008 on 'subtle sexism'), there remains a need for vigilance. Due to the wide circulation and recycling of many media texts, any gendered discourses in these can be seen as playing a role in the construction of gender (Sunderland 2004). Of course, the study of represented gender differences does not, and should not, preclude the exploration of *comparable* representations of women and men.

Students of gender and language

Students of Gender and Language are many and varied. I would here like to consider four 'social categories': discipline, age, gender and ethnicity. All pose certain challenges for the teacher; all thus raise questions about pedagogy. Below I briefly mention the first two, and then discuss the second two at greater length.

Gender and Language as a course is likely to attract students with a background in or currently studying some aspects of linguistics but who have little or no understanding of gender, *and* those with a background in gender (for example, from Women's Studies or Gender Studies departments or degree schemes) but with little or no understanding of the workings of language. While this can make for interesting class discussions, it can also leave some students feeling lost, and others feeling that they have heard it all before.

The presence of Gender and Language students of different *ages* raises not only questions of different life experiences (in particular, of parenthood), but also feminism. Prompted by the advent of the second wave of the women's movement, and politically underpinned by feminism, Gender and Language in some ways most directly addresses those sympathetic to, or at least familiar with the broad tenets of feminism. This was all very well in the 1980s. And while it is highly likely that a given teacher of language and gender in the early twenty-first century will have an interest in equal opportunities, gender relations and questions such as the beneficiary of gender-differential practices, and media representations of different 'types' of women, the same cannot be assumed of students. Young undergraduates (or at least those who have not yet had to juggle parenthood and career), in my experience, sometimes consider that we are now living in a 'Golden Age' as regards gender, that all the battles have been won, and that feminism is outdated. Such young women also sometimes equate feminism with man-hating, drawing on the notion of the 'battle of the sexes', which presupposes that if someone gains, someone else loses – which I would argue is *not* (and never was) an understanding of most forms of feminism.

Thirdly, classes often comprise both male and female students (although almost always a majority of the latter). This may be in part because, while adopting a critical stance on any form of discrimination against, or marginalisation or degradation of women, most Gender and Language courses these days nevertheless also address issues of masculinity *and* femininity. In this they parallel Gender Studies ('Women's Studies' now sounds distinctly dated and rather 'seventies') in the recognition that understanding women's situated struggles and progress requires a full understanding and exploration of masculinity, and of gender relations. For example, men need to be studied not as 'representatives of humanity' but as people who are often *seen as* representatives of humanity (see Johnson 1997). Nevertheless, and despite reassurances and exhortation in 'introduction to the course' sessions, Gender and Language (when taught as an optional module) still overwhelmingly attracts female students. Something to do with gender is clearly 'going on'. What is this? Presumably, 'gender' is perceived as being 'really about women', just as 'ethnicity' is perceived as being 'really about non-white people'. Even so, why would a course *about* women not attract men? Is it seen as 'for' as well as 'really about' women?

I will stick my neck out here and propose some reasons for this demographic imbalance, in terms of the possible motivations of those few men who do enrol for Gender and Language courses. A few (and I suggest a very few) may come for the 'social' opportunities offered in a class with a majority of women. Some may come because they are (or think they may be) gay, and expect (like some female students) to find useful insights about surviving, understanding or challenging the current (highly heterosexual) forms of hegemonic masculinity. Still others (I am not putting a number on it) may come with the 'macho' motivation of finding whether they can 'deal with' a course that they perceive as one that will challenge and perhaps undermine men, traditionally masculine practices, and perhaps men's desires and understandings. And a fourth group may come with genuine academic interest and with no baggage of feeling threatened. But whatever the reasons, over the many years I have been teaching Gender and Language as an 'elective', men have always been in a minority.

This demographic raises issues for pedagogy, not least whether the imbalance should be commented on or ignored. I use it as an example of 'gender relevance': with a gender-imbalanced class, as in any gender-imbalanced situation, clearly gender *is* relevant (although precisely how remains uncertain), and 'something to do with gender is going on'. What I have learned not to do is request a 'masculine' perspective from a particular male student: this is clearly not only unfair but also flies in the face of the need to challenge gender essentialism, a need that is likely to be seen as part and parcel of any twenty-first century Gender and Language course.

Can different things be achieved in mixed-sex and all-women Gender and Language classes? Do they work differently? To the extent that classes on gender can simultaneously function as *de facto* support groups and/or consciousness raising sessions, these may be more likely to come into play in all-women groups (but it is hard to know). As regards materials and teaching activities, I would make no distinction beyond a reservation about looking at pornographic texts (written and/or visual) with a mixed-sex class, given the possible difficulty heterosexual male students may have of separating desire from intellectual detachment – and here I include 'lad mags', an important modern topic, given our 'post-feminist' era and the prevalence of knowingness and irony in the media more widely. Both the possibility of consciousness-raising/support, and the reservation about pornography, of course, rest on an element of gender essentialism.

The fourth social category in terms of the demography of Gender and Language classes is that of ethnicity. Postgraduate courses, in the UK at least, are often highly multicultural in terms of the student body, undergraduate courses increasingly so, and Gender and Language courses are no exception. One issue here is, again, feminism. The 'man-hating' stereotype of feminism goes beyond young Western women: I have come across African students who share this notion, and who further see feminism as anti-family, responsible for single parents and anti-African (and 'imposed' from the West). Given the frequent association of women in certain societies with being 'cultural brokers' of (pre-colonial) tradition, feminism thus constitutes a many-dimensioned challenge, as well as a possible set of attractions for African women scholars.

The idea of feminism as associated with the West is exacerbated on Gender and Language courses by the fact that most of the research reported does indeed come from Western countries, for a range of reasons (not least that most journals require work in a very high standard of academic English), and the majority of work on linguistic sexism and language change in relation to gender has been on British and American English (for exceptions, see Pauwels 1998; Hellinger and Bussman 2001). This does not mean that we are stuck with this situation, but it does mean that teachers of Gender and Language need to try that bit harder to transcend these geographical and cultural boundaries. There is work out there on language and gender in non-Western contexts and on languages other than English (or other European languages; it is just harder to find; for example, see Sadiqi 2003; Okamoto and Shibamoto-Smith 2004; Majstrovic and Mandic 2011).

But what can be done in class? I conclude this article with a recorded and transcribed extract from a class in March 2010 in which I was the teacher. This was the last of nine sessions on a postgraduate (MA) course on Gender and Language at Lancaster University, UK; the session was called 'Gender and Language in Non-'Western' (or non-Anglo) Contexts'. My intention was that the group, which was extremely international, would develop a greater appreciation of how women's issues played out and were promoted in non-Western contexts, and also how the language of an unconventional 'text' (partly English, partly French) constructed women.

The 'text' was a 2009 International Women's Day dress from Cameroon[6] – magenta in colour, and bearing a range of visual images and words in French and English (Cameroon is a largely francophone country but many of its citizens speak both French and English), as shown below. The images were those of recognisably African women in a variety of occupational and domestic roles, all smiling. The occupational roles included driving a tractor and a bus, and operating a crane. The words include 'Actors of our future, building up together', 'Tolerant, peace-loving' *'altruiste'* (altruistic), and *'ingenieuse'* (ingenious).

I introduced the dress as a 'cultural object' (as well as a material one), then invited the students to the front of the class to examine its words and visual images more closely. Below are several extracts (reproduced chronologically) from the 'talk around the text' ('S' is 'a student' – they have not been differentiated; 'J' is myself):

J can you tell me something about it in general other than the fact that it's magenta OK we've got colour what else have we got

S what is it about the bus

S exactly

J OK we'll have a look at that in a minute in a minute it I think it's more to do with the sex of the driver

S there's colour text illustration and decoration

J yeah OK so it's quite flamboyant so it's one of those things it's not representing women as shy and retiring in that sense so if you

wear this you're sort of drawing attention to your womanhood
by the colours but what about the shape
S big
J it's non-revealing it's quite big so it's covering most of the body
it's covering the arms okay most of the legs
S women in Kuwait this this is the traditional dress in Kuwait
J yes yes exactly it's the same sort of thing so we can say it's woman
if you like as not shy and retiring but modest right it's not a little
tiny skimpy thing.

Here the students and I are constructively building on each other's
responses to develop an understanding of how this text is constructing gender. The observations continue, the students pointing out
what they see in terms of the images and written text (clearly, there
is a lot of overlapping text, so not all the voices, or entire utterances,
have been picked up). There is also some interpretation:

S tolerant peace-loving
S characteristics of women's ...
S is it he or she
S the driver's a woman
S all of the drivers are women
S and many doves like doves
S maybe they want to have the same jobs as men

The students also go beyond making observations to making
comparisons:

S can you see that the ones that are related to men are are smaller
I mean women are smaller than the ones related to women
S which one the other one
S all the jobs related to men (.) women is small
S this is a woman right
S what about this one – small
S you do need to fit a whole bus in that one
S but you could have done that
S what about this one
S in comparison with a machine its OK I mean it's like they try to
they try to
S and here they are in the similar size

Here it is proposed that the jobs traditionally associated with men are represented visually as smaller than those traditionally associated with women. There is some contestation of this, but an important gender-representational *possibility* has been raised. Equally importantly, this is coming from the students and not from me. (On a more basic level, this sort of activity encourages student rather than teacher talk).

After several minutes I try to pull the observations together:

J so in general terms how is this cultural object constructing women
S *extremely* positively
J you'd expect very positively so what's the range of constructions
S they're very they're varied aren't they
J so you've got the woman bus driver but what what else have you got or who
S doctors
S teachers
J so you've got all the professions but you've also got a strong emphasis on motherhood
S in the centre
S and the wife here
S so basically they're saying that saying that we [presumably: women] have all the qualities right
J I think they're saying we have all the qualities but they're also saying we're not driving buses at the expense of the family right
S yeah
J that's how I would interpret it they're saying it's OK for women to drive buses but they mustn't forget the husband the children you know and all this about the primary educator etcetera yeah

Here I am building on the observations to propose my own interpretation. In what I say next, however, I am roundly challenged, or at least reminded of my own apparent 'Western' bias:

J what I'm trying to say this whole emphasis on the family is a rather African thing yeah and I think in a lot of western countries if you had an International Women's Day dress which is a rather

bizarre concept but if you did I think the emphasis on the family
would be less yeah because I think if you're in Africa I think
there's a very big emphasis on the importance of the family
S it's not just in Africa
J no no no I know
S it's a universal thing
J absolutely absolutely

This enables me to link this textual representation of women with
wider social issues, namely feminism, and specific International
Women's Day practices:

J one of the issues a lot of countries have with feminism is
that it's seen as being anti-men and anti-family and anti-
child
S exactly
J now as far as I'm concerned it doesn't have to be any of those
things but there is a perception and therefore if you're promoting
International Women's Day which is basically a feminist idea if
you're in one of those countries then you have to show right
that it's not anti-men right and to do that you point out the
importance of the family as well
S but how is that pointing out the importance of family
J because there's a lot of representations with children
S but not with men
S yeah there is there's one dancing
S I would say it's saying that women can cope with their children
perfectly well without men

In the above, the students explore my claim that the dress is representing the importance of the family and the limitations of this, and
one student proposes her own interpretation. There is then further
discussion of International Women's Day, including an observation
concerning the *production* of this particular cultural object:

S also there's mentioned International Women's Day so the sign
here but this also gives me the kind of impression women can
do everything by taking different kinds of roles to make them in
harmony to make everything in harmony

J yes I think that's true so it's not it's supposed to be harmonious it's not supposed to be disruptive to the society

S yes not conflictive

S yeah but we do not know if it was more provocative it would be accepted so perhaps in order to be sell they should make it more like that for commercial reasons

The final extract shows students spontaneously identifying *different* gender representations (in particular, of men):

S I think he's holding a baby and that one [referring to a woman with a sewing machine] is stitching

J we have an example do we

S the husband is holding the baby

S that one is holding the baby

S yeah but it's not central it's here not very central

J it's very small

S yeah it's small

I hope this activity helped to attune the students to the practice of identifying and provisionally interpreting (multimodal) representations of women, including considerations of what/who is included and excluded, position and size, and that the activity also made the point about the global relevance of gender and language, mediated by cultural/context-specificity. In this sense, I feel confident that the activity 'worked'. In terms of systematic research practices, however, a further improvement would be to ask students (perhaps in pairs or groups) to note down *all* the words and phrases written on the dress (which could then be displayed on a screen), and short descriptions of all the visual images.

Of course, this is not the only way to encourage an appreciation of the global reach of gender and language issues, but an exercise like this constitutes a reminder of the way different contexts shape as well as reflect these issues. While English has provided a rich resource and indeed stimulus for research into gender and language (the language as a 'code', its use in naturally occurring talk and written text, and representations), it is not the only language to do so; nor do Western contexts have a monopoly on gender and language research. This is not just a question of looking at 'different linguistic and cultural contexts' across the globe, but also of designing curricula and teaching materials and activities to encourage students to identify links, similarities and echoes across those contexts.

Notes

1. For a list, see <http://www.lancs.ac.uk/fass/organisations/igala/Resources/On-line%20Materials.html>.
2. <http://www.lancs.ac.uk/fass/organisations/igala/Index.html>.
3. Otherwise known as 'native speaker intuition', that is, the 'feeling' for such things as the existence, grammaticality, appropriacy and relative frequency of different lexical and grammatical structures that someone has who has learned English, for example, as a first language (needless to say, this is a rather problematic concept).
4. I have simplified the transcription system from Wheeler's original. (.) means a short pause, [] indicates analyst comment; **** indicates 'unclear'; **hh** refers to breathiness or laughter.
5. See also <http://www.comm.umn.edu/faculty/sheldon/lgarchive.html>.
6. I am extremely grateful to Canisia Fontem, from whom I received this dress as a present.

Works Cited

Baxter, Judith (2003) *Positioning Gender in Discourse: A Feminist Methodology* (Basingstoke: Palgrave Macmillan).
Cameron, Deborah (1992) *Feminism and Linguistic Theory*, 2nd edn (London: Macmillan).
Cameron, Deborah and Don Kulick (2003) *Language and Sexuality* (Cambridge: Cambridge University Press).
Easton, Alison (1996) 'What Is Women's Studies?', *Women, Power and Resistance*, eds Tess Cosslett, Alison Easton and Penny Summerfield (Buckingham: Open University Press), 1–9.
Eckert, Penny and Sally McConnell-Ginet (1992) 'Think Practically and Look Locally: Language and Gender as Community-Based Practice', *Annual Review of Anthropology* 21: 461–490.
Edley, N. and M. Wetherell (2008) 'Discursive Psychology and the Study of Gender: A Contested Space', *Gender and Language Research Methodologies*, eds Kate Harrington, Lia Litosseliti, Helen Sauntson and Jane Sunderland (London: Palgrave Macmillan), 161–73.
Gray, John (1992) *Men Are from Mars, Women Are From Venus* (New York: HarperCollins).

Harrington, Kate, Lia Litosseliti, Helen Sauntson and Jane Sunderland, (eds) (2008) *Gender and Language Research Methodologies* (London: Palgrave Macmillan).

Hellinger, Marlis and Hadumod Bussman (eds) (2001) *Gender Across Languages: The Linguistic Representation of Women and Men*, Vols 1–3 (Amsterdam: John Benjamins).

Hollway, Wendy (1995) 'Feminist Discourses and Women's Heterosexual Desire', *Feminism and Discourse: Psychological Perspectives*, eds Sue Wilkinson and Celia Kitzinger (London: Sage).

Jespersen, Otto (1922) *Language: Its Nature, Development and Origin* (London: Allen and Unwin).

Johnson, Sally (1997) 'Theorising Language and Masculinity: A Feminist Perspective', *Language and Masculinity*, eds S. Johnson and U. Meinhof (Oxford: Blackwell), 8–26.

Labov, William (1972) *Sociolinguistic Patterns* (Philadelphia, PA: University of Pennsylvania Press).

Lakoff, Robin (1975) *Language and Woman's Place* (New York: Harper & Row).

Lazar, Michelle, ed. (2005) *Feminist Critical Discourse Analysis* (London: Palgrave).

Litosseliti, Lia (2006) *Gender and Language: Theory and Practice* (London: Arnold).

Litosseliti, Lia and Jane Sunderland, eds (2002) *Gender Identity and Discourse Analysis* (Amsterdam: John Benjamins).

Livia, Anna and Kira Hall, eds (1997) *Queerly Phrased: Language, Gender and Sexuality* (Oxford: Oxford University Press).

Majstrovic, Danijela and Maja Mandic (2011) *Living with Patriarchy: Discursive Constructions of Gender Across Cultures* (Amsterdam: John Benjamins).

Mills, Sara (2008) *Language and Sexism* (Cambridge: Cambridge University Press).

Okamoto, Shigeko and Janet Shibamoto-Smith (2004) *Japanese Language, Gender and Ideology* (Oxford: Oxford University Press).

Pauwels, Anne (1998) *Women Changing Language* (New York: Longman).

Sadiqi, Fatima (2003) *Women, Gender and Language in Morocco* (Amsterdam: Brill Academic).

Sauntson, Helen (2008) 'The Contributions of Queer Theory to Gender and Language Research', *Gender and Language Research Methodologies*, eds Kate Harrington, Lia Litosseliti, Helen Sauntson and Jane Sunderland (Basingstoke: Palgrave Macmillan), 271–82.

Sunderland, Jane (2004) *Gendered Discourse* (Basingstoke: Palgrave Macmillan).

Sunderland, Jane and Joan Swann (2007) 'Teaching Language and Gender', Lancaster University <http://www.llas.ac.uk/resources/gpg/2827>, accessed 20 March 2011.

Tannen, Deborah (1990) *You Just Don't Understand: Women and Men in Conversation* (London: Virago).

Trudgill, Peter (1972) 'Sex, Covert Prestige and Linguistic Change in the Urban British English of Norwich', *Language in Society* 1: 179–95.

Wheeler, Kay (2002) 'How do we know gender is being constructed? A discussion of the warrants from which gender construction may be claimed', MA dissertation, Lancaster University, UK.

Wodak, Ruth (2008) 'Controversial Issues in Feminist Critical Discourse Analysis', *Gender and Language Research Methodologies*, eds Kate Harrington, Lia Litosseliti, Helen Sauntson and Jane Sunderland (Basingstoke: Palgrave Macmillan), 193–210.

8
Teaching Gender and Popular Culture

Stéphanie Genz

The academic study and teaching of gender has had a relatively short history. Fuelled by the political and cultural emergence of second-wave feminism, gender – often under the aegis of Women's Studies – developed as a separate area of investigation as late as the 1960s, drawing attention to a range of inequalities that women face in both personal relationships and social positionings. Second-wave feminists also highlighted the fact that the academy itself was a deeply patriarchal structure with a number of academic disciplines acting to exclude the experiences, voices and identities of marginalised peoples, including women. Responding to second-wave critiques, English – along with other subjects in the humanities, arts and social sciences – began to focus on gender as a structuring principle and contest the supremacy of many classic, male-dominated/written texts of the literary canon. Questions were asked about the absence of 'great' women in this field and attempts were made to 'fill in the gaps' and undo the male bias – Kate Millett's influential *Sexual Politics* (1970), for example, identified patriarchy as a socially conditioned belief system whose attitudes and systems penetrate literature, philosophy, psychology, politics and life itself.

Early on, the connection with feminist politics and theory was concrete as many of these scholars were also engaged in gender-based struggles outside the academy and used their teaching as an act of consciousness-raising that directly drew on students' experiences of victimisation to politicise their personal outlooks as well as the classroom environment. As Jane Pilcher and Imelda Whelehan note, this had an effect on the formal characteristics of academic study, particularly the teacher–student link and assessment that were 'kept under scrutiny and other means of teaching and assessment than the formal lecture or seminar, the essay or examination were experimented with' (x–xi). Here, the central aim of education was emancipation and the politicisation of knowledge while the teacher–student relationship was one of political initiator and ally. This is concomitant with the aims and objectives of what Carmen Luke terms 'feminist pedagogy', which connects learning practices with the theoretical and political aims of feminism and seeks to change 'power, authority and the master (teacher) slave (student) dichotomy of pedagogical relations' in the hope of achieving a less authoritarian teaching mode (Luke 1998, 27–8). However, while the demystification of the teacher–student bond may have been one of the central tenets of feminist pedagogy, it is also an inherently problematic one, as feminist educators are without doubt institutionally authorised and exert power in a number of ways – by judging student work and assigning marks, for example. In our position as teachers, this could lead to a pedagogical/feminist predicament as, in our own classroom practice, we might experience the unworkable and slightly idealistic dimensions of this model of flattened hierarchy that in turn is counterbalanced by our continuing commitment to feminism's emancipatory project and our desire for inclusive content delivery and collaborative knowledge exchange. As Luke writes, there is a contradiction between 'the practical teaching project of academic feminism . . . and its professed theoretical and political standpoints' (32) – a paradox she aptly summarises as feminism's dilemma or 'trouble with authority' (30) and 'moral discomfort with claiming individual power' (33).

These concerns about feminist pedagogy have been further intensified by the changing nature of Gender Studies and the altered political/cultural landscape that feminism and feminist academics have encountered in recent decades. In line with postmodern/poststructuralist perspectives, feminism has diversified and moved beyond second-wave politics, asking broader questions about the impossibility of 'Woman' as an analytical category and the ensuing plurality and differences of 'women'. Moreover, academic institutions have themselves undergone a series of important changes in the last 30 years – not least a generational shift and inclusion of a younger group of feminist academics for whom feminist politics may no longer be a key motivating force. As Whelehan and Pilcher observe, 'many women's/gender studies academics now in the academy constitute the first generation to be educated in gender as students themselves and are correspondingly distant from the heady politics and campus activism of the 1960s and 1970s' (xiii). Nowadays, gender is often *taught* as part of an academic discipline – instead of being *lived* as a political identity – with gender theory for example permeating the English classroom as a key component of literary courses. These developments have not always been interpreted as a symptom of the vibrancy and productivity of Gender Studies, and fears reside among some commentators that a 'dangerous depoliticization' is taking place that results in the dilution and institutionalisation of the previously charged category of gender (Luke 1998, 29).

It is from this standpoint – as a post-second-wave feminist with a background in English Studies – that I approach the teaching and analysis of gender in the twenty-first century, well aware of the increasing complexity and diversity of this topic, as well as my own positioning within feminist history. Born in the mid-1970s, I did not witness the political excitement and activism of feminism's second wave – instead, I grew up and started my academic feminist journey in the backlash-ridden 1980s and 1990s when feminism itself became a dirty word for many and terms like 'equality' and 'emancipation' lost their innovative appeal and became part of our everyday vocabulary (see Faludi 1992). My introduction to feminism was not necessarily the result of a direct political engagement but, instead, was fuelled by critics like Sandra Gilbert and Susan Gubar whose influential *The Madwoman in the Attic* (1979) signalled a shift towards 'gynocritics' – a term invented by Elaine Showalter – which focused on literature by women. Given this generational/temporal distance and different positioning, some second-wave teachers have looked upon younger feminists with mistrust, often interpreting changes in feminist politics and ideology in familial terms as mother–daughter conflicts (Walker 1995). At the same time, feminist theories and teaching practices have also been re-examined by this post-second-wave generation of academics for whom the contradictions within feminist pedagogy – what Luke calls the 'not-said' (19) or 'hidden hegemony' of feminism (35) – have become apparent as they seek to engage in constructive and self-reflexive criticism of some feminist tenets.

Now, well into the new millennium, a third generation has embarked on gender-based analysis for whom not only patriarchy but feminism itself has become a kind of 'master' – or 'mistress' – discourse whose logic and principles they might not only be unfamiliar with, but also might actively resist. Indeed, as many of us teaching feminist theory or Gender Studies will have experienced, students are nowadays loath to engage with feminism or embrace the title of 'feminist', believing that it is either an anachronistic relic – something they no longer require in their supposedly emancipated lives and egalitarian careers – or a deeply unappealing attribute they associate with a number of stereotypes, from strident and quarrelsome to unattractive and 'hairy' (Douglas 1995, 7).[1] In this chapter, I will examine the contemporary role of feminism and status of gender theory within the humanities and, in particular, English Studies by reflecting on my experience of teaching gender-based courses. I will suggest that while gender analysis is now an inherent component of many literary theory modules, the position and understanding of feminism among teachers and/or students is more debatable and unsettled. Every year I start my introductory lectures on gender theory by asking my second-year students whether they identify with feminist goals or even define themselves as 'feminists' – usually only a handful of students are prepared to admit that they can relate to the dreaded 'F-word' (out of a cohort of almost 100) or they acknowledge that they espouse some feminist goals – such as 'equal pay for equal work' – but nonetheless disavow the actual label, in line with the often-cited refrain, 'I'm not a feminist, but...'.

While this complacency (and to some degree ignorance) on the part of modern-day students is intriguing – and, I have to confess, at times irritating – it also highlights another key feature of contemporary Gender Studies that we cannot ignore – namely, a lot of ideas about gender relations and perceptions of gender are no longer confined to the classroom but are perpetuated by other institutions and outlets, most notably the media. As many contemporary commentators recognise, feminism is now part of the cultural field and its meanings are increasingly mediated. Joanne Hollows and Rachel Moseley, for example, note that 'most people become conscious of feminism through the way it is represented in popular culture' (2). This is true for both post-second-wave feminist educators and students whose conception of feminism is often filtered through popular

discourses and images of ostensibly liberated and strong women –
Madonna and Buffy for some, Pink and Lady GaGa for others. Furthermore, feminist teachers now occupy a precarious middle ground,
having to combine their awareness and appreciation of feminism
with their own immersion in – and critical distance from – the
popular realm. This, of course, also has an effect on the content
and delivery of academic disciplines like English that have had to
respond to this changed cultural context and perception of gender.
The English classroom seeks to be dynamic and contemporarily relevant, which often means integrating non-canonical texts – such as
the chick-lit 'classic' *Bridget Jones's Diary* (1996) – with which students are familiar. As a result of this popularisation, the very tangible
link between feminist politics and teaching in the late 1960s and
1970s is no longer as apparent in a progressively more diverse media
culture saturated by information and communication technologies.
As Rosalind Gill has commented, 'the 'obviousness' of what it means
to do feminist intellectual work breaks down' (22) and we are left
with a 'messy contradictoriness' (2), a clear sign that gender relations
and media representations – as well as the feminist frameworks used
to interpret them – are constantly changing.

As might be expected, this also has important consequences for the
teacher–student relationship, as students are frequently more media-
savvy and knowledgeable than their teachers in this respect. Students
often have a pre-existing bond with popular culture that is perceived
as an 'authentic' part of their everyday life and experience. In this
context, we have to consider the intricate relationships between students' prior knowledge of the media and the knowledge that the
teacher makes available to them. This poses a number of practical,
pedagogical and ethical questions about the ownership of knowledge and the power relations in the post-millennium classroom: Is a
teacher's knowledge any more valuable or objective than that of their
students? How can she or he claim a standpoint of authority? Are students active or passive in their consumption and analysis of popular
culture and how can we successfully teach gender and/through popular culture in ways that use students' familiarity with the media while
also enhancing their understanding of feminist and gender theory?
Moreover, specifically in relation to English, is this popularisation
to be understood as a challenge to canonicity that either invigo-
rates or 'dumbs down' the curriculum? In what follows, I want to

address these issues by first examining the strenuous links between feminism and popular culture and then discussing the merits and pitfalls of using popular media texts as a means to engage with the English discipline and theoretical paradigms. The complex realities of the twenty-first-century classroom underline the fact that this is not going to be an easily resolvable debate but a pedagogical conflict that will keep us deliberating for years to come.

Uneasy companions: feminism and popular culture

As Gill has recently observed, 'most feminism in the West now happens in the media', emphasising the practical impossibility of experiencing and identifying an 'authentic' kind of feminism that is unadulterated by the hegemonic and often conservative forces of cultural representation (40). However, even if feminism – and our understanding of it – is now inextricably tied to media discourses, this does not mean that the idea of 'feminism in popular culture' or the concept of 'popular feminism' is straightforward and uncontested. Quite the contrary, what happens to feminism within the popular – and how popular culture reacts to the mainstreaming of feminism – has been a major concern of feminist critics ever since the second-wave's prime in the 1970s. In effect, the early days of second-wave feminism were characterised by a determinedly anti-media attitude, with the women's movement – along with other political groups at the time – conceiving of itself as 'outside' the dominant culture and offering an alternative to the predominantly stereotypical images perpetuated by/in the 1960s and 1970s media (see Genz 2009, 50–64). From this perspective, popular culture was criticised for its representation and reproduction of gendered inequalities and, as such, it was rejected as 'a sort of ideological machine which more or less effortlessly reproduces the dominant ideology' (Storey 1997, 12). It was seen as an inherently compromised and misogynist site, perpetuating both patriarchal and capitalist values and peddling 'false consciousness' to the masses. In order to counter this indoctrination, many second-wave critics employed what Ang calls 'the crude hypodermic needle model of media effects' that relies on the assumptions that 'mass-media imagery consists of transparent, unrealistic messages about women whose meanings are clearcut' and 'girls and women passively and indiscriminately absorb these messages and meanings as (wrong) lessons about "real life"' (111). This became known as the 'images of women' debate: the idea that media discourses socialise women/girls into consuming and accepting 'false' images of femininity and traditional sex roles. Accordingly, it was the feminist critic's responsibility to assume the social function of demystifier in an attempt to enlighten 'ordinary' women. As Whelehan advocates, the only way out of this media assimilation is to separate fact from fiction: 'the role of the feminist...is to prove herself equal to demythologising the powerful and ever-changing myths about the female self and nature perpetuated in the mass media and other state apparatuses' (Whelehan 1995, 229).

This focus on demystification also characterises many traditionalist approaches to media education that take up a protectionist stance that aims to 'inoculate' students against the effects of media manipulation. An often-cited starting point for this way of teaching and conceptualising popular culture is the work of literary critics F.R. Leavis and Denys Thompson, who offer a systematic set of suggestions for teaching about the mass media (Leavis and Thompson 1933). As David Buckingham summarises, the aims of the Leavisite perspective were to encourage students to 'arm themselves against the false and corrupting influence of the mass media and to move on to the self-evidently good and true values of the literary heritage' (Buckingham 1998b, 34). Here, the negative cultural influence of popular culture is opposed to the higher 'truth' of literature while students are seen as the unwitting victims of media influence who need to be rescued from the evils of popular culture by the superior comprehensive powers of their teachers. In this scenario, as Bazalgette aptly puts it, media education is 'the pedagogic equivalent of a tetanus shot' and the positions that students and teachers occupy remain relatively consistent: the former are seemingly unable to resist the control of popular culture, while their teachers are assumed to stand outside of this process, countering students' 'false' beliefs with their 'enlightened consciousness' (72).

This form of protectionism has been rightly criticised for the ways it fails to acknowledge the complexities of the twenty-first century classroom and for its instructor-focused outlook that may cause students to 'parrot' their teachers' interpretations (see, for example, Hobbs 1998, 16–32). As Buckingham among others has suggested, we need to adopt a more progressive, student-centred pedagogy that no longer views teachers' learning as a privileged site of knowledge, and instead takes into account students' – and educators' – experiences with the media and the genuine pleasures they may derive from it (Buckingham 1998a, 1–17). Following the development and insights of Cultural Studies in the 1960s and 1970s – in particular, a focus on audience research – the view of students as 'passive victims' has been steadily challenged and a shift towards a democratisation of the curriculum has taken place that stresses the possibilities presented by popular culture texts for moving beyond the limits of traditional disciplines and subject areas. In this case, the teacher is no longer seen to hold the key to liberation, and students' own relationship with popular culture is given emphasis – in the case of English, this could involve the academic study of popular texts such as Belle de Jour's *The Intimate Adventures of a London Call Girl* (2005) and Chuck Palahniuk's *Fight Club* (1997), both of which are taught on the interdisciplinary MA English programme at Edge Hill University. The kind of Leavisite defensiveness that hopes to disabuse students of 'false beliefs' has now given way to a more media literate pedagogy that involves teaching students the kinds of skills needed to become sensitive to the 'politics of representation' – a phrase often used by Stuart Hall that also doubles as the title of one of my second-year modules – not only of gender but also of race, sexuality, class and so on. As Omayra Cruz and Raiford Guins write, 'in order to best meet the needs of "media-saturated pupils", teaching practices should engage popular forms' (3).

Interestingly, with regard to gender and feminist theory, we have witnessed a corresponding move towards popular culture (and away from protectionism) with the introduction of the critical category of postfeminism that goes beyond the second-wave's anti-media stance and embraces the popular with much more willingness and enthusiasm.[2] From the 1990s onwards in particular, the notion of an elitist feminist 'club' that can illuminate the obfuscated and silent majority of women and the idea of an unadulterated, untainted feminism have been challenged by so-called postfeminists who argue for a different conceptualisation of popular culture and put forward the possibility of a popular kind of feminism. While the complexities of postfeminist standpoints are beyond the scope of this essay – specifically those facets of postfeminism that lie outside the popular realm and are situated as part of academia and politics (see Genz

2009, 50–64) – what characterises many of these new postfeminist voices is a re-articulation of popular culture that takes into consideration its intricate connections with feminism. In these accounts, the relationships between feminism and the popular have been reconfigured and new terms like popular feminism, postfeminism and third-wave feminism have started to appear to mark a changed social, cultural and political landscape (see 18–27, 156–65). While negative readings of the popular are still prominent – for example, Susan Faludi's description of postfeminism as backlash very much keeps alive the suggestion that representations of feminism within the popular are anti-feminist (Faludi 1992, 15) – there have also been concerted efforts to re-imagine popular culture as a potentially liberating and innovative site that puts forward the possibilities of active consumption and the popular consumer as a creative and productive agent. Postfeminist strands like Girl Power and 'new feminism', for example, contest the view of women as passive victims of an inevitably sexist media and acknowledge their insider position within popular culture by highlighting alternative modes of production/consumption (see Genz 2009, 64–90).

This kind of postfeminist agenda fits in well with the progressivist attitudes espoused by teachers who want to rethink established curricula and teaching strategies to make education viable for the technology-savvy and media-hungry generation of students who use digital media as a way to learn and be in touch with others and who view popular culture as a genuine expression of their identities. The emphasis on the popular has been accompanied by a technological, multimedia revolution that has had a profound impact on the ways that we work, communicate, spend our leisure time and, importantly, the ways that we learn and teach. A direct consequence of progressive media education has been a democratisation and broadening of the curriculum and the elimination of the high/low culture distinction that has structured more traditional, protectionist pedagogy. Nowadays, students are familiar with 'low brow' topics that are taught as part of their degree programmes – this applies both to media subject areas (which, due to their very nature, need to keep up to date with the revolution in information and communication technologies) as well as more 'established' disciplines like English that use media literacy concepts in cross-curricular ways. Teaching in both media and English departments, I have become well aware of the connections across disciplines and subjects and the increasing need to draw on multiple literacies – including reading, writing and (multi)media literacy (see Kellner 2000, 196–221). As such, I use both popular and literary texts when, for example, I give an introductory lecture on science fiction as part of a media module on 'Narrative and Genre'; similarly, I refer to advertisements and other media messages for my English MA module on 'Women and Popular Culture'. The advantages of teaching popular culture in this way are manifold: this student-centred and participatory approach teaches with or towards students' experiences and identities and allows for a personal engagement with the topic at hand. Moreover, it also foregrounds cooperative learning by challenging the hierarchical structure of the teacher–student relationship and taking seriously mass-cultural knowledges and students' different readings of popular culture. Taught in this cross-curricular way, the learning and teaching environment can be enhanced and revitalised and the power relations in the classroom can become more egalitarian and open.

However, as I have already mentioned, the ideal of a non-authoritarian classroom that draws on students' own experiences is often only realisable with difficulty as, in practice, we still continue to exert authority and lay claims to knowledge. In effect, as Buckingham notes, we need to be aware of the dangers and pitfalls of an 'easy progressivism' and uncritical 'media populism' that simply celebrates and validates students' culture and assumes that 'the kids are the experts' (Buckingham 1998b, 41). Such a conception of sophisticated, media-wise students romanticises their views and downplays the – very real – possibility that they may be uninformed, mistaken and superficial. In addition, we also need to account for the likelihood of conflicting knowledges, where the students' existing understanding of popular culture is at odds with the ideas that the teacher makes available to them. This is particularly evident in the tensions that arise in the teaching of gender theory as part of popular culture when students may resist the (often feminist) analyses that their teachers put forward and interpret these as part of feminism as a master discourse. At times, my media-accustomed students react in disbelief to my appraisals of a fashion advertisement or rap song and instead present their own (postfeminist) evaluations that underline the liberating aspects of popular culture. Emancipation is often conceived differently by students and teachers in postfeminist media cultures that highlight the importance of parodic gender performances and 'sexual subjectivity' that posits women (and men) as simultaneously active and passive, empowered and disempowered (see Genz 2009, 91–105). Here, for some critics – and given the second-wave's close ties with politics and activism – the risk of depoliticisation is tangible whereby, as William Christ and W. James Potter suggest, 'media literacy may degenerate into a substitute for action instead of a spur to it' (22). The situation is further complicated by the contradictory position that teachers themselves occupy as, on the one hand they are the bearers of 'truth' while on the other hand they seek to be equal partners in dialogue (11). Moreover, the complexity inherent in contemporary gender identities and representations may also prove testing for educators as it can undermine the fixity of theoretical models and paradigms, forcing the (feminist) teacher to revisit their own modes of analysis and interpretation. The challenge for teachers, then, is to remain self-critical with regard to their own positioning within the classroom and within popular culture/feminism whilst enabling students to politicise their own views and experiences by giving them the analytical tools to use media discourses critically.

Praxis: teaching gender and popular culture

I want to briefly illustrate some of the issues that I have discussed above by looking in greater detail at one of my postgraduate modules that combines gender theory and popular culture. 'Women and Popular Culture' is an option module that is run as part of an MA English pathway, and it examines the shifting representations of women in American and British popular culture from the 1960s to the present day. In particular, the module focuses on the repositioning of feminine images and language that range from second-wave feminist notions of the 'feminine mystique' and 1980s' backlash accounts of the 'superwoman' to postfeminism's re-embrace of femininity and 'Girl Power' in the 1990s. Each week, students are given a set of readings/viewings comprising of twentieth- and twenty-first-century popular texts – novels, films and television programmes – and a variety of (post-)feminist writings and theories. The module is taught in a three-hour slot, made up of a lecture and two hours of seminar/discussion. In devising the module, my intention was to not privilege one reading/interpretation over another but instead to bring to light the contradictions surrounding modern-day femininity and its complicated relationship with feminism and postfeminism. As such, the readings encompass a number of perspectives on gender/ feminist theory, from feminist classics like Betty Friedan's *The Feminine Mystique* (1963) and Sue Kaufman's *Diary of a Mad Housewife* (1967) to backlash films like *Fatal Attraction* (1987), postfeminist bestsellers (*Bridget Jones's Diary* (1996)) and Girl Power television (*Buffy the Vampire Slayer* (1997–2003)). The assessments for the module consist of a critical diary where students record their reflective responses to the literary, filmic and critical material studied on the module and a longer essay on a question formulated by the students themselves.

Student feedback was unanimously positive with regard to the content and delivery of the module, highlighting the relevance of popular culture for contemporary students' academic experience. The combination of feminist theory and media texts also proved successful as it provided students with theoretically grounded frameworks on which they could base their interpretations. One interesting observation was, in general, students found it easier to engage with more established feminist concepts and models as they were more familiar with second-wave readings of popular culture – which had been covered previously in introductory core modules on 'Critical Approaches to the Humanities'. This was especially evident in the critical diaries that students were asked to write to record their reactions to their weekly readings. In particular, students saw a direct correlation between Friedan's analysis of 1950s domesticity and Kaufman's (roughly) contemporaneous novel about a New York housewife who suffers a breakdown. However, the more contemporary media texts were viewed by students with much more scepticism and they were less willing to theorise the films, novels and television programmes with which they had grown up. The week on 'Girlies' and *Buffy the Vampire Slayer* was instructive in this way as students noted their own prejudices with regard to the series. As one student wrote in her critical diary, 'I had prejudged *Buffy* based on the assumption that, because it was a piece of hugely popular mass culture aimed primarily at teenagers, it was less worthy of discussion as a feminist text'.[3] Another student put it this way: 'my innate intellectual snobbery dismissed it [*Buffy*] as disposable, insubstantial "adolescent" fare – unworthy, perhaps, of critical scrutiny. My prejudice, I suspect, is indicative of my subconscious adherence to the

Leavisite dichotomy between "high" and "low" culture'. In this case, the cultural defensiveness inherent in protectionist approaches to popular culture was so deeply ingrained in students' understanding that they could not conceive of *Buffy* as a complex media text deserving of critical discussion and feminist interpretation. In addition, students seemed keenly aware of the 'silent authority' of academic feminism that kept them from engaging with and criticising popular culture in constructive ways (Luke 1998, 35). Here, the lecture and seminar were used to uncover conflicting readings of Girlie television and enable students to reflect on their own activity as media consumers and their propensity to adopt a feminist master discourse supposedly befitting the university environment. Specifically, we discussed the analogies between *Buffy* and the feminist project as a whole and the series' engagement with collective feminist activism and depictions of sisterhood. After a screening of the last episode, 'Chosen' – which sees Buffy defeat the forces of evil with the help of her slayer sisters – and a lecture on 'Girl Power' – which introduced the Butlerian notion of gender as performance and various definitions of postfeminism – students debated the cultural connotations of 'Girlie' and how Buffy fits the role of action heroine. In the ensuing discussion, students highlighted Buffy's contradictory characteristics – often described as a 'split between traditionally feminine and masculine traits' (Inness 1999, 149) – and her feminist credentials.

In this situation, my role was not so much to advance a (post-) feminist perspective but to open up different interpretive streams that students might not have contemplated beforehand. My intention was to generate self-reflexive knowledge and encourage students to become critical producers of meaning able to theorise/politicise popular culture texts. In spite of this, a slight caveat might be in order here as it is, of course, possible that students took on these readings of popular culture *because* they were presented to them in an academic context. While, as educators, we might aspire to implement a 'pedagogy of inquiry' that, as Christ and Potter propose, asks 'critical questions about what you watch, see, and read' (28), we cannot dismiss the fact that this pedagogy is still delivered within a locus of authority that invariably validates the subject at hand. Therefore, it is entirely possible that the module gave rise to a new postfeminist discourse that students accepted because it was endorsed by the academic context in which they were immersed, replacing one set of 'master's tools' with another. In this sense then, the study and teaching of gender within popular culture now has to address and incorporate a range of contradictions that apply to its subject matter as well as its teaching practice and strategies. What is essential, however, for students and educators alike is that we pre-serve a dimension for critique – that also encompasses self-criticism – in the midst of epistemological, practical and technological changes that will equip us with the intellectual tools to analyse and criticise popular (techno-)culture. It is this 'traditional' skill, coupled with a new awareness of the paradoxes emerging from popular culture, that will prove essential to the teaching of English and of gender theory in the twenty-first century.

Notes

1. As Douglas summarises, feminists are perceived to be 'shrill, overly aggressive, man-hating, ball-busting, selfish, hairy, extremist, deliberately unattractive women with absolutely no sense of humor who see sexism at every turn' (7).
2. While some commentators prefer the spelling 'post-feminism', I choose to omit the hyphen in my spelling of postfeminism in order to avoid any predetermined readings of the term that imply a semantic rift between feminism and postfeminism, instantly casting the latter as a negation and sabotage of the former. Also, by foregoing the hyphen, postfeminism is endowed with a certain cultural independence that acknowledges its existence as a conceptual entity in its own right.
3. I would like to thank all the MA students on my 'Women and Popular Culture' module for their hard work and engaging discussion.

Works Cited

Ang, Ien (1996) *Living Room Wars: Rethinking Media Audiences for the Postmodern World* (London and New York: Routledge).

Bazalgette, C. (1997) 'An Agenda for the Second Phase of Media Literacy Development', *Media Literacy in the Information Age*, ed. R. Kubey (New Brunswick, NJ: Transaction), 69–78.

Buckingham, David (1998a) 'Introduction: Fantasies of Empowerment? Radi-cal Pedagogy and Popular Culture', *Teaching Popular Culture: Beyond Radical Pedagogy*, ed. David Buckingham (London: UCL Press), 1–17.

——— (1998b) 'Media Education in the UK: Moving Beyond Protectionism', *Journal of Communication* 48(1): 33–43.

Buffy the Vampire Slayer (1997–2003) created by Joss Whedon (Twentieth Century Fox).

Christ, William G. and W. James Potter (1998) 'Media Literacy, Media Education, and the Academy', *Journal of Communication* 48(1): 5–15.

Cruz, Omayra and Raiford Guins (2005) 'Entangling the Popular: An Introduction to *Popular Culture: A Reader*', *Popular Culture: A Reader*, eds Omayra Cruz and Raiford Guins (London: Sage), 1–18.

De Jour, Belle (2005) *The Intimate Adventures of a London Call Girl* (London: Phoenix).

Douglas, Susan J. (1995) *Where the Girls Are: Growing Up Female with the Mass Media* (London: Penguin).

Faludi, Susan (1992) *Backlash: The Undeclared War against Women* (London: Vintage).

Fatal Attraction (1987) dir. Adrian Lyne (Paramount).

Fielding, Helen (1996) *Bridget Jones's Diary* (London: Picador).

Friedan, Betty (1963/1992) *The Feminine Mystique* (London: Penguin).

Genz, Stéphanie (2009) *Postfemininities in Popular Culture* (Basingstoke: Palgrave Macmillan).

Gilbert, Sandra M. and Susan Gubar (1979) *The Madwoman in the Attic: The Woman Writer and the Nineteenth-Century Literary Imagination* (New Haven, CT: Yale University Press).

Gill, Rosalind (2007) *Gender and the Media* (Cambridge: Polity).

Hobbs, Renée (1998) 'The Seven Great Debates in the Media Literacy Movement', *Journal of Communication* 48(1): 16–32.

Hollows, Joanne and Rachel Moseley (2006) 'Popularity Contests: The Meanings of Popular Feminism', *Feminism in Popular Culture*, eds Joanne Hollows and Rachel Moseley (Oxford: Berg), 1–22.

Inness, Sherrie A. (1999) *Tough Girls: Women Warriors and Wonder Women in Popular Culture* (Philadelphia, PA: University of Pennsylvania Press).

Kaufman, Sue (1967/2002) *Diary of a Mad Housewife* (London: Serpent's Tail).

Kellner, Douglas (2000) 'Multiple Literacies and Critical Pedagogies: New Paradigms', *Revolutionary Pedagogies: Cultural Politics, Instituting Education and the Discourse of Theory*, ed. Peter Pericles Trifonas (London: Routledge Farmer), 196–221.

Leavis, F.R. and Denys Thompson (1933) *Culture and Environment: The Training of Critical Awareness* (London: Chatto & Windus).

Luke, Carmen (1998) 'Pedagogy and Authority: Lessons from Feminist and Cultural Studies, Postmodernism and Feminist Pedagogy', *Teaching Popular Culture: Beyond Radical Pedagogy*, ed. David Buckingham (London: UCL Press), 18–40.

Millett, Kate (1970/1989) *Sexual Politics* (London: Virago).

Palahniuk, Chuck (1997) *Fight Club* (London: Vintage).

Showalter, Elaine (1977) *A Literature of Their Own: British Women Novelists from Brontë to Lessing* (London: Virago).

Storey, John (1997) *An Introduction to Cultural Theory and Popular Culture* (Harlow: Prentice Hall).

Walker, Rebecca, ed. (1995) *To Be Real: Telling the Truth and Changing the Face of Feminism* (London: Anchor Books).

Whelehan, Imelda (1995) *Modern Feminist Thought: From the Second Wave to 'Postfeminism'* (Edinburgh: Edinburgh University Press).

Whelehan, Imelda and Jane Pilcher (2004) *50 Key Concepts in Gender Studies* (London: Sage).

9
Bodies, Texts and Theories: Teaching Gender within Postcolonial Studies

Sarah Lawson Welsh

This chapter focuses on my experience of teaching gender theory as part of the undergraduate study of postcolonial literature. It considers some of the broader concerns of gendering the postcolonial, drawing on the specific context of teaching 'Writing the Caribbean', a final year English Studies module on Caribbean women's writing at York St John University. The module has a mixed generic focus (the discourses of the tourist brochure, oral and written literature, slave narrative, plantation owner's diaries, testimony, polemic and cultural criticism are all studied). Texts include Matthew Lewis's *Journal of a West Indian Proprietor* (1834), Jamaica Kincaid's *A Small Place* (1988), selected early twentieth-century Caribbean poetry, Grace Nichols' *I Is a Long Memoried Woman* (1986), V.S. Naipaul's *A House for Mr Biswas* (1961) and Shani Mootoo's *Cereus Blooms at Night* (1997). In commencing the module, I suggest to students that the study of postcolonial literatures might be productively complicated and interrogated by an engagement with gender theory. In turn, gender theory – specifically Western gender theories – might be usefully problematised and critiqued by literary and visual texts from postcolonial cultures.

Throughout the following discussion, I reflect on two sets of experiences: my own as an experienced postcolonial teacher and researcher of Caribbean literature, and those of my students, who have varying prior experience of Caribbean writing and postcolonial and gender theory.[1] 'Writing the Caribbean' provides an interesting study for considering some key pedagogical issues in the teaching of gender theory within postcolonial literary studies. How, for example, can particular teaching strategies, which foreground reflective learning, enable students productively to examine the complex imbrications of race, sexuality and gender in a range of literary and visual representations of the black female body? How might such strategies, translated into structured classroom activities, encourage students to consider overlapping spheres of power? What are the benefits – and perhaps the difficulties – of asking students to combine critical and theoretical approaches in this manner? What might be the most effective ways of introducing often complex theoretical concepts to undergraduate students? And does teaching gender theory within Postcolonial Studies present any particular challenges?

In an attempt to answer some of these questions, I developed a short questionnaire on undergraduate experiences of gender theory prior to taking the module. The questionnaire was supplemented by interviews with past and present students of the module. In reflecting on this feedback, my purpose is to identify pedagogic approaches that best facilitate student learning and encourage students to locate themselves reflexively – as reading subjects – within larger social contexts. I aim to consider how teaching strategies can actively promote student awareness of the implications of different reading practices (both individual and institutional) and the significance of location for reading, writing and wider representational practices. The following chapter outlines and considers the student responses to the questionnaire and interviews, and concludes with a case study in which I describe some approaches to teaching Grace Nichols' poem 'My Black Triangle'.

'Writing the Caribbean': teaching competing theories

In teaching gender theory within Postcolonial Studies, my aim is to raise student awareness of some important questions regarding the use of feminist theory in readings of black women's writing: the relation between texts and theory, the relative specificity or universalising tendencies of certain theoretical approaches, and some different ways of conceptualising the role and nature of theory itself. I ask students to discuss the problems (as well as potentialities) of using European-derived feminist models to read women's writing from other cultures. I encourage them to question whether there is such a thing as a 'universal' female experience, and consider the importance of the cultural specificity of texts and theories. Given that students often have greater familiarity with texts from an African-American female tradition, and the predominance of these texts on many Women's Studies and English Studies programmes, it is also relevant and timely to interrogate the use of concepts derived from an African-American tradition of black feminist criticism in the critical reading of Caribbean women writers.

In introducing theory on the 'Writing the Caribbean' module, I deliberately remind students of the 'whiteness' of much of the theory they have hitherto encountered as undergraduate students and the disproportionate visibility – and thus hegemonic position – of many Western feminist theorists on the curriculum in relation to indigenous theorists and to those who theorise in different ways. This reflexiveness about my own position and about the institutional politics of the canon and of the HE curriculum aims to engender a similar self-reflexivity in my students. To quote an often-cited passage by Caribbean-born, African-American feminist theorist, Barbara Christian, it is salutary to remember that the Western models we use are not the only available models for theorising:

> People of color have always theorized – but in forms quite different from the Western form of abstract logic. And I am inclined to say that our theorising...is often in narrative forms, in the stories we create, in riddles and proverbs, in the play with language, since dynamic rather than fixed ideas seem more to our liking. (Christian 1987, 457)

A question of context

At the heart of this enquiry is the question of context: how we contextualise literary texts in different ways; the difference context makes to our readings; and also how we contextualise ourselves as readers within a nexus of individual, disciplinary and other practices. Within the discipline of English Studies at least, it is often taken as axiomatic that students should be encouraged to place textual and visual representations within appropriate historical and cultural contexts. My own department's validated documents enshrine this principle as one of three key aims. While I broadly agree with this view, I still think we need to interrogate the assumption that context matters – especially in a non-canonical and/or postcolonial writing where the issue of 'context' is sometimes a fraught one.[2] A common response to the study of postcolonial literatures is that it is 'all about contexts' or 'ideology' rather than aesthetic and literary qualities. Furthermore, grasping contexts relevant to postcolonial literatures may prove especially difficult to students who are out of their cultural 'comfort zone', and my experience over almost 20 years of teaching, as well as students responses on this project, certainly bear this out.[3]

My interest lies in the difference that placing texts within appropriate contexts makes to students' learning experience. Why does context matter? Might it matter even more in the case of Postcolonial Studies? If students can be enabled to become 'active learners', agents in evaluating why context might matter to their readings (rather than being simply told that it does), their learning is likely to be considerably enriched. With this in mind, the questions I asked students aimed to encourage reflection on the process of teaching and learning, as well as on the content of the workshops. Specifically, students were prompted to consider *why* they were asked to undertake certain tasks.

The questionnaire

This project began with my asking final year students how well their previous undergraduate study had prepared them for discussions of gender, sexuality and theories of race in a range of contexts; which modules and theories they had already studied; and which teaching and learning strategies they felt had best facilitated an understanding of often complex theoretical material.

Final year undergraduate study is often posited on levelness and learning outcomes, anticipating an increasingly sophisticated handling and understanding of relevant critical theories. Within the context of the teaching and study of postcolonial literatures it also presents further challenges for both tutor and students. In my experience, final year undergraduates have often established a typically Eurocentric approach to theory, and can struggle to contemplate and apply such theories in new global contexts. I would suggest that establishing the cultural assumptions that students hold, often unconsciously, is as crucial – if not more so – than the learning outcomes upon which a module is predicated. A journey must have a beginning as well as an end, and I believe we are sometimes too goal-orientated around outcomes, especially when it comes to assessment matters. I have long regarded undergraduate students as *already* theorisers, even if they do not consider themselves to be so, and I believe that enabling understanding and increasing confidence in handling and using relevant theoretical insights is at the core of what we do as English practitioners.

So how prepared are final year students for thinking about theories of gender, sexuality and race? Of 32 students taking the module, 19 responded to an initial questionnaire. Sixty-six per cent of those were single honours English students and 33 per cent joint honours. The vast majority of respondents (83 per cent) were female; this reflects the gender composition of literature modules in the institution and indeed, nationally but also presents some interesting dynamics in workshops (discussed below). Students were asked to list any modules they had previously taken at degree level and that had included the study or discussion of theories of feminism; gender; sexualities or queer theory; race and ethnicity; or a combination of the above:

Table 9.1   Previous modules with gender-related content

First year modules:
- 'Women and Writing' (15 responses)

Second year modules:
- 'Literatures of Childhood' (11)
- 'Researching Genre Fictions' (10)
- 'Literature, Space & Place' (8)
- 'Gothic and Horror' (7)
- 'Literary Theory' (4)

Third year modules:
- 'Writing the Caribbean' (9)
- 'Shakespeare' (7)
- 'Sex and the City [eighteenth century in basis]' (6)
- 'Early twentieth-century writing' (6)
- 'Post World War II American Literature' (6)
- 'Nineteenth-century writing' (4)
- 'The Romantics' (4)

The most cited module at any level was 'Women and Writing'. The inclusion of this module in the first year seems to suggest a front-loading of gender study in the curriculum in order to set up pathways for embeddedness throughout the degree, or at least suggests that gender study is deemed a core area of introductory-level study. Literature survey modules also scored significantly, and those from other programmes (American studies: 'Screening the Modern Immigrant'; history: 'Race and Revolution'; film studies: 'Introduction to Film Studies'; media: 'Gender, Sexualities & Popular Culture') also featured in a smaller number of joint honours responses. However, the most cited modules were thematically organised second year modules.

Students were then asked to choose graduated responses to a further four statements:

Table 9.2   Guided self-reflection on previous learning

From your degree study so far, do you consider yourself well equipped to engage with feminist theories?

- strongly agree: 26%
- agree: 58%
- slightly agree: 16%

From your degree study so far, do you consider yourself well equipped to engage with theories of gender (masculinities and femininities, etc.)?

- strongly agree: 32%
- agree: 47%
- slightly agree: 21%

From your degree study so far, do you consider yourself to be well equipped to engage with theories of sexuality/queer theory?

- strongly agree: 16%
- agree: 53%
- slightly agree: 21%
- don't know: 5%
- slightly disagree: 5%

From your degree study so far, do you consider yourself to be well equipped to engage with theories of race and ethnicity?

- strongly agree: 21%
- agree: 53%
- slightly agree: 21%
- don't know: 5%

In order to tease out prior knowledge and expectations, students were asked to list any relevant theorists or texts they had studied (or of which they were aware) that might be considered examples of gender theorising, with the following results:

Table 9.3   Theorists and/or texts seen as engaging with gender theory

- Judith Butler, *Gender Trouble*: 39%
- Virginia Woolf, *A Room of One's Own* and other Woolf texts: 32%
- Laura Mulvey, 'Narrative Film and Visual Pleasure': 21%
- Sandra Gilbert and Susan Gubar, *The Madwoman in the Attic*: 16%
- Elaine Showalter, selected writings: 16%
- Kate Chopin, *The Awakening*: 16%
- Sigmund Freud, selected writings: 11%
- Ursula Le Guin, *The Left Hand of Darkness*: 11%
- Charlotte Perkins Gilman, *The Yellow Wallpaper*: 11%
- Simone de Beauvoir, *The Second Sex*: 5%
- Mary Eagleton, *The Feminist Reader*: 5%
- Donna Haraway, 'A Cyborg Manifesto': 5%
- Gertrude Stein, selected writings: 5%
- Toni Morrison, *The Bluest Eye* and *Beloved*: 5%
- Alice Walker, *The Color Purple* and 'Everyday Use': 5%
- John Cleland, *Fanny Hill*: 5%
- Charlotte Bronte, *Jane Eyre*: 5%
- Bram Stoker, *Dracula*: 5%
- Jackie Kay, *Trumpet*: 5%
- The Beat Poets and Alan Ginsberg, *Howl*: 5%

When asked whether they had ever studied/discussed feminist theories, theories of gender and theories of sexuality from a non-European/white American perspective as undergraduates, 53 per cent of students answered yes and named the following modules:

Table 9.4   Modules that discuss non-European/white American gender theories

First year modules:

- 'Women and Writing': 11%
- Introductory module, 'Reading Texts': 5%

Second year modules:

- 'Literature, Space & Place': 11%

Third year modules:

- 'Writing the Caribbean': 16%
- 'Post-War American Literature': 16%

Recalled texts included Jean Rhys' *Wide Sargasso Sea*, poetry by Grace Nichols and Jean Binta Breeze, Alice Walker's *The Color Purple* and 'Everyday Use', and Toni Morrison's *The Bluest Eye* and *Beloved*. The Caribbean/American bias here may well reflect individual tutor interests, but it also reinforces the notion that undergraduate study of black writers is still largely American in focus (rather than African or aboriginal Australian, for example).

The interviews

How do students react to Caribbean women's writing? What impact does gender theory have on their readings? What are the challenges of learning about gender theory as part of Postcolonial Studies? These were just a few of the questions that I wanted to ask past and current 'Writing the Caribbean' students. The student-centred nature of a pedagogical project such as this required student input, and I was lucky enough to have two postgraduate students who had both previously taken the module work with me on the project, helping to compile the initial questionnaire and interview questions and undertaking and transcribing the interviews. Although only a small number of students were interviewed (six), their responses were illuminating.

Discussing their engagement with theory on the module, the primary concern for the students was the complexity of the texts. Asked about the challenges of reading theoretical texts, one male mature student commented: 'the theories themselves can be very complicated... the main challenge is trying to put a theory into practice'. He cited the difficulty of Cixous's language, compounded by its being translated from the French. He was most attracted to theories proposing equality, and spoke of context as being very important: 'Wordsworth for example, was very much a product of his time; he doesn't know much about queer theory!' A younger female student reflected that she had experienced difficulties with the language and/or style of theoretical texts as well as the theoretical concepts therein, and the abstraction of some of the gender theory taught on the module. Another female student gave the specific example of Butler's *Gender Trouble* as a text that was 'difficult to understand': 'It was recommended in a first year module, "Narrative Cultures", and was referenced throughout the degree but I don't really think I ever fully understood the theory and felt that Butler made the concept unnecessarily difficult'.

When asked about the main challenges of combining race and gender theories, the male mature student spoke of this challenge in terms of 'an extra paradigm shift. [It's] a challenge because it's come from the Caribbean culture. [It's] something unfamiliar'. He observed a 'sense that the West has got an interest in the female body, that [it] thinks of Caribbean people as highly sexualised', and reflected: 'that can be unsettling – for both men and women'.

The students were also asked about their previous awareness of gendered racial stereotypes and their responses differed significantly. One female student admitted that she was unaware of these stereotypes, but added: 'there is an innate sense of stereotyping within us all and we are not necessarily aware of it... To me, gendered racial stereotypes are two separate concepts and, up to a point, we are not aware of using them'. For her, awareness of the long cultural history of stereotypical representations 'very much alters understanding of the Nichols poems but... also the Matthew Lewis text. It helped me to understand the context in which the texts were written and also the viewpoints of the writers'. Another female student agreed: 'Definitely, we all have/use the stereotypes but don't [always] realise. These characters and images are so familiar to us that we don't really consider them or deconstruct them. An awareness of the racial stereotypes certainly altered my understanding of the Nichols poem, and led me to consider the relevance and significance of the title *"i is a long memoried woman"'*. The mature male student was aware of the Hottentot Venus from eighteenth- and nineteenth-century studies, but not the Mammy or Aunt Jemima figure:

> However when I saw the images I recognised them and had not made a connection, and that's why the course has been useful to me. Clearly we have these stereotypes, we just aren't aware of them. I remember playing cricket and if there was a tall West Indian . . . he must be a terribly fast bowler. [I thought: 'he's] going to be superior at cricket'. [Awareness of these stereotypes] adds depth and a historical perspective to the reading of the Nichols poem ['My Black Triangle'] – and her other work. It made me aware of how difficult it must be to have such a heritage in that you want to celebrate it. Rather like queer theory [it suggests a need] to reappropriate the territory – and to look forward.

When asked which learning and teaching strategies best facilitated their understanding and application of gender theory, all but one respondent preferred the workshop with structured worksheet given out by the tutor beforehand. The mature male student valued the student interaction, commenting: 'This is more important for a mature student perhaps: nice to hear other people's comments and it's easier to discuss and argue in small groups – even if there is no consensus – and then report back'. A female student concurred in favouring the workshop: '[it] gives more responsibility for learning and is more helpful and beneficial to me than simply reading or taking notes in a lecture'. Another female student observed: 'the tutor giving preparatory reading in handout form, and discussing it in a workshop format . . . feels a more comfortable environment to ask questions in, rather than a lecture'. She favoured tutor-led explication and discussion of how a theory might be applied to a text, done in a workshop setting.

Regarding content, students were asked whether they had ever felt uncomfortable or anxious as a result of reading or discussing any of the course texts. The same young female student had felt guarded in her responses, although she admitted this was 'mainly because of a fear that I have misunderstood or misinterpreted the texts! . . . I find that after a group discussion has taken place my response is more structured than it was initially and I am more confident to share it with the class'. The male mature student commented that he found Cixous 'too polemical, not balanced – as a man I felt a bit of a target'. He continued: 'If you're studying Matthew Lewis, he uses terms such a creole/negro and sometimes you have to think about what the appropriate "theoretical term" may be.' He cited the 'use of the word "queer" ' as just one example of 'Theory [as] a field in which language is always shifting'. On the issue of correct terms, he responded:

> Yes, I have a concern not to be seen as sexist, and yes I have a concern not to be seen as racist. But on the other hand, by actually reading the theoretical texts and understanding the position, that gives you the equipment and the information not to be sexist or racist. [It's] a double edged sword.

The same student cited Shani Mootoo's *Cereus Blooms at Night,* a novel that explores rape and childhood sexual abuse and its lifetime effects, amongst other topics, as 'an uncomfortable text' to read and noted: 'Slavery is an uncomfortable topic – in a film [we saw, there is mention of a slave owner] pissing on their slave. [It was] really hard to take.' On the issue of not knowing how to respond at all, he commented: 'It's hard sometimes to point out literary merit in an article where you find the content completely disturbing. For example – I wrote an essay on Lewis and I was concerned that my essay didn't come across as flippant, yet I wanted to acknowledge that there was humour in his text and that needed to be balanced with the awful truth about slavery.'

Men in class: the burden of representation?

In an early planning discussion on the project, my research students and I reflected on the 'burden of representation'. The module itself deals with the politics of representation in Caribbean texts and culture, but this term may also, of course, apply to minorities within the classroom. We decided to ask students whether the fact that men are in a minority on the module altered the dynamic of the workshops; whether men are ever expected to speak for their gender in class or in assignments; and whether the gender discourses studied (or indeed the tutor) had represented men in any particular way.

In response, the male mature student commented that he was 'very much in a minority [yet it had been] a life changing experience for me...Discussing gender theory has been the most challenging thing I've done at university'. He continued: 'Often in feminist texts I feel like a target: the "white, middle class man"', and he described the discomfit of reading Matthew Lewis: '[It made me want to say:] "he doesn't represent me, so I don't represent him"'. He did not, however, regret the text's inclusion: 'The tutor has represented a historically accurate account of gender – men *were* in power. But in terms of more recent writing studied there has been an emphasis on female texts. [This is] a corrective and a celebration. [I found this a] good mix from the context to the celebration.' Another female student made the interesting point that 'Often it seems that female students are able to speak regarding gender issues from both a female *and* male perspective – but perhaps men are unable or perhaps unwilling to give strong opinions on female experience.' The same student commented: 'I think the module fully addressed the concept of "double colonisation", yet I think the module remained balanced. For instance, when looking at the history of slavery, [the tutor] used a variety of texts. [Lewis's] journal and Nichols's collection *i is a long memoried woman* worked well together. The texts were well selected – overall a balanced module.'

Case study: teaching Grace Nichols' poetry

The following case study aims to give an indication of the type of learning activities that the above students were engaged in on this module. As preparation for the workshops on selected Caribbean women's poetry, students were asked to read Grace Nichols' poem cycle, *I Is a Long Memoried Woman*, alongside Helene Cixous's feminist manifesto for *écriture féminine*, 'The Laugh of the Medusa', and key poems from Nichols' *The Fat Black Woman's Poems* and *Lazy Thoughts of a Lazy Woman* alongside Audre Lorde's essay 'The Uses of the Erotic'. They were also asked to research a number of key terms relevant to the poems: 'the Black Atlantic', 'Black Triangle', 'the Dark Continent', 'Steatopygous', 'The Hottentot Venus', 'Aunt Jemima'/'the Mammy' figure, '*écriture féminine*' and 'patriarchal binary oppositions'. Noting the source of the information (or difficulties in sourcing the same) was deemed as important as the definitions themselves, and the students were invited to provide feedback in small groups on both aspects of their research.

In the workshop, selected poems and extracts were read aloud and students were encouraged to comment on their first responses to the texts and on how an understanding of a term such as 'Steatopygous'[4] and its long history in representing the black woman's body could enrich a reading of the poems. This exercise was then repeated in terms of a series of visual representations of the Hottentot Venus that I sourced from anthropological studies, political cartoons, press coverage and contemporary art works and installations. The aim is to foster not only focused research skills in reading poems in context, but to encourage the kinds of reading strategies that might illuminate the complex intersection of race and gender issues in many of Nichols' poems. Using visual resources adds another dimension to teaching, and students can be asked to research the images further or respond to them in creative ways (through writing, painting, installation) as a means of encouraging thinking around the topic and student ownership of the project.

'My Black Triangle'

I often use this Nichols' poem as a way of getting students to think about the intersection of racial and gender concerns in Nichols' poetry. Historically, the 'black triangle' referred to the three-way traffic of raw materials, manufactured goods and human bodies of the Atlantic slave trade; in Nichols' poem – as students are quick to point out – it also becomes a reference to the female pudenda. This introduces the idea of physicality; the body, its erotic desires and its creative as well as procreative potential. I ask students to think about how this changes our reading, as we move from historical and cultural contexts to an intimate focus on the black female body. I ask students to think about the yoking of gendered body and historical context. What does it suggest? How are black female bodies linked to the wider context of the 'triangular trade'? An exploration of other poems from *I Is a Long Memoried Woman* can illuminate the point that the slave experience was importantly also a gendered experience, encompassing quite specific experiences for the female slave. In short, 'The black woman was situated at the (re)productive core of the slave system with a unique legal status' (Beckles 1998, 37). This discussion builds on our previous study of a number of texts and extracts that demonstrate how children born to slave mothers automatically took on slave status, irrespective of their paternity, thus providing additional economic incentive to the widespread sexual abuse of slave women by white overseers and plantation owners. For example, the Matthew Lewis text describes how the economic imperative to get one's female slaves to 'breed' became still more urgent once the abolition of the slave trade in 1807 ended the importation of new slaves to replace those who had escaped, grown sick or died.

Finally, I encourage students to share their findings on the term 'the dark continent' in relation to this poem, and to think about how this nineteenth-century imperial concept bled into late nineteenth- and early twentieth-century psychoanalytic discourse on female sexuality. Freud famously defined female sexuality as 'the dark continent'; students are less familiar, however, with the ways in which his statement reflected racial and sexual discourses of the time, combining both colonial and gendered concerns in his image of female sexuality as the ultimate darkness and otherness. I find it useful at this point to raise the idea of spatial metaphors (female sexuality as unchartered space; the female body as a territory that can be mapped, penetrated, invaded). Contemplating the racial, as well as the gender implications of Freud's construction demands consideration of the limitations of reading from a Western or Eurocentric perspective. As the eponymous protagonist of Jamaica Kincaid's 1990 novel, *Lucy*, puts it in response to the Western feminist tome her white employer shows to her: 'My life could not really be explained by this thick book... My life was at once something more simple and more complicated than that' (132).

If, for Freud, the 'dark continent' of the female body signifies difference and 'lack', in Nichols' poem it signifies a specific racial and gendered history as well as an empowering black female sexuality and (pro)creative potential. Discussing this with students, it is useful at this point to bring in 'The Laugh of the Medusa', in which Cixous challenges the same Freudian metaphor. She declares: 'As soon as [little girls] begin to speak, at the same time as they're taught their name, they can be taught that their territory is black: because you are Africa, you are black. Your continent is dark. Dark is dangerous. You can't see anything in the dark, you're afraid...' (318). Pursuing the connections between the suppression of women's sexuality and women's writing, she counters: 'the Dark Continent is neither dark nor unexplorable. It is still unexplored only because we've been made to believe that it was too dark to be explorable. And they [men] want to make us believe that what interests us is the white continent, with its monuments to Lack' (325).

I ask students to consider how Cixous's essay might speak to black women and to black women writers, who seem largely excluded here, and for whom the metaphorical ascription 'the Dark Continent' is altogether more complex and multilayered than it is for a white woman. The collusion of whiteness and phallocentrism/patriarchy in Cixous's phrase, 'the white continent, with its monuments to Lack', is also problematic when considered within this new context. These critiques are often beyond the grasp of all but the brightest under-graduates, but the notion that theory is a discourse open to debate and critique is not. Not all theories 'fit' all writing, and I encourage students to engage with theoretical discourse as they would liter-ary texts: with a critical eye. Perhaps more importantly, students are encouraged to think about their position as readers, how they locate themselves – and how they are located – by a range of factors, including the critical and theoretical discourses they use.

Workshop discussion on 'My Black Triangle' often concludes with a reading that sees Nichols' black female persona exercising a sim-ilar kind of appropriation and abrogation of the metaphor of the 'Black Triangle'. She seizes control over the process of signification, by personalising the metaphor ('*My* black triangle') and by stressing its close connection to the female body, allowing it to signify wider possibilities and more positive attributes: the ability to 'experience the world [and one's own history] through [the] body' (Webhofer 1996, 14), to celebrate the creative potential for growth and the empowering nature of confident female sexuality, self-affirming and approving.

Conclusions and reflections

From the teaching of this workshop to different cohorts over two years, the following conclusions have emerged in tutor-led discus-sion. Context clearly matters and students can see more clearly how bodies are located, and how they have cultural as well as biological meanings. Students can also see how Nichols' poems participate in and interrogate a longer history of literary and visual cultural representation of the black female body. We interrogate universalism and discuss the importance of cultural specificity in speaking and writing of women, their bodies and experiences, and how some of the representations we researched do the opposite: they fix, homogenise, limit. Alice Walker's observation that she sees 'her brothers and sisters doing time in images not of their own making'[5] is very useful here. It is possible to connect this to Nichols' poems, which invoke representations of black women's bodies in order to question and subvert them.[6] Students come to recognise that location matters: that where a body is born, where it's located, can define the world that is seen.[7] Moreover, location also affects readers – we usually sum up our discussion by thinking about the intended audiences of the theoretical essays and the Caribbean women's poems we have studied. Students are hopefully much more aware at the end of the sessions that reading texts within relevant contexts is not enough: we need to be aware of the 'blindspots', limitations and pitfalls of our reading practices too.

Finally, in this concluding session, we also discuss how certain feminist approaches may 'fit' some poems better than others. I try to encourage equal critical interest in those approaches that don't seem to 'fit' quite so well. We ask: does this have implications for the poetry itself – for its incorporation into academic courses, literary anthologies and so on? Might we see Nichols' poems as resisting or even critiquing the feminist theoretical concepts that may (and have been) used to read them?[8] In my experience, the most capable students can feel liberated and excited by the interpretive possibilities opened up by this session, while less confident students end sessions more secure in their use of gender theory and more aware of the complexities of using it in relation to postcolonial writing. Both groups ultimately benefit from the shared sense of a non-hierarchical and supportive learning community that student-centred, self-reflective/reflexive learning strategies and carefully structured workshopping activities can engender.

I strongly believe that learning is a process that takes place both in and outside of the classroom; the 'gaps' around teaching contact time can be as important as the workshop time itself. It is clear from the student responses that the module offers an immersive experience that empowers as well as challenges: students begin, to greater and lesser extents, feeling 'at sea' in this non-Eurocentric (textual) space, but they soon learn to adopt and to experiment with new vocabularies and new ways of seeing as they progress through this rich terrain. One finding of special interest is the respondents' emphasis on collaborative learning, supported by pre-seminar reading and preparation. The praise for this evolving learning strategy in turn echoes the Caribbean oral tradition itself, and speaks to Christian's insistence that for the Caribbean subject 'dynamic rather than fixed ideas seem more to our liking'.[9]

It is clear that a programme of study that offers engagement with feminist theory, queer theory and debates surrounding masculine representations in literature, in addition to the issues surrounding the representation of race and ethnicities, works to prepare students for a module such as 'Writing the Caribbean' – a module containing literary texts and historical subject matter that British students are unlikely to have encountered previously. It is something to celebrate when students highlight the appearance of these culturally interrogating perspectives on a number of their modules. However, it is also clear, given the students' observations that many prominent gender theory texts (for example, Butler's *Gender Trouble*) are extremely dense, and arguably alienating to the undergraduate, as well as the students' developing awareness that the gender theory under study is overwhelmingly Western in origin, that it might be timely to review and revise the texts we use to explore gender in literary studies provision. bell hooks' title, *Ain't I a Woman?: Black Women and Feminism* (1981), reminds white feminists and gender theorists in Higher Education that our textual choices – both critical and creative – count. In this way, the module itself aims to encourage tutors as well as students to 'write back' to the HE contexts in which we operate. Not only have these respondents commented on and interrogated the complex and intertextual journey that the course inspires, but they have worked to comment on macro-level pedagogical practice. So out of the seeming chaos of text and context, of Eurocentric and non-Eurocentric theory, of the contradictory maelstrom that is postmodern arts and humanities education, comes this observation: gender study at undergraduate level needs to diversify, and to bring itself up to date in global terms.[10]

Acknowledgements

Thanks are due to Charlotte Craig and Alice Cowell for all their input as student researchers on this project, to York St John University for granting me a 'Students as Researchers' bursary, to my colleague Dr Liesl King for her careful reading and incisive comments, but most of all to my 'Writing the Caribbean' students, especially those such as Terry Kay, Sheetal Dandiker, Katie McNicholas and Helen Lonsdale, who were generous enough to give their time to be interviewed for the project.

Notes

1. The typical literature student at York St John University is full-time, white British, female and in their 20s, but about a third of the student body at any one time are mature students or returning learners, and we have small numbers of students of other British ethnicities. An important minority of our students each year are visiting us from overseas institutions, usually from Europe and North America.
2. See, for example, Elleke Boehmer and John McLeod, 'The Challenges of Teaching Postcolonial Literature' for an excellent overview of this and related issues.
3. See David Dabydeen, 'Teaching West Indian Literature in Britain'; Evelyn O'Callaghan, ' "It's all about ideology: there's no discussion about art": Reluctant Voyages into Theory in Caribbean Women's Writing'; and section 3 of Wilson, Sandru and Lawson Welsh (eds), *Re-routing the Postcolonial,* for further discussion of these issues.
4. The *Oxford English Dictionary Online* (2nd edn, 1989) defines 'steatopyga' as: 'A protuberance of the buttocks, due to an abnormal accumulation of fat in and behind the hips and thighs, found (more markedly in women than in men) as a racial characteristic of certain peoples, esp. the Hottentots and Bushmen of South Africa'.
5. Alice Walker, source unknown.
6. I direct students to further reading here, especially Tiffin, 'Postcolonial Literatures and Counter-Discourse'.
7. I usually direct students to further reading, especially Adrienne Rich's essay 'Notes toward a Politics of Location' at this point.
8. Here I direct students to further reading, especially Christian (1987).
9. I'm indebted to Dr Liesl King for this observation and for the basis of my concluding comments.
10. Ideally, with more contact time, I would set a third theoretical text on gender for preparatory reading, one by a Caribbean feminist theorist such as Sylvia Wynter, Evelyn O'Callaghan, Patricia Mohammed, Rhoda Reddock, Bridget Brereton or Olive Senior, in order to show how a

growing indigenous body of Caribbean feminist theory is disrupting the simple polarities of 'the West and the rest' and proving that the Caribbean can have its own traditions of feminist and gender analyses that draw upon but are not necessarily complicit with, uncritical of or unresistant to, dominant Anglo-American approaches. However, students can also use this as follow up material with considerable effectiveness.

Works Cited

Beckles, Hilary (Summer 1998) 'Historicizing Slavery in West Indian Feminisms', 'Rethinking Caribbean Difference', ed. Patricia Mohammed, special issue of *Feminist Review* 59: 34–56.

Boehmer, Elleke and John McLeod (Winter 2004) 'The Challenges of Teaching Postcolonial Literature', *CCUE News, Teaching Postcolonial Literature & Anglo America* Special Issue 18: 4–8.

Christian, Barbara (1987) 'The Race for Theory', *Cultural Critique* 6: 51–63, reprinted Bill Ashcroft, Gareth Griffiths and Helen Tiffin (eds) (1995), *The Post-colonial Studies Reader*, 1st edn (London & New York: Routledge), 457–60.

Cixous, Helene (1975/1990) 'The Laugh of the Medusa', *Literature in the Modern World*, ed. Dennis Walder (Oxford University Press), 316–26.

Dabydeen, David (1997) 'Teaching West Indian Literature in Britain', *Studying British Cultures*, ed. Susan Bassnett (London and New York, Routledge), 135–51.

hooks, bell (1981) *Ain't I a Woman?: Black Women and Feminism* (London: Pluto).

Kincaid, Jamaica (1988) *A Small Place* (New York: Farrar, Strauss & Giroux).

———— (1990) *Lucy* (New York: Farrar, Straus & Giroux).

Lewis, Matthew (1834) *Journal of a West Indian Proprietor Kept During a Residence in the Island of Jamaica* (London, John Murray).

Lorde, Audre (1981) 'Uses of the Erotic: the Erotic as Power', *Sister Outsider – Essays and Speeches* (Freedom, CA: The Crossing Press), 53–9.

Mohammed, Patricia (1998) 'Towards an Indigenous Theorizing in the Caribbean', ed. Patricia Mohammed, Special Issue of *Feminist Review* 59: 6–33.

Mootoo, Shani (1997) *Cereus Blooms at Night* (London: Granta).

Naipaul, V.S. (1961) *A House for Mr Biswas* (London: Andre Deutsch).

Nichols, Grace (1986) *I Is a Long Memoried Woman* (London: Karnak).

———— (1989) 'My Black Triangle', *Lazy Thoughts of a Lazy Woman* (London: Virago), 25.

O'Callaghan, Evelyn (1992) ' "It's all about ideology: there's no discussion about art": Reluctant Voyages into Theory in Caribbean Women's Writing', *Kunapipi* 14(2): 35–44.

Rich, Adrienne (1984/1987) 'Notes toward a Politics of Location', *Blood, Bread, and Poetry: Selected Prose (1979–1985)* (London: Virago), 210–31.

Tiffin, Helen (1987) 'Postcolonial Literatures and Counter-discourse', *Kunapipi* 9(3), reprinted Bill Ashcroft, Gareth Griffiths and Helen Tiffin (eds) (2006), *The Post-colonial Studies Reader*, 2nd edn (London and New York: Routledge), 99–101.

Webhofer, Gudrun (1996) *'Identity' in the Poetry of Grace Nichols and Lorna Goodison* (Lewiston, NY: Edwin Mellen Press).

Wilson, Janet, Cristina Sandru and Sarah Lawson Welsh eds (2010) *Re-routing the Postcolonial: New Directions for the New Millennium* (London and New York: Routledge).

10
The Space between Submission and Revolution: Teaching Gender in China

Caryn M. Voskuil

The social role and cultural expression of gender in China today is shaped by the nation's unique five thousand-year history. The two dominant ideologies in contemporary China remain Confucianism and Communism, the former of which does much to entrench ancient and traditional gender ideologies within the modern social fabric. In the mid-twentieth century, Mao's regime decreed that women in a Communist state should be equal to men. While Communist doctrine sought to overturn conventional gendered ways of thinking, the societal effects of Communist ideology have in many ways proved somewhat less tenacious than those of Confucianism. Furthermore, the adoption of a market economy has challenged both dominant national ideologies in recent years, and the English classroom, to remain relevant, must contend with this evolution as well.

For four years I taught English and culture courses at two universities in Beijing, China. The first institution I taught at is a smaller city university of approximately 10,000 students and is primarily concerned with foreign language training. The second, at which I taught for three years, is a large national university of approximately 25,000 students, which specialises in journalism, film, television, radio and other forms of communication media. Both universities are internationally oriented, traditional in degree and course structure and competitive in their admissions policies. Both are considered primarily 'Liberal Arts' universities. The language of instruction in my courses was English. My experience of teaching in a Chinese class-room was, in many ways, similar to that of teaching in America. Nevertheless, inevitable cultural and social differences drove me to seek out information and pedagogical tools that would help me to make English texts and Western gender theory more accessible to this particular group of learners. Of course, four years' experience of teaching in this context, though significant and unusual, is by no means definitive, and its discussion here involves some inevitable shorthand when it comes to dealing with cultural differences. This shorthand is no doubt as revealing of my own particular cultural assumptions as it is of those belonging to the students that I taught. Nonetheless, I did find a pedagogic method that utilised more gen-eral ideas about contrasting cultural attitudes between East and West to open up the discussion of texts in the classroom, and this is offered here as a means of sharing my reflections, as well as providing a dif-ferent perspective on teaching English for those with a solely Western experience.

The social construction of the gendered subject in the Chinese uni-versity setting is based upon that culture's underlying system of social values – a system that blends two very different gender ideologies: an ancient one in which women are constructed primarily as submis-sive subjects, and a modern one in which women both symbolise and pose a threat to the revolutionary values of an emergent repub-lic. Somewhere between submission and revolution, I hoped to find a place in which I could discuss Western theories of gender with my Chinese students in a credible and constructive manner.

Reflecting on cultural difference

The average Chinese student is, in many ways, remarkably similar to the average British, American or European student. They wear simi-lar fashions, watch many of the same movies, and hum many of the same tunes as their Western counterparts. This is a relatively recent phenomenon. I first travelled to China in 1980, the year I gradu-ated from high school in St. Louis, Missouri. At that time, Beijing's often unpaved streets were navigated by few cars and buses, and were instead filled with bicycles and pedestrians. Both women and men wore unisex 'Mao' suits, and shorts and other types of 'immodest' clothing were strictly banned by our group leader. When we walked down the streets we were often stared at by locals who had seen few foreigners. While the ruling Communist Party stressed the equality of the sexes, daily life seemed to reflect traditional attitudes towards gender roles.

In 2005 I made my second trip to China – this time as a professor – and saw much more evidence of the growing cultural influence of the West. My students wore mini-skirts, t-shirts and Reeboks, and carried folders depicting Western rock stars. At first glance, they resembled any student I had taught over the past decade in the USA, but there were certain significant differences in life style and culture. The students lived in six-person dormitories without air-conditioning or en-suite showers, and had to walk to a central location to collect boiled water each day to use for drinking water and tea. While classrooms were usually (but not always) fitted with computers and projectors, and most students had Internet access, web browsing was strictly limited by the 'Great Firewall' of the Chinese government. While Chinese students regularly watch R-rated movies, those I encountered were typically much more reluctant to discuss sexual issues compared with the American students I had previously taught. My Chinese students were typically extremely polite and respectful: a pleasure and a boon to classroom management, but an aspect that sometimes made it difficult to instigate critical debate. These anecdotal differences, although incidental in some ways, had an inarguable impact on my experience of approaching and discussing theories of gender and ideology in the classroom.

China has opened up in recent years, but only in particular ways (the most dominant being economically), and only in fits and starts. As a Westerner living there, China often appeared to be philosophically remote from the Western world, even as it was growing in power and influence, and I was aware that cultural difference must be carefully addressed in order to teach there successfully as a foreign national.

Chinese and Western cultural values serve as ideological underpinnings for many of the attitudes each society holds towards gender roles and gender differences. While individual members of society may hold quite different attitudes, it is necessary to understand widespread, common cultural variances to better adapt teaching techniques within the Chinese classroom. Paraphrasing the work of Niels Noorderhaven and Loek Halman, Kathy Durkin states: 'One of the aims of a lecturer should be to encourage understanding, respect and tolerance of cultural groups and alternative viewpoints through education.' She continues, 'This highlights the need for lecturers themselves to acquire intercultural competency, so that they can provide a safe environment for students, where intercultural dialogue, reflectivity and courage to think can be nurtured' (16). To address gender in the classroom, then, one must first address general issues of cultural variance.

During the years I taught in China, a regular workshop in my Western and American culture courses consisted of asking each student to make a list of what they considered to be the 'top ten Chinese cultural values'. This was then compared to the list of American/Western cultural values presented first in the research of Edward D. Steele and W. Charles Redding, whose seminal 1960s study – a foundational text in the field of American Cultural Studies – identified and analysed core values portrayed in American political speeches from the 1940s and early 1950s (many of which are arguably still valid today, though to varying degrees). While certainly not strictly 'scientific' in approach, I adhered to the methodology supported by more contemporary cultural theorists in that I encouraged students not to identify their own personal values, but rather the perceived values of their society or of the 'average' Chinese person. This seemed a useful way to get a picture of the students' general notions of Chinese cultural ideology, while still acknowledging that individual values may of course differ greatly from the 'average' or societal norm. A 2007 article in the *Journal of Personality and Social Psychology* by Ching Wan *et al.* endorses the value of identifying cultural generalisations without discounting individual variances, and asserts that 'cultural values are those that are strongly endorsed by *most* members of the culture' (quoted in Vauclair 2009, 10; emphasis added). This introductory pedagogical task developed a similar approach.

The workshops provided me with abundant data written by Chinese university students from all over the country, between the ages of 19 and 21, outlining their perceptions regarding the value system of their own culture. The hundreds of responses I received were remarkably consistent in content. By asking students to work in small groups to describe what they might identify as their own culture's values, and then come together as a class to compare these to documented ideas about Western cultural values, I was able to change the gender dialogue from one centred on morality to one focused on cultural variances. This seemed more acceptable to students than teaching Western attitudes towards gender as if they were absolute 'truths' that students were expected to adopt. One function of this task was to articulate stereotypes so that they might be confronted and explored. It essentially opened a window of tolerance that permitted more uninhibited dialogue in the classroom.

While cautioned to keep in mind the inevitable element of generalisation, the students identified the most striking cultural differences between Chinese and Western cultures as follows:

1. *Unity vs. Individuality* – for the students, these terms described what they saw as a Chinese privileging of collectivism over a more typically Western cultural emphasis on the individual.[1]
2. *Harmony vs. Competition* – while the students saw social harmony rather than social competitiveness as a typical Chinese aspiration, we also noted the cultural changes brought about by an emergent and highly competitive Chinese economy.
3. *Tradition vs. Progress* – students articulated this contrast in terms of respect for tradition and for one's elders, which they saw as quintessentially Chinese.
4. *Extended Family vs. Nuclear Family* – the Chinese extended family, and sense of familial duty, was contrasted with a perceived Western emphasis on the nuclear family.
5. *Respect for Authority vs. Equality* – most students pitted a Chinese respect for authority and social hierarchies against what they saw as a Western liberal discourse of equality.
6. *Humility vs. Pride* – this rather interesting opposition identified 'pride' as something condemned in China and broadly valued in the West.
7. *'Face' vs. Candour* – the Chinese concept of 'face' encapsulates ideas of restraint, reserve and self-control, and was contrasted by the students to a Western privileging of self-expression.
8. *Patience vs. Action* – patience, highly valued by Confucianism, was contrasted to a Western (specifically American) impatience and aggressive pursuit of personal happiness.
9. *Risk Aversion vs. Risk Taking* – the students suggested that Western society rewards risk-takers, whereas Chinese society advocates stability.

10. *Confucian Morality vs. Christian Morality* – finally, the students attempted to articulate a distinction between a Judeo-Christian moral discourse of 'good' and 'bad', and a less rigid, more situational and evolving Chinese moral system, grounded in Confucianism.[2]

By introducing this activity at the beginning of the course, I aimed to encourage my students to articulate and think critically about their own perhaps unconscious cultural values, and how those values might inform gender constructions and gender criticism in both China and the West. By commencing with stereotypes that might readily be challenged, we were able to proceed to ideas of difference and dissent.

Teaching gender in China: from Chekhov to *Desperate Housewives*

Classes at the first university at which I taught in China took place primarily in large lecture halls and consisted of anywhere from 50 to almost 100 students. I also taught a few smaller classes, which contained about 30 students each. At the second university I had a few large lecture classes, but most consisted of approximately 40 students. Women generally outnumbered men – dramatically so in some cases (as in America, this is particularly the case in liberal arts and language departments, and the situation is reversed in the sciences). My students came from a variety of social classes, although the highly competitive university entrance test system in China does tend to privilege those whose parents can afford to pay for additional lessons and tutoring. Among my colleagues, gender issues and gender theory did not seem to be a primary concern within their teaching practice. One university at which I taught had a Gender Studies Institute (under the auspices of UNESCO), and even sponsored some conferences, but information about their activities was not readily available, and joint projects were not encouraged.

In China, students are still largely taught by lectures based around textbooks, with few student-led activities. A Chinese colleague who has studied in the West summarised the traditional Chinese teaching model in this way:

> Traditional Chinese teachers who have not had Western influences tend to do a lot of lecturing.... They might ask questions of students, but they often only expect students to conform to standard answers. Students are not encouraged to think for themselves and to ask questions of their own. This is because China has the test-based education system. Students have to train for exams as early as they enter primary school.... In English classes, teachers spend a lot of time talking about language points, grammar, and sentence making, but not enough time using English to discuss ideas. (Wang 2010)

Thus students were initially somewhat unprepared for my use of audio and video texts, in-class workshops, requests for presentations and interactive class format. And in addition, of course, the students were also dealing with the difficulties of being taught in English.

In my classes, I adopted the student-centred pedagogic models with which I was familiar from my teaching in the US, and I used an interactive approach that stressed analysis and cultural comparison. My purpose was not only to teach English language and literature to my students, but to introduce analysis of Western and English-speaking cultures through the texts studied, and to practice reading cultures as texts themselves. It is widely accepted that '[s]tudying literature, one of the products of a culture, one of its forms of cultural discourse, can enhance intercultural education. Literature portrays its culture implicitly' (Einbeck 2002, 62). Within English Studies, my students had little or no training in literary theory or textual analysis; most of their previous experience had consisted of close-readings of texts for language study and translating vocabulary. I tried to address this issue first, prompting them towards a literary rather than purely linguistic study, and encouraging them to identify and analyse themes and theses in literary works. In practical terms, this was done through demonstrations followed by group and individual workshops. Students were required to present their findings to the class, an exercise that was initially difficult for many, but which I think helped to affirm the importance of individual contribution.

As part of this shift from form to content, I attempted a representation of some basic concepts of Western cultural gender ideology in the context of these classes by selecting a number of texts that were written by women, as well as texts by male authors that grappled with themes important in Gender Studies. These texts included short stories such as 'A Jury of Her Peers' by Susan Glaspell, 'Lady with Lapdog' by Anton Chekhov, and Kate Chopin's 'The Storm' and 'The Story of an Hour'. Other canonical Western literary texts were also regularly analysed from a gendered perspective, and in sections on postmodernism, audio and visual texts were brought into the classroom to stimulate discourses centring on contemporary gender representation. Lyrics by Pink, Madonna and Eminem, television shows such as *Desperate Housewives*, and recent Hollywood films proved to be extremely effective in touching on the popular culture sensibilities of the students. While my Chinese students had read, listened to or seen many of the same texts as my Western students, and often found them enjoyable, their understanding of the culturally specific gender issues in these texts could be limited. One student, for example, informed me that she had just finished watching *Desperate Housewives*; when asked what she thought of it, she replied: 'I don't really understand it'. I found that students were often baffled, not only by what they described as the excessive and unconventional sexual behaviour exhibited by female characters in television and film texts, but that women depicted in this way would be privileged by Western viewers. Some were also surprised that governments in the West would permit such depictions to be broadcast. One student informed me that on other literature courses 'topics such as premarital sex, homosexuality and politics...were barely touched upon by Chinese teachers' (Li 2010). My concern was therefore to address matters of gender and sexuality – which might more typically be considered unsuitable for the classroom – in a critically productive but non-confrontational manner.

A focus upon Western texts and an analysis of, for example, character, setting, plot, symbolism and theme, paved the way for detailed discussions of 'difference' in the cultural values the texts expressed, together with a broader consideration of the manner in which societies construct concepts of gender and gender roles. Like many of the Western students I have encountered, most of my Chinese students had not previously considered the possibility that beliefs about gender might be 'constructed' as opposed to 'organic'. Undergraduates were generally perplexed by this idea, often pointing to social norms as their guide to defining concepts such as 'gender' and 'sex'. Feminist ideas, in particular, were likely to be judged as suspect – again, this is not by any means unusual in a Western undergraduate classroom, but their rejection by Chinese students tended, notably, to be on the grounds of selfishness. By returning to our earlier discussions of cultural values, however, I was able to couch this discussion in terms of how Western feminism might be understood as actually embodying common cultural preoccupations in the West with individualism, social equality and the pursuit of liberty and happiness. In this way, taking the time to work with students to explore Western cultural contexts encouraged them to be more receptive to ideas that might have otherwise been dismissed on moral terms, and made critical dialogue possible.

Although I identified many similarities between my Chinese and American students, one palpable consequence of the cultural differences identified above was evident in the specific issues I faced around classroom management. 'Speaking up' in class or disagreeing with others seemed to be generally viewed disapprovingly, as an expression of pride and a desire to stand out. I found that, at least in the formal setting of the classroom, my students were reluctant openly to question socially accepted norms. Most students would listen to my propositions with respect and, when urged, reply with courtesy, but would typically see any unconventional ideas I expressed as 'foreign' eccentricities. Not wanting openly to disagree with a professor, students would sit quietly, offering little or no input or feedback. What I found effective in this situation was to place students in small groups and ask them to evaluate the cultural beliefs or values being presented *in the text* – encouraging them to carefully steer clear of expressing their personal beliefs. Was a character or situation acting against the status quo of their society or culture? What was the tone of the work? Did the author seem to view the situation as negative, positive or indifferent? What vocabulary indicates this? Focusing on literary and cultural analysis encouraged students to consider and discuss the ideas present in the text while maintaining a psychological distance from those ideas, and permitted them to think about and discuss new and perhaps controversial ideas without losing 'face'.

Once participation became less intimidating, cultural roadblocks in the classroom most commonly occurred when discussing female literary characters who were unconventional or who resisted traditional gender roles and beliefs, such as Mrs. Mallard in Chopin's 'The

Story of an Hour', or Calixta in 'The Storm'. As one Chinese student explained, 'Chinese teachers would indicate that divorce is imperfect and unfortunate; we should not sleep with a person unless we feel certain that he/she is the one we are going to marry [and] a person who has experienced several relationships before marriage is not a moral person' (Iris 2010). Indeed, I had to be careful to explain that, while I had selected the texts we were studying in class, these texts did not necessarily depict my personal views or morals, and that I expected the students to analyse and understand the texts, but not necessarily to agree with the ideas expressed in them. This was readily accepted by most students, and many became increasingly more comfortable with discussing gender theory beyond the realms of the purely textual. For example, one graduate student described her own experience of gender discrimination in this way at the end of the semester:

> I have been laughed at and interrupted by men many times when talking about politics just as if what I was saying was nonsense. It's weird and ridiculous! ...

> Again and again, I hear my girlfriends complaining about their unfair treatment during job-hunting (But none of my male friend has ever said that they were treated unfairly compared to female in job market.) I can't help wondering: are we born to be a weaker gender? Well, I think, actually we are constructed – especially by the MEDIA – to be a weaker gender [*sic*].[3]

It was gratifying to see this student begin to utilise a theoretical framework to articulate her own experiences of cultural gender difference.

Despite such developments, many of my literature students still had difficulty accepting the portrayal of Mrs. Mallard in 'The Story of an Hour' – a woman who finds hope for a brighter future while reflecting on her husband's death, and is mortally disappointed when she discovers he is still alive. The students typically expressed strong disapproval of this character. Critic Yongbing Liu helps us to understand this reaction, explaining:

> [A]ny preoccupation with one's own interests is strongly equated ... with the concept of egotism and selfishness. The value of the

self or individuality is totally ruled out of the discourse of 'collective spirit'. An extreme version of collective spirit was in fact selected and reconstructed by the government throughout Mao's rule. It is evident in the slogans 'serving the people', 'pursuing selflessness', and 'sacrificing for the people and the country' that dominated the public media of that time. (Liu 2005, 28)

Mrs. Mallard, in flouting social conventions and privileging her own happiness, threatens social harmony and the traditional family structure so often privileged by Chinese culture. Again, asking students to focus on analysing the text from a standpoint of wider cultural values provided the necessary intellectual distance and made critical classroom dialogue possible.

Finally, an additional obstruction to the discussion of gender theory unexpectedly arose due to the difficulty of translating the now-familiar distinction between 'gender' and 'sex', which both overlaps and contrasts with the Chinese opposition of *'nuxing'* and *'funu'*. As Tani Barlow explains, 'The term *nuxing* (literally *female sex*) came into use during the 1920's ... [B]efore this time, women were described by the relational term *funu*, emphasizing familial and gender roles rather than biological sex' (quoted in Stevens 2003, 85). Without a corresponding binary conceptualisation of sex and gender, I found that a clear and precise dialogue on Western gender theorists such as Judith Butler was made difficult, although an approximation using the Chinese terms was certainly possible. Barlow continues: 'the formation of this oppositional term involved the adoption of a universal, scientistic, personal identity based on biological attributes rather than familial or gender roles. This construction also allowed "woman" to become the Other of "man" in the Westernized binary' (Stevens 2003, 85). As Mayfair Mei-hui Yang explains, in China, 'gender was not intertwined with modern discourses of sexuality in a sustained way until the 1980s, the effect of which is yet to be fully understood' (quoted in McWilliams 2005, 40). Keeping in mind the existence of such conceptual differences, and the continuing importance of tradition within Chinese culture, it is no wonder that gender theory has been reluctant to follow a Western trajectory in China. At present, nascent ideas about performativity coexist with more traditional, relational ways of thinking about men and women.

For example, as one of my graduate students wrote in an exam paper:

> [The] man is ... the center of a family. A man should be powerful and able to make a lot of money to feed his family. At present, women are accepted to work outside. However, the most important tasks are also traditional, such as to give birth to a child, doing housework, nursing the family and so on. In public eyes, a good woman should be sweet, patient, a good mother and a good daughter.

> Though improved a lot, the society is still patriarchal. Man still stands for the authority, power and rationality. ... Contrarily, woman is subordinate, [weak] and irrational. She should contribute mostly to her family and husband.

While many Westerners certainly hold similar beliefs, I found that it proved particularly difficult, for many complex and interrelated reasons, for students to voice oppositional opinions to such views within a classroom setting. Discussing alternative gender roles within the context of the independence and self-direction of female literary characters, however, provided a powerful forum for the exploration of such ideas.

The material reality of gender difference, and its impact on the lives of many Chinese women, was described in an exam by another graduate student in this way:

> I come from [the] countryside, things are worse there. In most families, the wives don't have jobs. They just cook, wash and take care of their husbands as well as babies. When they want to buy something, they must ask the husband for money. ... They don't know how to change their fate and earn respect from the family members. Housework is the main subject in their daily life.

> There are two or more children in each family. And there is an interesting phenomenon that the youngest baby is usually a boy. That's because all of the families in the rural areas want to have a boy baby. If the first baby is a girl, they will give birth to another or more until a boy [is] born. The government in China advocates the policy of 'one family, one baby' to control the birth.

If one family has more children than the family planning policy allows, it will be punished and fined. But there are still a lot of people secretly give birth to several children. They pay much emphasis on boys and they think boys are the unique successors of the family fortune. So the boys will get more care and have better education.

On the contrary, the girls are a little bit miserable. They do much housework everyday and they often get punishment and scorn [if] they make a small mistake. Some of my friends in my childhood left school when they were twelve or thirteen. They got married early and are repeating the same thing as their mothers. Now, I'm sitting in the classroom to get knowledge while they may be cleaning the house messed up by their husbands or babies. So the inequality between men and women is still a problem in our society.

As this student recognises, gender inequalities are deeply embedded, and it is little wonder, then, that young people in Chinese universities adhere to the tenets of the system in which they were raised; after all, most Western students do the same. Yet critical thinking about gender issues can be introduced into the classroom, if cultural contexts are both foregrounded and respected.

Conclusion

While both Chinese and Western values are highly regarded in their own settings, friction may occur when East meets West in the classroom. The study of gender in China must be approached with an awareness of what it means to be a gendered individual in Chinese culture. As a Western professor engaged in gender discourses with Chinese students, I was forced repeatedly to reflect on my own acculturated assumptions. Whether in America, Europe or China, as educators we must focus on cultural stereotypes, and seek to 'break them down by confronting, analysing, and challenging them, first in literature and then in reality' (Einbeck 2002, 64). Teaching gender in China, however, I found that the cultural assumptions with which I was most familiar differed greatly from those by which my Chinese students had been raised, and thus theoretical concepts created within a Western value system could not be readily adopted. Introducing the notion and practice of cultural literacy into the classroom was, in my experience, an effective method of coping with this dilemma.

Whether in literature, media, or within HE institutions, 'cultural displays do both reflect and create reality' (Stevens 2003, 100–1). While the cultural displays in China have historically varied greatly from those of the West, Chinese students are today faced with a collision of cultures. In the classroom, they study foreign ideas, including those dealing with gender issues, within a culture that remains resistant to outside influence. To find a space between submission and revolution in which to meet these learners, one must both appreciate and tackle cultural difference, and open one's own assumptions up to critical enquiry. Only in this way can East and West move towards a productive pedagogic discourse on the role of gender theory within the classroom.

Notes

1. This view has been supported by recent studies that reveal 'an emerging consensus in personality and social psychology that cultures vary in the extent to which either independence or interdependence is sanctioned' and that 'Western cultural contexts emphasize a view of the self as independent [...while] in Eastern civilizations, a contrasting view of the self as interdependent, interpersonally connected, and socially embedded has been elaborated' (Kitayama *et al.* 2009, 237).
2. Kitayama *et al.* (2009) help to clarify this idea: 'This general [East Asian] view of self can be found in the ontology of Buddhism (which emphasizes a unity of the universe including all creatures, both past and present); Confucian ethics (which is grounded in the central significance given to hierarchical relationships at both societal and personal levels); and a variety of indigenous holistic beliefs, such as Bushido and Taoism. Of course, the relational, interdependent view of the self acknowledges *one's internal attributes such as desires, intentions, and attitudes*. However, these attributes *are not considered primary*. Instead, they are seen as coexisting with, contingent on, and often to be *subordinated to the social order*. These broad views of the self as relational provide an important epistemic basis for a social ideology of *collectivism* and have become a major *cultural mandate*' (237, emphasis added).
3. This quotation, and the subsequent direct quotations from students, have been taken from written work submitted to me as part of the assessment requirements for the course. I have removed all names in order to protect the anonymity of the students.

Works Cited

Durkin, Kathy (2008) 'The Adaptation of East Asian Masters Students to Western Norms of Critical Thinking and Argumentation in the UK', *Intercultural Education* 19(1) (February): 15–27.

Einbeck, Kandace (2002) 'Using Literature to Promote Cultural Fluency in Study Abroad Programs', *Die Unterrichtspraxis/Teaching German* 35(1) (Spring): 59–67.

Kitayama, Shinobu, A. Timur Sevincer, Hyekyung Park, Mayumi Karasawa and Ayse K. Uskul (2009) 'A Cultural Task Analysis of Implicit Independence: Comparing North America, Western Europe, and East Asia', *Journal of Personality and Social Psychology* 97(2): 236–55.

Iris (29 July 2010), personal interview via e-mail.

Li, W. (29 July 2010), personal interview via e-mail.

Liu, Y. (2005) 'The Construction of Chinese Values and Beliefs in Chinese Language Textbooks: A Critical Discourse Analysis', *Discourse: Studies in the Cultural Politics of Education* 26(1) (March): 15–30.

McWilliams, S. (2005) 'Critical Fictions, Critical Spaces: Teaching Multicultural and Queer Women's Literature in China', *Transformations: The Journal of Inclusive Scholarship & Pedagogy* 16(1) (Spring): 32–50.

Steele, E.D. and W.C. Redding (1962) 'The American Value System: Premises for Persuasion', *Western Speech Symposium* (Spring): 83–9.

Stevens, Sarah E. (2003) 'Figuring Modernity: The New Woman and the Modern Girl in Republican China', *NWSA Journal* 15(3): 82–103.

Su, H. (2005) 'Reinserting Woman into Contemporary Chinese National Identity: A Comparative Reading of Three "New Immigrant" Plays from 1990s Shanghai', *Theatre Journal* 57: 229–46.

Vauclair, C. (2009) 'Measuring Cultural Values at the Individual-Level: Considering Morality in Cross-Cultural Value Research', *RAM – Revista de Administracao Mackenzie* 10(3): 60–83.

Wang, H. (30 July 2010), personal interview via e-mail.

11
Teaching Gender in a Turkish Context

Rezzan Kocaöner Silkü

More than half a century has passed since Simone de Beauvoir's state-ment in *The Second Sex* that 'One is not born, but rather becomes, a woman' (295), and despite some significant cultural differences between nations, gender roles are still essential 'foundations of every existing social order' (Lorber and Farrell 1991, 1). At the same time, while there has been a widespread growing interest in gender issues, the emergence of Gender Studies in different cultural contexts – from Great Britain, Germany and France, to the United States and Turkey, Australia, India and Africa – varies from one country to another. Thus, each country has its own experiences of critically engaging with gen-der, and this chapter aims to examine the rise and development of Gender Studies in Turkey, and discuss, from my own experience, strategies for teaching gender theory to Turkish students.

In her article, 'Emancipated but Unliberated? Reflections on the Turkish Case', Deniz Kandiyoti questions the 'applicability' of 'Western feminist theory... to non-Western contexts' due to its 'eth-nocentrism', and also emphasises 'the possible role of religion in legitimating women's oppression' in the Middle East (317). The Turkish case, however, is considered to be distinct from that of the Middle East, and Kandiyoti suggests that 'Turkey may be singled out as a republic that has addressed the question of women's emanci-pation early, explicitly, and extensively... through a series of legal reforms following the war of national independence (1918–1923)' (320). For example, as a result of 'the Law for Unification of Instruc-tion', which came into force in 1924 to provide 'equal opportunity for education' between genders, Turkish women were admitted to

Higher Education programmes and became 'visible in the area of academia, the liberal professions, art and literature' (Abadan-Unat 1981, 5, 13). In particular, in the Western Languages and Literatures departments of Turkish universities, the number of female students and scholars has always been relatively high, largely because the teaching profession – especially in the humanities – has long been associated with women (reminding the English literature student perhaps of the role of governess as a rare female profession in the Victorian period).

Accordingly, in the process of teaching gender in English departments in Turkey, students are introduced to feminist theory, with examples ranging from Mary Wollstonecraft to Elaine Showalter, Simone de Beauvoir to Judith Butler. The students approach these various literary and critical texts in different ways. 'the Woman Question' in the Victorian period, for example, is often stimulating for Turkish female students because they can easily empathise with Victorian characters and their conflicts within a conservative patriarchal society. Alternatively, the difficulties that female characters experience in postcolonial novels also offer good opportunities for English Studies students in Turkey to develop a more nuanced awareness of their own gendered cultural identity. To encourage a fuller appreciation of different representations of gender, examples from a wide spectrum of writers, including Jane Austen, George Eliot, Virginia Woolf, Doris Lessing, Arundhati Roy, Flora Nwapa, Jean Rhys, Daniel Defoe, Oscar Wilde, Joseph Conrad, D.H. Lawrence, Chinua Achebe and Caryl Phillips, are typically studied on undergraduate and graduate courses in English Language and Literature departments in Turkey.

In this light, this chapter aims to discuss the experience of teaching gender through literature within a specifically Turkish Higher Education context. To fulfil this aim, I will firstly describe something of the rise and influence of Gender Studies in Turkey, with reference to the Turkish modernisation process that followed the Tanzimat (Reorganisation) Period (1839–1876) as the harbinger of a new, modern era. I will discuss how, after this secular transformation of Turkish society, gender theory was increasingly taught through literature as part of English Studies, and I will consider how students respond to these literary and theoretical texts today. The chapter will also investigate how reading texts from a gender-conscious perspective with an additional awareness of cultural representations can provide students with an experience of self-identification and, potentially, a sense of liberation. Finally, my concern is to examine how Gender Studies translates from an Anglo-American context into a Turkish environment within the Department of English Language and Literature of my own institution, Ege University.

The rise of Gender Studies in Turkey

As Sibel Bozdoğan and Reşat Kasaba state, the Turkish experience of modernisation can be traced back 'to the institutional reforms of the late Ottoman era and epitomized by the establishment of a secular nation-state under Kemalism in 1923' in accordance with 'Western norms, styles, and institutions, most conspicuously in education, law, social life, clothing, music, architecture, and the arts' (3–4).[1] For Ayşegül Yaraman, the declaration of the Tanzimat Edict in 1839 gave impetus to the transformation and modernisation of nineteenth-century Ottoman society (17). For example, the Ottoman Land Law of 1858 allowed women to claim property rights alongside their male counterparts (25), while the 1876 Education Reform Act made primary school education compulsory for both boys and girls, paving the way for the amelioration of women's legal rights in the following years. High schools for girls were first opened in Istanbul in 1913–1914, followed by women's admission to Higher Education. Thus, under the impact of education reforms and women's rights movements, women started to gain access to universities. Institutionalised gender discrimination in Higher Education officially ended in the 1920s, when women were given the right to share the same classroom with men (34–5).

Accordingly, the evolution of the women's movement in Turkey since the Republican era can be discussed in two complementary phases: the Kemalist 'project of modernity' and the feminist phase since the 1980s. Yeşim Arat explains that, 'For the founding fathers, the "woman question" was part of the populist project', whereas for the feminists, 'the problems they [women] themselves experienced' were significant (104). Thus, 'the republican project of modernity' mainly focused on liberating women from the manacles of patriarchy as a major component of the Republican reforms, rather than as a specifically feminist goal (105).

In her study, 'The Turkish Woman and the Public Sphere', Nazife Şişman suggests that in the Republican era women's legal expectations were fulfilled without struggle, as part of a Republican governmental policy which could also be described as a 'state feminism' (55). At that time, women's rights were not gained by force but by the imposition of the state through the principle of 'laicism', which can be defined as the separation of religious and secular matters. Kandiyoti also underlines 'the absence' of the women's suffrage movement in Turkey, since reforms were planned as part of the state ideology within the framework of the Turkish modernisation project (323). On the other hand, the second wave of feminism, which emerged in the 1960s and continued throughout the 1970s in North America and Europe, was not to have an impact in Turkey until the 1980s. During this period, many protests and demonstrations were organised by Turkish feminists, feminist journals and periodicals were published, and Women's Studies departments were established in universities (Şişman 1996, 57). In order to liberate women from the confinement of domesticity, contemporary Turkish feminism has sought more egalitarian gender relations. From the 1990s onwards, many campaigns have encouraged the revision of Turkish law in order to further improve women's position in society. The unfair situation between the sexes started to change 'with the adoption of the law on protection orders aiming to prevent domestic violence in 1998, followed by the reform of the Civil Code in 2001, and most recently the Turkish Penal Code Reform in 2004' (Anıl *et al.* 2009, 3). Thus, through such legal improvements, Turkish women have become increasingly visible in the public sphere and gained greater personal rights and freedoms.

In this regard, as a natural outcome of the employment of female teaching staff in many educational institutions, and the socio-political developments within Turkey in the 1970s and 1980s, Women's Studies and Gender Studies programmes began to open in major Turkish universities in the 1990s, both as interdisciplinary programmes in research centres and as postgraduate and undergraduate programmes in university departments.[2] Among these various gender-based programmes were research and implementation centres for the employment of women, women's research and education centres, Women's Studies departments, Gender and Women's Studies centres and Women's Studies postgraduate programmes

(Birkalan-Gedik *et al.* 2006, 1). As Birkalan-Gedik notes, gender theory is also implemented into the curricula of other disciplines and departments, including sociology, anthropology and literature (2). European and American theoretical models played a significant role in the establishment of Gender and Women's Studies programmes in Turkey. Birkalan-Gedik cautions, however, that '[p]articular issues related to Turkey need to be developed rather than borrowing paradigms from abroad' (2).

In evidence of the ongoing institutionalisation of Gender Studies and Women's Studies programmes in Turkish academia, the syllabi of Western Languages and Literatures departments in most Turkish universities now include a variety of gender-related courses, at both graduate and undergraduate level. Courses such as 'Studies in Women's Literature', 'Gender and Literature' or 'Gender and Language' are now common, and gender theory is a popular subject of study in Turkish Higher Education. Accordingly, I would like to draw here upon my own third- and fourth-year undergraduate teaching in the English Language and Literature Department of Ege University,[3] and discuss three courses – 'The Victorian Novel', 'Colonial Literature' and 'Postcolonial Literature' – as case studies in order to elaborate on the way in which gender theory is transferred from an Anglo-American context into a Turkish classroom.

Student attitudes to gender

As part of the process of analysing and reflecting on gender within my teaching, I give my third- and fourth-year English students a questionnaire to complete, in order better to understand their attitudes towards gender at the start of the course. The following findings are taken from the spring semester of 2010, when the questionnaire was answered by 74 students (82 per cent female and 18 per cent male). The responses are enlightening. For example, the statement 'In marriage, a wife must shoulder more responsibilities than a husband, even if they both work' was not approved by most of the female participants (82 per cent); while 31 per cent of the male students were indecisive, and only 39 per cent did not agree with the statement. Moreover, the statement 'Most men seem to be defending gender equality, but they never consider women equal to themselves' was agreed by 85 per cent of female students, whereas 62 per cent of male participants approved the same statement. In another statement, 'Women can have a career, but marriage and family should have priority', there was a closer correlation between the answers of male and female students; 75 per cent of female students did not agree with the given statement, whereas 62 per cent of male students disagreed with the same statement. Another question was closely related to the conservation of the family unit; 78 per cent of female students did not agree with the statement 'To protect the family unit, men must be the head of the family', while 46 per cent of male students agreed with the same statement. The suggestion that 'gender discrimination in society is getting worse every year' was approved by 41 per cent of female students, while 34 per cent of them were indecisive; however, 85 per cent of male students disagreed with the same statement. Lastly, the statement 'In general, society is fairly constructed to provide men and women with equal rights' was refuted by 72 per cent of female students, while 10 per cent fewer male students disagreed with the same statement.

Within its limits, the questionnaire shows that it is still very difficult to assume a consensus on gender equality within Turkish society. Female students appear to be very much aware of gender discrimination and support gender equality, whereas male students seem to retain certain conservative attitudes towards gender issues, presumably because of the nature of the students' traditional upbringing. In general, gender equality seems to be deemed theoretically desirable, but practically inapplicable within a patriarchal society. Most of the students support a woman's right to work, either for principles of gender equality or for economic reasons, yet there is still disagreement with regards to the distribution of power between the sexes. Thus, teaching gender theory, or applying gender as a key issue to the teaching of literature, can provide students with a variety of representations of gender and demonstrate how gender roles are practised in different parts of the world. In this way, students can learn to reflect on their own gendered position in society, and perhaps even be moved to improve gender equality. Accordingly, the practise of distributing and analysing the questionnaire has proved useful in helping me to revise and shape my course syllabi, and to develop new strategies in order to familiarise my students with gender issues and broaden their horizons.

Teaching gender and the Victorian novel

In designing my course syllabi, gender has always been a significant factor; literature provides students with stimulating and often provocative examples that encourage the discussion of women's positions within patriarchal societies. I find that it can particularly improve female students' awareness of gender politics, and even encourage self-awareness, as they often identify with female characters in given literary texts. In my course on the Victorian novel, for example, students are introduced, not only to the social, political, economic and literary characteristics of the Victorian period in Britain through examples from Emily Brontë, Charles Dickens, Elizabeth Gaskell and Oscar Wilde, but also to the dominant patriarchal ideology of Victorian morality from the perspective of gender theory. The students gain knowledge of certain major literary trends of the period, such as realism and naturalism, develop basic critical reading and writing skills, and also learn to elaborate on the selected texts, both thematically and analytically, with an emphasis on gender issues.

'The Victorian Novel' is a third-year compulsory course offered in the spring term with an average class size of 60 students, approximately two-thirds of whom are female (as in Europe and the United States, the proportion of female students in the English Language and Literature Department of Ege University is relatively high). After equipping students with the necessary theoretical and social background through lectures, wider reading and films, I facilitate a number of student-centred learning activities such as class discussions, student presentations and group work, in order to encourage active participation. My aim is to encourage students better to construct and articulate their own synthesis of some of the problems related to transferring 'the Woman Question' from an Anglo-American context into a Turkish one. Before the class, students are introduced to various critical perspectives through reading set essays about the assigned novels. I find, for example, Terry Eagleton's 'Myths of Power in *Wuthering Heights*' particularly useful when discussing class and gender issues in Brontë's novel. For broader contextual information, students also read Herbert F. Tucker's *A Companion to Victorian Literature and Culture*, Gail Marshall's *Victorian Fiction: Contexts* and

Deirdre David's *The Cambridge Companion to the Victorian Novel*. During seminars, certain arguments and positions from gender theory are discussed with reference to excerpts from the literary texts.

In class discussions of *Wuthering Heights*, for example, the conversation between Nelly Dean and Catherine Earnshaw on marriage often provides a striking opportunity to discuss students' responses to the same subject matter in Turkish society. As Catherine, the daughter of a landowning family, receives a proposal from Edgar Linton, son of the local elite, she seeks Nelly's confirmation of her choice of Edgar over the penniless Heathcliff, declaring: 'I shall like to be the greatest woman of the neighbourhood, and I shall be proud of having such a husband' (60). At this point, recognising the aspects of social, cultural and familial expectations rooted within Catherine's dilemma, students commonly express empathy for the character, although some denounce her as selfish or weak for capitulating to social mores rather than defending her love for Heathcliff. In Turkish society, 'marriages of reason' are still favoured by traditional families. Daughters of such families are expected to respect the decisions of their parents and marry to maintain their status within a patriarchal society. With increasing rates of education and with economic liberation, however, women have started to question social norms that demand their submission. Analysing Brontë's novel provides a way in to discussing these expectations and their socio-cultural origins within the classroom.

Teaching gender with colonial and postcolonial literatures

'Colonial Literature' is a fourth-year elective course offered in the fall semester and designed to complement the spring term elective, 'Postcolonial Literature'. The 'Colonial Literature' course, with an average of 30 students, provides a good opportunity to discuss the concept of womanhood from the perspectives of colonialist and patriarchal ideologies. During the initial sessions of the course, students are introduced to British colonial ideology and literature through reading Doris Lessing, E.M. Forster and Rudyard Kipling.

The basic objective of this undergraduate course is to create a student-oriented learning environment in which students are encouraged to develop their own critical responses to gender issues as well as to colonialist ideology and discourse. To introduce students to the theoretical framework of the course, I use Edward W. Said's *Orientalism* (1978) as a key reference text. Reading significant quotations from Said's text, students learn about Orientalism as a Western institution, and stereotypical representations of the East under the Western gaze. Due to Turkey's specific geopolitical position between the East and the West, and their experiences of the Western-oriented Turkish education system, students commonly identify with both Eastern and Western cultures. Through reading essays, class discussions, presentations, personal contributions and writing response papers, students develop awareness about the background of the British colonial period. For instance, character analysis of Adela Quested in Forster's *A Passage to India* (1924), Mary Turner in Lessing's *The Grass is Singing* (1950) or Kipling's Lispeth in his short story, 'Lispeth' (1888) provide good opportunities for students to develop critical questions and responses towards gender-related problems in a colonial and patriarchal British society. As Teresa McKenna argues, 'We internalize and perpetuate old systems by not asking questions, by accepting a situation as if it were the natural order of things' (436). Thus, at the start of each session, I raise some short questions on the issues of womanhood, marriage, gender and sexuality pertaining to the assigned texts, designed to encourage students to think critically, formulate further questions to explore and begin to draw their own conclusions. For example, the function of Adela Quested or Mary Turner as Western colonising women in India and Africa respectively is a good starting point. In this way, students can translate fictional examples to real life, and evaluate their own situations in a patriarchal society in order to transfer this experience from an Anglo-American context into a Turkish one.

While discussing *A Passage to India*, students are encouraged to reflect not only on colonial issues, but also on issues of gender in a colonial society. When British Adela is taken by the Muslim Indian doctor Aziz to see 'the real India', her curiosity about his life, so alien to hers, leads her to ask whether Aziz has 'one wife or more than one', thus irritating Aziz and leading him, with significant consequences, to enter a cave to overcome his confusion (164). Discussing this scene, students are encouraged to think about marriage practice in their own culture, where polygamy is not commonly practised, and to then contemplate questions of cultural relativism and difference.

This critical process aims to encourage students to consider cultural specificity and cultural impact on the formation of human behaviour.

Finally, discussing Lessing's *The Grass is Singing* provides further opportunity to contemplate the politics of marriage from both gendered and colonial perspectives. As 30-year-old Mary Turner over-hears gossipers declaring her too old for marriage, she decides to marry Dick Turner. Soon after her marriage, however, she realises that Dick expects the previously independent Mary to adopt a stereotypical housewife role. Discussing this scenario, students are faced with narrative statements such as: '[Mary] had inherited from her mother an arid feminism, which had no meaning in her own life at all', and '[Dick] was lonely, he wanted a wife, and above all, children' (33, 48). I find that students typically respond to such quotations by relating them to their own life experiences, translating them into the contemporary context of a still traditional and patriarchal Turkish society. They often describe their ready comprehension of the manner in which social pressures can direct and limit individual choices, as they do for Mary, who was 'leading the comfortable carefree existence of a single woman in South Africa' (33) before her disappointing marriage. Perhaps most striking in these classroom conversations is the manner in which students commonly privilege gender issues over the racial and colonial issues offered by the text, indicating perhaps that gender is a more readily recognisable and applicable phenomenon than race and colonialism for many Turkish students today.

The 'Postcolonial Literature' course is similarly popular, with an average of 35 students each year. It introduces students to postcolonial literary theory and encourages them to consider a variety of cultures distinct from their own. The objective of the course is to discuss the characteristics of postcolonial writing, with an emphasis on gender, race and ethnicity, through readings from Chinua Achebe, Flora Nwapa and Arundhati Roy. During the early sessions of the course, I find that students are often hesitant to take an active part in class discussions because they are unfamiliar with the culture under consideration. Another problem for students typically arises from the difficulty of relating the theory to the selected texts. One strategy that I find useful is to assign tasks that encourage students to digest and rearticulate complex theories in their own words, and then ask them to explore their own views on gender, ideology, race, identity or politics of power and resistance. In this process, students are motivated to consider different and overlapping aspects of postcolonial issues, including gender, race, ethnicity and cultural difference, and hopefully to develop a more nuanced mode of analysis.

Unlike established and predominantly Western ideological approaches, which Western students commonly employ to interpret any given text 'according to the criteria they have used for everything they have ever read', Turkish students are arguably more likely to develop multiple reading strategies, combining Eastern and Western ideological approaches (McWilliams 2000, 253). As Sally McWilliams says, ' "we are one" is another colonizing approach', through which 'the students see only differences and hold at arms' distance any influence the text might exert on their interpretive knowledges' (253). In contrast, Turkish students are perhaps better placed to recognise the cultural situatedness of Western criticism and theory. Accordingly, Turkish students are not only required to read examples of postcolonial gender theory commonly used in the West (texts by critics such as Ketu Katrak, Ania Loomba and Gayatri Spivak), but also the work of Turkish scholars such as Deniz Kandiyoti, Nermin Abadan-Unat and Yeşim Arat, who have published variously on gender, Islam and the Middle East.[4] Turkey's geographical and philosophical positioning between the East and the West gives Turkish students an opportunity to evaluate various literary examples of different cultures from both Eastern and Western perspectives.

Again, much of this module is concerned with addressing gender roles; students are often interested, for example, in Achebe's representations of women in *Things Fall Apart* (1958) and his positioning of his male-chauvinistic tragic hero, Okonkwo, as a representation of traditional Igbo society. Living in an extremely patriarchal society, Achebe's women are confined to a life of domesticity and restricted within the confines of their regional customs relating to polygamy, dowry or bride price, childbirth and subservience to men. In addition, Roy's *The God of Small Things* (1997), with striking female characters such as Baby Kochamma, Ammu, Mammachi and Rahel, alongside Nwapa's female characters, Dora, Agnes, Rose and Comfort in *Women Are Different* (1986), all provide further opportunities for students to contemplate the impact of culture on gender, often through comparing and relating the concerns of these texts to their own position in Turkish society. Students are encouraged to trace the historical development of postcolonial writing through examples from male and female writers, and with reference to different decades and nations, reflecting the transformation of women's position across various postcolonial societies.

Students are also invited to consider the manner in which a single text can voice multiple positions on gender. *Women Are Different*, for example, describes a Nigerian culture in which female education is still uncommon, and girls are expected to fulfil traditional female domestic roles. Nwapa articulates multiple perspectives through various characters; Comfort, a young woman attending a missionary school, voices traditional values: 'she believed that their parents were wasting their money educating them. They would eventually marry, have children and forget all they learnt in school' (12), while Rose, representing an alternative view of female power, responds to Comfort: 'the hand that rocked the cradle ruled the world' (12). Agnes instead is determined to sit the Cambridge School Certificate Exam and attend university, but is forced to marry a man 'who had wanted to marry [her] when she was a little girl of ten years old'; as the narrator notes, 'Once [fathers] are given money, they sell their daughters' (53–4). Challenging stereotypical representations of poorly educated 'Third World' women, Agnes continues to study for her exams after her marriage. During a seminar on Nwapa's novel, students are asked to elaborate on the concept of alternative modernities, with reference to postcolonial societies, and consider the multiple pressures acting on women moving to claim independent identities free from the manacles of both patriarchal and colonial forces. I ask students to consider the narrator's statement that Dora's daughter Chinwe's 'generation was doing better than her mother's own ... They have a choice, a choice to set up a business of their own, a choice to marry and have children, a choice to marry or divorce their husbands' (118–19). Contemplating this optimistic, progressive statement, students are asked to apply their reading of postcolonial theory to critically analyse the historical and cultural factors impacting on the processes of global gender equality.

As noted above, in teaching postcolonial literatures, I often find that the complexity of many theoretical texts can cause some anxiety in students, particularly when asked to apply theoretical readings to literary texts. Further practical solutions that I find helpful include requiring students to articulate as questions things that they are struggling to understand; asking students to prepare presentations and response papers to particular critical and literary extracts; and also posing exploratory questions aimed at encouraging participation. For example, a student might be asked to prepare a PowerPoint presentation addressing excerpts from Ketu Katrak's 'Postcolonial Women Writers and Feminisms', and then to raise some questions about 'the shared gender concerns' of postcolonial women writers, in order to initiate a student-led class discussion (Katrak 2000, 232). Such directed tasks aim to overcome any initial concerns about the difficulty of addressing literatures from quite different cultures, and also to encourage students to compare and contrast literatures written in English by writers writing from the margins and to reflect on the interrelatedness of both patriarchal and colonial ideologies.

Throughout the course, I seek to build on such learning tasks. With reference to Katrak's views on gender, colonialist education and the shared experience of African, Indian and Caribbean women writers, students are then asked to apply these ideas to extracts from Nwapa's novel. One strategy I find productive is to have the students draw a list of comparisons between Nigerian and Turkish societies. Discussing these cultural differences, we consider the manner in which ideological constructions and social pressures can affect one's life in a positive or negative way; these ideas are then related to both the students' wider critical reading and other literary examples, such as Ammu's case in *The God of Small Things*. At this point, I also find Mohit Kumar Ray's article on *The God of Small Things* useful in discussing issues of gender in the text. Contemplating Ammu's situation within the strict Indian caste system, Ray notes: 'Ammu had been humiliated and cornered by her father, ill-treated and betrayed by her husband, insulted by the police and rendered destitute by her brother. Each of them voiced the patriarchal ideology which commanded that she should have no right anywhere – as daughter, wife, sister and citizen' (54). I ask the students to discuss this statement alongside the text, and to draw analogies – historical and contemporary – between Indian, Anglo-American and Turkish societies from multiple perspectives. With this, students are being asked to consider not just global cultural differences but also the persistence of common stereotypical gender constructions across patriarchal societies of all types. As always, my aim is to encourage students critically to deconstruct the ideological gender roles and discursive strategies of patriarchy, to better understand the dialectics between ideology and gender, and to participate in and contribute to a more democratic and questioning classroom environment.

Notes

1. Kemalism is the nation-building ideology of the Turkish Republic, based on Mustafa Kemal Atatürk's principles of republicanism, nationalism, statism, populism, secularism and reformism.
2. For example: the Department of Women's Studies in the Ankara University Social Sciences Graduate School was established in 1996 and offers courses at MA and PhD level; the Department also collaborates with Ankara University Women's Centre, which was established in 1993; the Women's Studies Department of Istanbul University was founded in 1993 to offer courses for graduate students; the Gender and Women's Studies Centre at Middle East Technical University has promoted research and education since 1994; while the Women's Studies Graduate Programme of Ege University was established in 2000. There are also other Women's Studies research and implementation centres in many Turkish universities, such as Hacettepe, Atılım, Başkent, Çankaya, Çukurova, Gaziantep, Marmara, Gazi, Mersin and Yüzüncü Yıl Universities.
3. Ege University is a typical large Turkish public university, established in 1955 to promote research and education at both undergraduate and postgraduate levels. The university is composed of 11 faculties, 27 research and implementation centres, 7 vocational schools, 6 schools and 8 graduate schools. It has 50,000 students, most of whom are Muslim Turkish undergraduates and graduates, from different social classes. Some international students also attend the university, both within the framework of the Erasmus Programme and as part of other bilateral agreements with non-Turkish universities.
4. Key critical texts used on the 'Postcolonial Literature' course include *The Empire Writes Back* (1989) by Ashcroft, Griffith and Tiffin, *Colonialism/Postcolonialism* (1998) by Ania Loomba and *Orientalism* (1978) by Said. In addition, I also ask students to read 'Postcolonial Women Writers and Feminisms' by Ketu Katrak, "'Locusts Stand I": Some Feminine Aspects of *The God of Small Things*' by Mohit Kumar Ray, and 'First Things First: Problems of a Feminist Approach to African Literature' by Kirsten Holst Peterson.

Works Cited

Abadan-Unat, Nermin (1981) 'Social Change and Turkish Women', *Women in Turkish Society*, ed. Nermin Abadan-Unat (Leiden: Brill), 5–31.
Achebe, Chinua (1958/1994) *Things Fall Apart* (New York: Anchor Books, Doubleday).

Anıl, Ela, Canan Arın, Ayşe Berktay Hacımirzaoğlu, Mehveş Bingöllü, Pınar İlkkaracan, Liz Erçevik Amado (2009) *Turkish Civil and Penal Code Reforms from a Gender Perspective* (Istanbul: WWHR-New Ways).

Arat, Yeşim (1997) 'The Project of Modernity and Women in Turkey', *Rethinking Modernity and National Identity in Turkey*, eds Sibel Bozdoğan and Reşat Kasaba (Seattle and London: University of Washington Press), 95–112.

Ashcroft, Bill, Gareth Griffiths and Helen Tiffin (1989) *The Empire Writes Back: Theory and Practice in Post-colonial Literatures* (London and New York: Routledge).

Birkalan-Gedik, Hande A., Dinara Alimdjanova and Farideh Fahri (2006) 'Women's Studies Programs in Muslim Countries', *Encyclopedia of Women & Islamic Cultures*, gen. ed. Suad Joseph (Brill online) <http://www.brillonline. nl/public/womens-studies>, accessed 13 March 2010.

Bozdoğan, Sibel, and Reşat Kasaba (eds) (1997) *Rethinking Modernity and National Identity in Turkey* (Seattle and London: University of Washington Press).

Brontë, Emily (1990) *Wuthering Heights* (New York and London: Norton).

David, Deirdre (ed.) (2001) *The Cambridge Companion to the Victorian Novel* (Cambridge and New York: Cambridge University Press).

De Beauvoir, Simone (1997) *The Second Sex*, trans. and ed. H.M. Parshley (London: Vintage).

Eagleton, Terry (1993) 'Myths of Power in *Wuthering Heights*', *Wuthering Heights: Contemporary Critical Essays*, ed. Patsy Stoneman (Basingstoke: Palgrave Macmillan), 118–30.

Forster, E.M. (1924/1981) *A Passage to India* (Harmondsworth: Penguin).

Kandiyoti, Deniz A. (1987) 'Emancipated but Unliberated? Reflections on the Turkish Case', *Feminist Studies* 13(2) (Summer): 317–38.

Katrak, Ketu H. (2000) 'Postcolonial Women Writers and Feminisms', *New National and Post-colonial Literatures*, ed. Bruce King (Oxford: Clarendon Press), 230–44.

Kipling, Rudyard (1888/1994) 'Lispeth', *Plain Tales from the Hills* (London: Penguin), 7–11.

Lessing, Doris (1950/1978) *The Grass Is Singing* (New York: Plume Books).

Loomba, Ania (1998) *Colonialism/Postcolonialism* (London and New York: Routledge).

Lorber, Judith and Susan A. Farrell (eds) (1991) *The Social Construction of Gender* (Newbury Park, CA: Sage).

Marshall, Gail (2002) *Victorian Fiction: Contexts* (London: Arnold).

McKenna, Teresa (2003) 'Borderness and Pedagogy: Exposing Culture in the Classroom', *The Critical Pedagogy Reader*, eds Antonia Darder, Marta Baltodano and Rodolfo D. Torres (New York and London: Routledge Falmer), 430–9.

McWilliams, Sally (2000) 'Trajectories of Change: The Politics of Reading Postcolonial Women's Texts in the Undergraduate Classroom', *Going Global: The Transnational Reception of Third World Women Writers*, eds Amal Amireh and Lisa Suhair Majaj (New York and London: Garland), 252–83.

Nwapa, Flora (1986/1992) *Women Are Different* (Trenton, NJ: Africa World Press).

Peterson, Kirsten Holst (2002) 'First Things First: Problems of a Feminist Approach to African Literature', *The Post-colonial Studies Reader*, eds Bill Ashcroft, Gareth Griffiths and Helen Tiffin (London and New York: Routledge).

Ray, Mohit Kumar (1999) "'Locusts Stand I": Some Feminine Aspects of *The God of Small Things*', *Arundhati Roy: The Novelist Extraordinary*, ed. R.K. Dhawan (London: Sangam Books), 49–64.

Roy, Arundhati (1997) *The God of Small Things* (London: Flamingo).

Said, Edward W. (1978) *Orientalism* (London and Henley: Routledge and Kegan Paul).

Şişman, Nazife (1996) *Global Konferanslarda Kadın Politikaları* (Istanbul: Iz).

Tucker, Herbert F. (ed.) (1999) *A Companion to Victorian Literature and Culture* (Oxford: Blackwell).

Yaraman, Ayşegül (2001) *Resmi Tarihten Kadın Tarihine* (Istanbul: Bağlam).

12
Women's Studies, Gender Studies, Feminist Studies? Designing and Delivering a Course in Gender at Postgraduate Level

Ros Ballaster

This chapter begins with an account of designing and developing a taught course at postgraduate level in Women's Studies at Oxford University, one of Britain's oldest and most elite universities; it draws out from that history wider implications and considerations for those teaching gender today, especially within humanities faculties or departments in higher education.

Introducing Women's Studies at Oxford

'Women's Studies: Oxford's cheapest faculty' was the text sported by the badges printed by the Oxford University Women's Studies Committee in 1993. The committee mounted termly lecture series across the disciplines (mainly those in humanities and social sciences) and was funded through the small sums received from royalties from a series of publications based on those series.[1] There were and are no salaried university posts at Oxford in Women's Studies, and our committee was not part of the formal university structure. Nonetheless, we regularly received correspondence from supervisors and doctoral students suggesting we might supervise interdisciplinary work in Women's Studies. One of our number pointed out that in undergraduate curricula some visibility and security had been gained for the exciting work in feminist theory and gender analysis then underway through the establishment of examined courses. An obvious example at Oxford University was the option in 'women's writing' added to the English Language and Literature syllabus – relatively, if unsurprisingly, late by comparison with other, less traditional universities – in the early 1990s.

British universities, unlike their North American counterparts, have not been quick or numerous in designing and developing degree programmes in 'Women's Studies' or 'Gender Studies'. Undergraduate degrees in Britain tend to be taken in subjects, faculties or disciplines at a high level of specialism, rather than in liberal arts or general sciences. However, tutors at Oxford were aware of numbers of students seeking to go on to postgraduate study who sought to further an understanding of feminist and gendered theoretical frameworks developed through interdisciplinarity, or to make a transition from one discipline to another (from social sciences to humanities especially) in order to pursue research in the fields of Women's Studies, Feminist Studies and Gender Studies.

A subcommittee was established to design a proposal for a nine-month taught Masters degree from within humanities faculties, with representatives from four faculties: Literae Humaniores, English Language and Literature, Modern Languages and Modern History. We consulted extensively with colleagues in the Centre for Cross-Cultural Research in Women based at Queen Elizabeth House, Oxford University. While the initiative for the course came from within the humanities, discourses and methods traditionally associated with the social sciences were and remain powerful in Gender Studies: political theory, Legal Studies, Anthropology. We aimed to deliver a team-taught core course grounded in lectures and seminars as well as offer a long list of options that made visible the extraordinary strength in the field across the contributing faculties.

Our first cohort of ten students was admitted in October 1995. Over the more than 15 years of the programme's existence, I have taught options and core courses, supervised dissertations, examined, and acted as chair of the organising committee. These experiences have been immensely enriching for me, fostering interdisciplinary conversations with my co-leaders in the feminist theory seminar and the students of very different cultural and academic backgrounds who undertake the course. They consistently raise questions for me about the extent to which one can 'teach' politically or, indeed, avoid doing so. They also require consistent investigation of the relationship between theory and practice, and the balance between the acquisition of skills or the understanding of methodologies and the central requisite of study in the humanities of familiarity with powerful written arguments.

The Quality Assurance Agency for Higher Education (QAA) of 2001 made explicit the expectation that outcomes of Masters-level work be at a higher level than those at the honours level:

> Much of the study undertaken at Masters level will have been at, or informed by, the forefront of an academic or professional discipline. Students will have shown originality in the application of knowledge, and they will understand how the boundaries of knowledge are advanced through research. They will be able to deal with complex issues both systematically and creatively, and they will show originality in tackling and solving problems.
>
> They will have the qualities needed for employment in circumstances requiring sound judgement, personal responsibility and initiative, in complex and unpredictable professional environments.[2]

Two important distinctions for our purpose of considering the different demands of a Masters course from an honour's programme are first, the requirement for a creative as well as systematic approach to complex issues, and second, the advancement of the boundaries of knowledge through research. While honours students might be expected to show understanding of significant arguments about the nature of 'gender', the creative application of such understanding within the context of a research project, albeit a confined one achievable within the time constraints of a Masters dissertation, raises the expectations and demands.

In the early years of the course, the majority of students who applied did so because they felt it was an area overlooked in their first degree. In recent years students more often undertake the course to seek out interdisciplinary ways of thinking and to gain access to high-level research resources in the field (which a magnificent copyright and manuscript library such as the Bodleian inevitably holds, regardless of the 'gender-friendliness' of its acquisition policies).

The first degrees held by our incoming students have proved to be enormously various and students have hailed from every populated region of the globe, the majority nonetheless from North America and Great Britain. Interestingly, the shared focus on the acquisition of knowledge and research skills in a designated field of Women's Studies tends to make these differences less a source of conflict or inequality than a genuine asset. Discussions in seminars drew and draw on an immense variety of experience and understanding by comparison with discipline-specific Masters teaching. This kind of teaching teaches people to communicate their understanding in ways that do not simply conform to the discipline-specific models they have come to learn as undergraduates, or the high-level theoretical languages that may be valued in some fields but not in others.

In what remains of this chapter I address three issues that have proved both intractable and stimulating in the design and delivery of an interdisciplinary and multidisciplinary course in 'gender' in the humanities. First, nomenclature and the very different valences and expectations (academic and political) associated with certain kinds of analytic practice in the field of what has (too loosely) come to be called 'gender'. Second, the teaching of theory and methodology for a core assessed course and especially the necessary but often unhelpful divisions between theory and practice that trouble and should trouble our understanding of 'gender' and its performances. And third, the design and delivery of single-discipline options that enable graduates to undertake independent high-level research drawing on the theoretical understandings of Gender and Women's Studies that inform their Masters studies as a whole.

Naming the terms

Feminist writers and thinkers have often focused on gaining entry into institutions of learning and access to the resources there. Or they have shaped alternative feminist visions of those institutions, in particular those of higher education. We can trace the expression of such ambitions and the Utopian project for women's education in English women's writing from Mary Astell's proposal for an Anglican seminary for genteel women in 1694 (*A Serious Proposal to the Ladies*) to Virginia Woolf's demand for *A Room of One's Own* (1929); in the latter,

Woolf's musings on the relations between women and fiction are prompted by her experience of exclusion from the green spaces and the library of a male-only 'Oxbridge' college. Women are now admitted to the institutions of learning and knowledge from which they were previously excluded, and feminists need to think carefully how to transform them, not least because more often than not women do not appear to have entered those institutions on the same terms, with the same privileges and the same sense of ownership as experienced by their male counterparts.

When we were planning our nine-month taught graduate course, we inevitably spent some time debating what it should be called. One structural given that produced an unconscious and magnificent irony for the semiotic theorist to contemplate is that all humanities-taught graduate courses are called 'Masters': that is, our students were studying for a masculine gendered qualification. (And let us not delude ourselves that the term is understood to be used in a purely adjectival sense, as in that of 'mastering' an area of study!) How though should we nominate the 'study' itself: Women's Studies? Gender Studies? Or, most radically of all, Feminist Studies?

A variety of approaches fall within 'Women's Studies'. It is, of course, possible to 'do' Women's Studies without taking a feminist approach. The social organisation of women's lives can and has been studied with no analysis of women's oppression or brief to address change that might achieve freedom for women. Indeed, feminism has been one of the driving forces in the challenge to the anthropological myth of observation without engagement.[3] Equally, it is possible to produce feminist work outside of the field of Women's Studies. Feminist political theory is a good example here, in which trenchant analysis of the gender assumptions that underlie modern concepts of the civil subject has been produced by authors such as Carole Pateman, but in relation to texts and ideas produced, disseminated and consumed by men.[4] 'Feminist Studies' has the virtue of making explicit the politics of academic analysis, demanding political analysis of a group defined politically (rather than biologically or socially or culturally). Feminism proposes ways of transforming society in order to liberate women. However, academic 'disciplines' tend historically, and for good reason, not to define themselves by political objectives or interests, partly to retain their relative autonomy from state power, partisan politics and interest groups. The objective analysis of 'identities' (racial, sexual, class) can find a place among the disciplines, but the interested pursuit of liberation, it appears, cannot be supported by government funding nor form the foundation of an individual student's qualification for a future career. Feminism in academic fields always runs the risk of being designated as or demoted to an 'approach', marked as suspect by its political interest. 'Women's Studies' or 'Gender Studies' remain more popular terms for fields that have been defined by a feminist *political* argument, precisely because the academic is understood to need to be in some way outside of or untouched by the political. We might schematise the understanding as follows:

Gender = the study of a structure.

Women = the study of a group/person.

Feminist = the study of a system seeking redress/justice/equality.

We chose 'Women's Studies' on a number of grounds. First, because it was indeed a more accurate descriptive title for what the course and the research strengths of those contributing to it could offer. Options were designed to make visible the historical and political agency of women: in literary texts of different European cultures (classical and modern languages and literature), in history (from antiquity to the present day) and as philosophers and the interlocutors of philosophy. We were not developing a 'politically neutral' course that gave 'equal' attention to masculinities and femininities historically. 'Gender Studies' was a sub-category or a contributing discourse to the understanding of 'Women's Studies' rather than vice versa. The debate over 'Women's Studies' and the category 'woman' is at the heart of the discussions held with each new cohort of students and with the contributing lecturers and seminar leaders.

The final point to make with regard to the choice to name the course 'Women's Studies' is that the nomenclature made explicit the concentration on women's voices, experiences and lives. Core courses that identify key readings always have to make hard choices about inclusion and exclusion. Our decision in the 1990s was not to require students to undertake extensive primary reading in those male theorists whose writings had been so influential for feminist writers: from Thomas Paine and John Locke to Sigmund Freud, Jacques Derrida,

Michel Foucault, Jacques Lacan. Although these writers do feature in reading lists, concentration was to be on the writings and work of women 'theorists'.

Troubling distinctions

Distinctions between gender and sexuality, between men and women, between 'Gender Studies', 'Women's Studies' and 'Feminist Studies' have been and continue to be the subject of overt classroom debate. Other distinctions, which are common to academic research and often go unchallenged, are equally significant for the teaching of gender and yet often go unexamined. One such distinction is that of 'theory' and 'method': the framework of ideas that inform the interpretation of evidence as opposed to the ways in which that evidence is handled. This distinction chimes with and has proved as troublesome as the distinction drawn in radical politics between 'theory' and 'practice'. The history of feminism in academia has been one of a necessary questioning of abstraction, generalisation or 'theorisation', often seen as a means of avoiding 'practice' and 'real life' constraints or as the preserve of a certain kind of self-aggrandising masculinism. Yet, the recognition that the 'personal is political' of second-wave feminism also sought to identify and expose forms of behaviour and expression (the exclusion of women from positions of power; violence against women) as systematic and structural rather than incidental or personal. In designing this course in the early 1990s we identified these two separate areas for teaching as part of the core course and built into the course design the expectation that skills in the core courses would be subject to assessment that counted qualitatively towards the final degree. We were mindful that core courses were too often given insufficient attention by students and teachers if the work undertaken there did not count towards final assessment. We were also keen to ensure that our students were reflective about the methodologies they employed, derived from a variety of disciplines, as well as self-conscious about the theoretical models and the need for such models in analysing the material they encountered.

These debates proved very troublesome and often marked the distinctions between disciplines and disciplinary training about which we had not needed to be self-conscious in our own single-disciplinary experiences. The Masters degree was to provide not only a freestanding course but also a research preparation course for students to progress into doctoral work in any one of the contributing faculties. Yet, some faculties/disciplines had much firmer ideas about the kind of skills and methods that students needed to become confident practitioners in the 'subjects' of doctoral work. Historians were, for instance, much more committed to the notion of skills training than literature specialists: for them, training in handling archival materials, identifying statistically meaningful samples, drawing conclusions based on appropriate evidence, were an absolute prerequisite of research preparation. Philosophers were most committed to training students in 'ways of thinking' and relatively unconcerned about archives, the status of particular texts and their authority as sources; for the philosophers among us, theory is a method, or, to put it another way, method is nothing more than critical thinking. For literary critics the act of interpretation is a method, whereas, for historians, interpretation seemed to belong to the category of 'theory'. One of three pieces of written work for assessment was an essay on 'theory and/or method', expected to be developed from content covered either in a theory course (a series of lectures and seminars based on a set of key and core 'theoretical' feminist texts, from Christine de Pizan's *Book of the City of Ladies* to Judith Butler's *Gender Trouble* and Karen Barad's *Meeting the Universe Halfway: Quantum Physics and the Entanglement of Matter and Meaning*), or in the method course (a series of seminars introducing reflective methodologies common to feminist work in different disciplines, such as canon-formation, the ethics of enquiry, archives and digital resources, and ethnographic research methods). Students could also write an essay that bridged the two courses and brought together 'theory' and 'method'.

Core courses are a source of perennial anxiety for tutors and students alike, and these courses were no exception. Students seek to have a clear definition of the kind of work required, while course designers and tutors want to provide sufficient latitude for students to do more than simply 'reflect back' an understanding achieved through attendance at lectures and seminars. Students often over-exaggerate the requirement, moving well beyond an already demanding core course to find a topic. Others are baffled by a new rhetorical exercise which requires them to see materials they have previously viewed as 'secondary' or 'contextual' as of primary significance in and of themselves, and subject to the same standards of proof, investigation and interpretation as more obviously literary or historical or sociological 'primary' materials. The most significant challenge for the Masters student is to move beyond response to a question posed and observation of 'set' materials to a writing and research regime in which they identify, pose and seek to address research questions of their own devising based on self-directed and selective reading in an archive.

Again, one specific example may serve. One of the essays I recently supervised concerned the politics of translations from French to English of works by women in the 1980s and the shaping or marketing of a 'canon' of works in English criticism or theory by Luce Irigaray, Julia Kristeva and Helene Cixous. The student had the advantage of a background in combined honours in French and English, which allowed her to move between 'original' and 'translation' to measure and consider specific textual decisions made by translators. The essay drew on materials from both the 'theory' and 'method' elements of the course. A 'methods' session had considered the politics of 'canon-formation' in Literary and Language Studies (inclusions and exclusions of texts in anthologies, ways in which disciplines identify new fields via publishers' lists and essay collections). A 'theory' lecture and accompanying seminar as part of the history of Western feminism had considered 'poststructuralist feminisms' and the same key texts, but only in their English translations (Helene Cixous's *Le rire de la Méduse*/ [The Laugh of the Medusa], 1975/1976; Julia Kristeva's *Stabat Mater* [Stabat Mater], 1976/1987; Luce Irigaray's *Ce sexe qui n'en est pas un* [This sex which is not one], 1977/1981). In terms of method the essay offered close readings of individual translation decisions concerned with wordplay, the language of gender and metatextual reference. These readings were also, however, framed by a wider theoretical debate within feminism about the limits of a deconstructive method which celebrates free play and indeterminacy of meaning in order to expose the malleability of linguistic constructions of gender at the expense of acknowledging the local historical, social and cultural conditions that contain such play. This kind of work, typical of the best practice of able students on the course, not only demonstrates the ways in which theoretical insights are informed by method and vice versa, but also – and perhaps more importantly – that the theoretical separation of the two activities (theory and method) is a necessary first step to making visible that mutual interdependence.

Freedoms within disciplines

The 'MSt in Women's Studies' requires students to produce three pieces of assessed work: an essay in theory/method, a dissertation and an essay in a single option chosen from a list of over 20 possibilities. These options are an indication of the diversity and strength across the humanities disciplines in a large elite university. The option I have offered since the course's inception is in 'Women's Writing 1660–1789'. It is also offered to students undertaking the 'MSt in English Literature' and has attracted numbers from one to seven students. Students who undertake this course have often also written dissertations on early women's writing in English and a number have progressed to doctoral work in the area. The academic shorthand of 'aims' and 'objectives' with which all students are provided may help to explain the thinking behind this course:

Women's Writing 1660–1789
Aims:

1) to develop an awareness of a range of writing by women in different genres and the historical specificity of generic norms in the period
2) to encourage critical engagement with dominant interpretations, mainly in feminist criticism
3) to explore relevant contexts and intertexts of a 'women's tradition' (as well as question the category)
4) to provide a grounding that will make possible independent and original work in the field.

Objectives:

1) to encourage debate and discussion between participants and collaborative research work
2) to provide opportunities for critical writing in the field
3) to promote the discovery and shaping of research agendas on an individual/collective basis.

This option has seen profitable exchanges between students with feminist interests enrolled in an English Masters course and students with English interests enrolled in a Women's Studies Masters course. In any one group the majority of students hold honours degrees in English Literature – whatever the Masters programme in which they were enrolled – one assumes because they were seeking to strengthen and build on prior disciplinary knowledge. Nevertheless, the vantage point of the students who are taking the Women's Studies Masters degree is significantly different. For Women's Studies students, the texts considered provide the opportunity to address issues within feminism and feminist literary history in particular: essays have been concerned, for instance, with collaborative writing between women; the representation of sexual choice and volition in rape narratives of the eighteenth century; and feminist biographies of women's writing of the early modern period. By contrast, and unsurprisingly, the English Masters students have been more inclined to explore issues of genre, theme, and the work of individual writers, fielding essays on women's prophetic writing; the idealisation of monarchy in women's writing; labouring class women's writing; literary debts to male predecessors; and Utopian writing by women. Classes often centred on a single author or group of writers or writings, and participants presented short papers that posed research questions and suggested ways of proceeding to pursue solutions.

In these classes, students repeatedly challenge each other to defend both the validity of the questions asked and the method employed to pursue them. One especially energetic classroom controversy, which translated in turn into a fine piece of scholarship, comes to mind. One two-hour seminar explored women's contribution to the early novel and turned to a discussion about the representation of seduction and/or rape in the 1720s' fiction of Eliza Haywood. Reading Haywood's *Love in Excess* (1719–1720) in the context of Thomas Hobbes' mechanical theory of the will as explained in *Leviathan* (1651) led one of the presenters to point out that in this novel's representations of male characters, will is seen as a necessary consequence of desire (sexual attraction to women leads to a will to possess), whereas in the representation of female characters desire is more often seen as at odds with the will (women find themselves responding to male sexual advances while wanting to refuse them). She in turn suggested that Haywood's novel offers, among other things, a critique of Hobbesian libertinism. Nonetheless, she expressed her own dissatisfaction as a feminist reader with the elision of rape with seduction in the novel and was unhappy with an historically relativist explanation that sees rape as a discursive category with different meanings for the eighteenth than the twenty-first century (as a property crime rather than a crime against the person). Closer attention to the narrative voice, in turn, alerted us to the careful anticipation and manipulation of readerly response by Haywood which requires readers, often carefully differentiated in terms of their gender, to attempt to confront rather than evade ethical questions of sympathy and judgement at stake in such representations.[5] The discussion progressed to a wider debate about the ethical role of the critic and the material she addresses. To what extent are our current understandings of rape and seduction and the politics of the representation of the female body inadequate or anachronistic vehicles for 'understanding' early texts? Or, conversely, could we identify in the anticipated responses charted by Haywood and the philosophies of will and desire with which she is working the sources of some of our own current confusions and inconsistencies? Is the object of our study a better, or more accurate, or more proximate, understanding of the meanings available to its contemporaneous readings? Or are there more urgent and relevant political concerns that should drive our interpretations while paying due attention to the specificity of the literary objects we study? Gender is not here seen just as a further 'tool' or 'method' to explicate the meanings of a text; rather, the intellectual and institutional framework in which Gender Studies is pursued ensures that questions are posed for the academy and researchers within it that they *should* be vigilant to keep alive in their writing and research activity: Whose interests does this research serve? And why? To what end? We have to be equally vigilant not to resort to answers that are crudely instrumental ('my research will change the way women think') nor wholly abstract ('research for its own sake escapes the determinations of power in other institutional forms of acquiring knowledge').

To 'teach gender' in these classes has been to question and explore the object of analysis in the broadest sense: to consider what ends or outcomes are being sought as well as the nature of the materials under discussion. The course has led me to question the assumption that interdisciplinarity is always a necessary good. There is a freedom in teaching gender from within a single discipline if the questions we ask are sufficiently generous and rigorous. And it is enabling for students also who can expand their disciplinary horizons and knowledges and shift the terms of the questions asked of course content, while building on prior competencies and skills.

Coda: the future

Courses undergo constant revision and alteration in response to changed academic, intellectual and political climates – local, national and international. The Women's Studies Masters programme continues to attract a strong and varied application, despite the decline or closure of Women's Studies programmes in anglophone education, itself we hope the effect of increasing integration of feminist theory and method into mainstream courses and teaching. This is not to say that the programme has not been responsive to changes in political ideology and educational practice, especially in the value placed on inter- or multi- or cross-disciplinary study. Two significant choices have been made in the ways that we teach gender in this course from 2011:

1) Due to institutional barriers at postgraduate level (research councils' 'subject' divisions and the impossibility of cross-funding between different councils such as the ESRC and the AHRC; the difficulty of teaching credit being transferred from one division or school to another), Women's Studies courses in Britain have habitually fallen under the provenance of one or other field: humanities-based courses such as the one described here, informed by literary and historical methods/theories and preparing students for archival and/or theoretical research, or social sciences-based courses, informed by models from ethnography, anthropology and most recently Development Studies. While graduate students are precisely seeking opportunities to import skill sets and understandings from very different fields and disciplines, tutors and institutions may not be equipped to enable such variety and flexibility while defending the intellectual coherence and maintaining the high level of expertise that informs their courses. The Women's Studies masters at Oxford has become more explicitly defined as a humanities

course and the 'core course' assessments have become focused on preparation for research in the humanities. Social science methods have in the last decade moved far closer to those of the hard sciences and economics, and preparation for such research at doctoral level would require a shift of emphasis not possible within the existing teaching disposition of the course.

2) All students are required to undertake a bespoke core course in key readings and research training, but work in this field is no longer assessed through a single essay. Assessment is now based on option work and dissertations. This is a response to anxieties on the part of tutors and students about the level of expertise required in Gender Studies or Women's Studies as disciplines to assess and produce such work. Assessment anxieties appeared to have become a positive inhibition for students in making creative connections between the research materials they selected and the theoretical and methodological insights they encountered in the course.

The tensions within an academic institution and its disciplines, and the questioning of institutional and intellectual boundaries, make graduate courses in 'gender' stimulating, challenging and significant within Higher Education. The shifting sands of interdisciplinarity and multidisciplinarity, alongside the increasing professionalisation and specialisation of individual disciplines, have posed a challenge to the practice of teaching gender in Higher Education. While teaching gender and Gender Studies demands that we question distinctions, boundaries and categories, it can and should enrich the work conducted within single disciplines. This is nowhere more evident than within English Studies, where the study of both language and literature has been transformed by an attention to discourses of gender and sexuality. Moreover, students who graduate from courses that explicitly and consistently pay such attention – precisely by virtue of having to address these tensions and recognise that knowledge is never free from the contexts of power in which it is produced, although not necessarily constrained or confined thereby – contribute productively in their future careers to the transformation of the intellectual models that inform feminist and academic practice.

Notes

1. *Women in Society: A Feminist List.* Includes Sharon McDonald, Pat Holden and Shirley Ardener, eds (1987) *Women in Peace and War: Cross-Cultural and Historical Perspectives* (Houndmills, Basingstoke: Macmillan); Ros Ballaster, Margaret Beetham, Elizabeth Frazer and Sandra Hebron (1991) *Women's Worlds: Ideology, Femininity and the Woman's Magazine* (Houndmills: Macmillan).
2. See the descriptions of five levels of Higher Education (certificate, intermediate, honours, masters, doctoral), QAA (2001) <http://www.qaa.ac.uk/academicinfrastructure/fheq/ewni/default.asp>, accessed 25 July 2010.
3. See Henrietta Moore (1988) *Feminism and Anthropology.*
4. See Pateman, *The Disorder of Women, Democracy, Feminism and Political Theory*, and *The Sexual Contract.*
5. For Haywood's fiction and contemporary philosophy, see Kramnick, 'Locke, Haywood and Consent', and Potter, ' "A God-like Sublimity of Passion": Eliza Haywood's Libertine Consistency'.

Works Cited

Barad, Karen (2007) *Meeting the Universe Halfway: Quantum Physics and the Entanglement of Matter and Meaning* (Durham, NC: Duke University Press).

Butler, Judith (1999) *Gender Trouble: Feminism and the Subversion of Identity* (London: Routledge).

De Pizan, Christine (1999) *The Book of the City of Ladies (1405)*, trans. Rosalind Brown-Grant (Harmondsworth: Penguin).

Haywood, Eliza (1719–1720/2000) *Love in Excess*, ed. David Oakleaf (Peterborough, ON: Broadview).

Kramnick, Jonathan Brody (2005) 'Locke, Haywood and Consent', *English Literary History* 72: 453–70.

Moore, Henrietta (1988) *Feminism and Anthropology* (Cambridge: Polity).

Pateman, Carole (1989) *The Sexual Contract* (Stanford, CA: Stanford University Press).

——— (1990) *The Disorder of Women: Democracy, Feminism and Political Theory* (Stanford, CA: Stanford University Press).

Potter, Tiffany (2001) ' "A God-like Sublimity of Passion": Eliza Haywood's Libertine Consistency', *The Eighteenth-Century Novel* 1: 95–126.

Quality Assurance Agency for Higher Education (2001) <http://www.qaa.ac.uk/academicinfrastructure/fheq/ewni/default.asp>, accessed 25 July 2010.

Guide to Further Reading

Teaching gender

Knights, Ben (2008) *Masculinities in Text and Teaching* (Basingstoke: Palgrave Macmillan).

Spurlin, William J. (ed.) (2000) *Lesbian and Gay Studies and the Teaching of English: Positions, Pedagogies and Cultural Politics* (Urbana, IL: NCTE).

Gender studies

Butler, Judith (1990) *Gender Trouble: Feminism and the Subversion of Identity* (London: Routledge).

—— (1993) *Bodies that Matter: On the Discursive Limits of "Sex"* (London and New York: Routledge).

Colebrook, Clare (2004) *Gender* (Basingstoke: Palgrave Macmillan).

Cranny-Francis, Anne (ed.) (2003) *Gender Studies: Terms and Debates* (Basingstoke: Palgrave Macmillan).

Essed, Philomena, David Theo Goldberg and Audrey Kobayashi (2009) *A Companion to Gender Studies* (Chichester: Wiley-Blackwell).

Foucault, Michel (1990) *The History of Sexuality, Volume 1: An Introduction*, trans. Robert Hurley (Harmondsworth: Penguin).

Glover, David and Cora Kaplan (2000) *Genders* (London: Routledge).

Holmes, Mary (2007) *What Is Gender?* (London: Sage).

Richardson, Diane and Victoria Robinson (eds) (2007) *Introducing Gender and Women's Studies* (Basingstoke: Palgrave Macmillan).

Sarmento, Clara (ed.) (2007) *Eastwards/Westwards: Which Direction for Gender Studies in the 21st Century?* (Newcastle: Cambridge Scholars).

Whelehan, Imelda and Jane Pilcher (2004) *50 Key Concepts in Gender Studies* (London: Sage).

Gender and literature

Bertram, Vicki (2005) *Gendering Poetry: Contemporary Women and Men Poets* (London: Pandora).

Gilbert, Sandra M. and Susan Gubar (1979) *The Madwoman in the Attic: The Woman Writer and the Nineteenth-Century Literary Imagination* (New Haven, CT: Yale University Press).

Goodman, Lizbeth (1996) *Literature and Gender* (London: Routledge).

Morris, Pam (1993) *Literature and Feminism: An Introduction* (Oxford: Blackwell).

Pykett, Lyn (1995) *Engendering Fictions: The English Novel in the Early Twentieth Century* (London: Edward Arnold).

Showalter, Elaine (1977) *A Literature of Their Own: British Women Novelists from Brontë to Lessing* (London: Virago).

Gender and language

Cameron, Deborah (1992) *Feminism and Linguistic Theory* (London: Macmillan).

Cameron, Deborah and Don Kulick (2003) *Language and Sexuality* (Cambridge: Cambridge University Press).

Coates, Jennifer (2004) *Women, Men and Language* (Harlow: Pearson).

Litosseliti, Lia and Jane Sunderland (eds) (2002) *Gender Identity and Discourse Analysis* (Amsterdam: John Benjamins).

Livia, Anna (2001) *Pronoun Envy: Literary Uses of Linguistic Gender* (Oxford: Oxford University Press).

Livia, Anna and Kira Hall (eds) (1997) *Queerly Phrased: Language, Gender and Sexuality* (Oxford: Oxford University Press).

Mills, Sara (2008) *Language and Sexism* (Cambridge: Cambridge University Press).

Speer, Susan (2005) *Gender Talk: Feminism, Discourse and Conversation Analysis* (London and New York: Routledge).

Sunderland, Jane (2010) *Language, Gender and Children's Fiction* (London: Continuum).

Feminisms

Brooks, Ann (1997) *Postfeminisms: Feminism, Cultural Theory and Cultural Forms* (London: Routledge).

Bulbeck, Chilla (1998) *Re-Orienting Western Feminisms: Women's Diversity in a Post-Colonial World* (Cambridge: Cambridge University Press).

Digby, Tom (ed.) (1998) *Men Doing Feminism* (London: Routledge).

Gamble, Sarah (ed.) (2001) *The Routledge Companion to Feminism and Postfeminism* (London: Routledge).

Humm, Maggie (ed.) (1992) *Feminisms: A Reader* (London: Harvester Wheatsheaf).

Marks, Elaine and Isabelle de Courtivron (eds) (1981) *New French Feminisms: A Reader* (Brighton: Harvester).

McRobbie, Angela (2009) *The Aftermath of Feminism: Gender, Culture and Social Change* (London: Sage).

Moi, Toril (1985) *Sexual/Textual Politics: Feminist Literary Theory* (London: Methuen).

Masculinities

Baker, Brian (2006) *Masculinity in Fiction and Film, Representing Men in Popular Genres, 1945–2000* (London and New York: Continuum).

Clare, Anthony (2000) *On Men: Masculinity in Crisis* (London: Chatto and Windus).

Connell, R.W. (1995) *Masculinities* (Cambridge: Polity).

Faludi, Susan (1999) *Stiffed: The Betrayal of Modern Man* (London: Vintage).

Kimmel, Michael (1987) *Changing Men: New Directions in the Study of Men and Masculinity* (London: Sage).

—— (1996) *Manhood in America: A Cultural History* (New York: Free Press).

Knights, Ben (1999) *Writing Masculinities* (Basingstoke: Palgrave Macmillan).

Robinson, Sally (2000) *Marked Men: White Masculinity in Crisis* (New York: Columbia University Press).

Schoene-Harwood, Berthold (2000) *Writing Men: Literary Masculinities from Frankenstein to the New Man* (Edinburgh: Edinburgh University Press).

Whitehead, Stephen M. and Frank J. Barrett (eds) (2001) *The Masculinities Reader* (Cambridge: Polity).

Queer theory

Hayes, Jarrod, Margaret R. Higonnet and William J. Spurlin (eds) (2010) *Comparatively Queer: Interrogating Identities across Time and Cultures* (Basingstoke: Palgrave Macmillan).

Jagose, Annamarie (1996) *Queer Studies: An Introduction* (Melbourne: Melbourne University Press).

Morland, Iain and Annabelle Wilcox (eds) (2005) *Queer Theory* (Basingstoke: Palgrave Macmillan).

Sedgwick, Eve Kosofsky (1985) *Between Men: English Literature and Male Homosocial Desire* (New York: Columbia University Press).

—— (1995) *The Epistemology of the Closet* (London: Penguin).

Sönser Breen, Margaret (2009) *Narratives of Queer Desire: Deserts of the Heart* (Basingstoke: Palgrave Macmillan).

Stryker, Susan and Stephen Whittle (eds) (2006) *The Transgender Studies Reader* (New York: Routledge).

Sullivan, Nikki (2003) *A Critical Introduction to Queer Theory* (Edinburgh: Edinburgh University Press).

Gender, media and popular culture

Douglas, Susan J. (1995) *Where the Girls Are: Growing Up Female with the Mass Media* (London: Penguin).

Gauntlett, David (2008) *Media, Gender and Identity: An Introduction* (Abingdon: Routledge).

Genz, Stéphanie (2009) *Postfemininities in Popular Culture* (Basingstoke: Palgrave Macmillan).

Gill, Rosalind (2007) *Gender and the Media* (Cambridge: Polity).

Hermes, Joke (2005) *Re-Reading Popular Culture* (Malden, MA and Oxford: Blackwell).

McRobbie, Angela (1994) *Postmodernism and Popular Culture* (London: Routledge).

Pailer, Gaby, Andreas Böhn, Stefan Horlacher and Ulrich Scheck (eds) (2009) *Gender and Laughter: Comic Affirmation and Subversion in Traditional and Modern Media* (Amsterdam: Rodopi).

Index

Note: The letter 'n' preceded by the locators refers to notes cited in the text.